Amazon Elasticsearch Service Developer Guide

A catalogue record for this book is available from the Hong Kong Public Libraries.

Published in Hong Kong by Samurai Media Limited.

Email: info@samuraimedia.org

ISBN 9789888408313

Contents

What Is Amazon Elasticsearch Service?

Amazon Elasticsearch Service (Amazon ES) is a managed service that makes it easy to deploy, operate, and scale Elasticsearch clusters in the AWS Cloud. Elasticsearch is a popular open-source search and analytics engine for use cases such as log analytics, real-time application monitoring, and clickstream analytics. With Amazon ES, you get direct access to the Elasticsearch APIs so that existing code and applications work seamlessly with the service.

Amazon ES provisions all the resources for your Elasticsearch cluster and launches the cluster. It also automatically detects and replaces failed Elasticsearch nodes, reducing the overhead associated with self-managed infrastructures. You can scale your cluster with a single API call or a few clicks in the console.

To get started using the service, you create an Amazon ES domain. An Amazon ES domain is an Elasticsearch cluster in the AWS Cloud that has the compute and storage resources that you specify. For example, you can specify the number of instances, instance types, and storage options.

Additionally, Amazon ES offers the following benefits of a managed service:

- Cluster scaling options
- Self-healing clusters
- Replication for data durability
- Enhanced security
- Node monitoring

You can use the Amazon ES console to set up and configure your domain in minutes. If you prefer programmatic access, you can use the AWS SDKs or the AWS CLI.

There are no upfront costs to set up clusters, and you pay only for the service resources that you use.

Topics

- Features of Amazon Elasticsearch Service
- Supported Elasticsearch Versions
- Getting Started with Amazon Elasticsearch Service
- Signing Up for AWS
- Accessing Amazon Elasticsearch Service
- Regions and Endpoints for Amazon Elasticsearch Service
- Choosing Instance Types
- Scaling in Amazon Elasticsearch Service
- Using Amazon EBS Volumes for Storage
- Related Services
- Pricing for Amazon Elasticsearch Service

Features of Amazon Elasticsearch Service

Amazon ES includes the following features:

Scale

- Numerous configurations of CPU, memory, and storage capacity, known as *instance types*
- Up to 1.5 PB of instance storage
- Amazon EBS storage volumes

Security

- AWS Identity and Access Management (IAM) access control
- Easy integration with Amazon VPC and VPC security groups
- Encryption of data at rest
- Amazon Cognito authentication for Kibana

Stability

- Multiple geographical locations for your resources, known as *regions* and *Availability Zones*
- Dedicated master nodes to offload cluster management tasks
- Automated snapshots to back up and restore Amazon ES domains
- Cluster node allocation across two Availability Zones in the same region, known as *zone awareness*

Integration with Popular Services

- Data visualization using Kibana
- Integration with Amazon CloudWatch for monitoring Amazon ES domain metrics and setting alarms
- Integration with AWS CloudTrail for auditing configuration API calls to Amazon ES domains
- Integration with Amazon S3, Amazon Kinesis, and Amazon DynamoDB for loading streaming data into Amazon ES

Supported Elasticsearch Versions

Amazon ES currently supports the following Elasticsearch versions:

- 6.2
- 6.0
- 5.5
- 5.3
- 5.1
- 2.3
- 1.5

Compared to earlier versions of Elasticsearch, the 6.x versions offer powerful features that make them faster, more secure, and easier to use. Here are some highlights:

- **Index splitting** – If an index outgrows its original number of shards, the _split API offers a convenient way to split each primary shard into two or more shards in a new index.
- **Vega visualizations** – Kibana 6.2 supports the Vega visualization language, which lets you make context-aware Elasticsearch queries, combine multiple data sources into a single graph, add user interactivity to graphs, and much more.
- **Ranking evaluation** – The _rank_eval API lets you measure and track how ranked search results perform against a set of queries to ensure that your searches perform as expected.
- **Composite aggregations** – These aggregations build composite buckets from one or more fields and sort them in "natural order" (alphabetically for terms, numerically or by date for histograms).
- **Higher indexing performance** – Newer versions of Elasticsearch provide superior indexing capabilities that significantly increase the throughput of data updates.
- **Better safeguards** – The 6.x versions of Elasticsearch offer many safeguards that are designed to prevent overly broad or complex queries from negatively affecting the performance and stability of the cluster.

For more information about the differences between Elasticsearch versions and the APIs that Amazon ES supports, see Supported Elasticsearch Operations.

If you start a new Elasticsearch project, we strongly recommend that you choose the latest supported Elasticsearch version. If you have an existing domain that uses an older Elasticsearch version, you can choose to keep the domain or migrate your data. For more information, see Migrating to a Different Elasticsearch Version.

Getting Started with Amazon Elasticsearch Service

To get started, sign up for an AWS account if you don't already have one. For more information, see Signing Up for AWS.

After you are set up with an account, complete the Getting Started tutorial for Amazon Elasticsearch Service. Consult the following introductory topics if you need more information while learning about the service.

Get up and Running

- Signing Up for AWS
- Accessing Amazon ES
- Getting Started with Amazon ES Domains

Learn the Basics

- Regions and Endpoints for Amazon ES
- Amazon Resource Names and AWS Namespaces
- Choosing an Elasticsearch Version

Choose Instance Types and Storage

- Choosing an Instance Type
- Scaling in Amazon ES
- Configuring EBS-based Storage

Stay Secure

- Amazon Elasticsearch Service Access Control.
- Signing Amazon ES Requests

Signing Up for AWS

If you're not already an AWS customer, your first step is to create an AWS account. If you already have an AWS account, you are automatically signed up for Amazon ES. Your AWS account enables you to access Amazon ES and other AWS services such as Amazon S3 and Amazon EC2. There are no sign-up fees, and you don't incur charges until you create a domain. As with other AWS services, you pay only for the resources that you use.

To create an AWS account

1. Open https://aws.amazon.com/, and then choose **Create an AWS Account**. **Note**
   This might be unavailable in your browser if you previously signed into the AWS Management Console. In that case, choose **Sign in to a different account**, and then choose **Create a new AWS account**.

2. Follow the online instructions.

   Part of the sign-up procedure involves receiving a phone call and entering a PIN using the phone keypad.

You must enter payment information before you can begin using Amazon ES. Note your AWS account number, because you will need it later.

Accessing Amazon Elasticsearch Service

You can access Amazon ES through the Amazon ES console, the AWS SDKs, or the AWS CLI.

- The Amazon ES console lets you create, configure, and monitor your domains. Using the console is the easiest way to get started with Amazon ES.
- The AWS SDKs support all the Amazon ES configuration API operations, making it easy to manage your domains using your preferred technology. The SDKs automatically sign requests as needed using your AWS credentials.
- The AWS CLI wraps all the Amazon ES configuration API operations, providing a simple way to create and configure domains. The AWS CLI automatically signs requests as needed using your AWS credentials.

Regions and Endpoints for Amazon Elasticsearch Service

Amazon ES provides regional endpoints for accessing the configuration API and domain-specific endpoints for accessing the Elasticsearch APIs. You use the configuration service to create and manage your domains. The regional configuration service endpoints have this format:

```
1 es.region.amazonaws.com
```

For a list of supported regions, see Regions and Endpoints in the *AWS General Reference.*

Domain endpoints have the following format:

```
1 http://search-domainname-domainid.us-east-1.es.amazonaws.com
```

You use a domain's endpoint to upload data, submit search requests, and perform any other supported Elasticsearch operations.

Choosing Instance Types

An instance type defines the CPU, RAM, storage capacity, and hourly cost for an *instance*, the Amazon Machine Image (AMI) that runs as a virtual server in the AWS Cloud. Choose the instance type and the number of instances for your domain based on the amount of data that you have and number of requests that you anticipate. For guidance, see Sizing Amazon ES Domains.

For general information about instance types, see Amazon Elasticsearch Service Pricing.

Scaling in Amazon Elasticsearch Service

When you create a domain, you choose an initial number of Elasticsearch instances and an instance type. However, these initial choices might not be adequate over time. You can easily accommodate growth by scaling your Amazon ES domain horizontally (more instances) or vertically (larger instance types). Scaling is simple and requires no downtime. To learn more, see Configuring Amazon ES Domains and About Configuration Changes.

Using Amazon EBS Volumes for Storage

You have the option of configuring your Amazon ES domain to use an Amazon EBS volume for storing indices rather than the default storage provided by the instance. An Amazon EBS volume is a durable, block-level storage device that you can attach to a single instance. Amazon ES supports the following EBS volume types:

- Magnetic
- General Purpose (SSD)
- Provisioned IOPS (SSD)

For an overview, see Amazon EBS Volumes in the Amazon EC2 documentation. For procedures that show you how to use Amazon EBS volumes for your Amazon ES domain, see Configuring EBS-based Storage. For information about the minimum and maximum size of supported EBS volumes in an Amazon ES domain, see EBS Volume Size Limits.

Related Services

Amazon ES commonly is used with the following services:

AWS CloudTrail
Use AWS CloudTrail to get a history of the Amazon ES API calls and related events for your account. CloudTrail is a web service that records API calls from your accounts and delivers the resulting log files to your Amazon

S3 bucket. You also can use CloudTrail to track changes that were made to your AWS resources. For more information, see Auditing Amazon Elasticsearch Service Domains with AWS CloudTrail.

Amazon CloudWatch
An Amazon ES domain automatically sends metrics to Amazon CloudWatch so that you can gather and analyze performance statistics. You can monitor these metrics by using the AWS CLI or the AWS SDKs. For more information, see Monitoring Cluster Metrics and Statistics with Amazon CloudWatch (Console).
CloudWatch Logs can also go the other direction. You might configure CloudWatch Logs to stream data to Amazon ES for analysis. To learn more, see Loading Streaming Data into Amazon ES from Amazon CloudWatch.

Kinesis
Kinesis is a managed service that scales elastically for real-time processing of streaming data at a massive scale. For more information, see Loading Streaming Data into Amazon ES from Amazon Kinesis.

Amazon S3
Amazon Simple Storage Service (Amazon S3) provides storage for the internet. You can use Amazon S3 to store and retrieve any amount of data at any time, from anywhere on the web. Amazon ES provides Lambda sample code for integration with Amazon S3. For more information, see Loading Streaming Data into Amazon ES from Amazon S3.

AWS IAM
AWS Identity and Access Management (IAM) is a web service that you can use to manage users and user permissions in AWS. You can use IAM to create user-based access policies for your Amazon ES domains. For more information, see the IAM documentation and Amazon Elasticsearch Service Access Control.

Amazon ES integrates with the following services to provide data ingestion:

AWS Lambda
AWS Lambda is a compute service that lets you run code without provisioning or managing servers. Amazon ES provides Lambda sample code to stream data from DynamoDB, Amazon S3, and Kinesis. For more information, see Loading Streaming Data into Amazon Elasticsearch Service.

Amazon DynamoDB
Amazon DynamoDB is a fully managed NoSQL database service that provides fast and predictable performance with seamless scalability. To learn more, see Loading Streaming Data into Amazon ES from Amazon DynamoDB.

Pricing for Amazon Elasticsearch Service

With AWS, you pay only for what you use. For Amazon ES, you pay for each hour of use of an EC2 instance and for the cumulative size of any EBS storage volumes attached to your instances. Standard AWS data transfer charges also apply.

However, a notable data transfer exception exists. If you use zone awareness, Amazon ES does not bill for traffic between the two Availability Zones in which the domain resides. Significant data transfer occurs within a domain during shard allocation and rebalancing. Amazon ES neither meters nor bills for this traffic.

For full pricing details, see Amazon Elasticsearch Service Pricing. For information about charges incurred during configuration changes, see Charges for Configuration Changes.

If you qualify for the AWS Free Tier, you receive up to 750 hours per month of use with the `t2.micro.elasticsearch` or `t2.small.elasticsearch` instance types. You also receive up to 10 GB of Amazon EBS storage (Magnetic or General Purpose). For more information, see AWS Free Tier.

Getting Started with Amazon Elasticsearch Service

This tutorial shows you how to use Amazon Elasticsearch Service (Amazon ES) to create and configure a test domain. It walks you through the basic steps to get a domain up and running quickly. For a detailed walkthrough, see Creating and Configuring Amazon Elasticsearch Service Domains and the other topics within this guide.

You can complete the following steps by using the Amazon ES console, the AWS CLI, or the AWS SDK:

1. Create an Amazon ES domain
2. Upload data to an Amazon ES domain for indexing
3. Search documents in an Amazon ES domain
4. Delete an Amazon ES domain

For information about installing and setting up the AWS CLI, see the AWS Command Line Interface User Guide.

Step 1: Create an Amazon ES Domain

Important

This process is a concise tutorial for configuring a *test domain*. It should not be used to create production domains. For a comprehensive version of the same process, see Creating and Configuring Amazon Elasticsearch Service Domains.

An Amazon Elasticsearch Service domain encapsulates Elasticsearch itself, your indexed data, snapshots of the domain, access policies, and metadata. You can create an Amazon ES domain by using the console, the AWS CLI, or the AWS SDKs. If you don't already have an account, see Signing Up for AWS.

To create an Amazon ES domain (console)

1. Go to https://aws.amazon.com, and then choose **Sign In to the Console**.

2. Under **Analytics**, choose **Elasticsearch Service**.

3. On the **Define domain** page, for **Elasticsearch domain name**, type a name for the domain. In this Getting Started tutorial, we use the domain name *movies* for the examples that we provide later in the tutorial.

4. For **Version**, choose an Elasticsearch version for your domain. We recommend that you choose the latest supported version. For more information, see Supported Elasticsearch Versions.

5. Choose **Next**.

6. For **Instance count**, choose the number of instances that you want. For this tutorial, you can use the default value of 1.

7. For **Instance type**, choose an instance type for the Amazon ES domain. For this tutorial, we recommend `t2.small.elasticsearch`, a small and inexpensive instance type suitable for testing purposes.

8. For now, you can ignore the **Enable dedicated master** and **Enable zone awareness** check boxes. For more information about both, see About Dedicated Master Nodes and Enabling Zone Awareness.

9. For **Storage type**, choose **EBS**.

    1. For **EBS volume type**, choose General Purpose (SSD). For more information, see Amazon EBS Volume Types.

    2. For **EBS volume size**, type the size in GB of the external storage for *each* data node. For this tutorial, you can use the default value of 10.

10. For now, you can ignore **Enable encryption at rest**. For more information about the feature, see Encryption of Data at Rest for Amazon Elasticsearch Service.

11. For **Automated snapshot start hour**, use the default value. For more information, see Configuring Automatic Snapshots.

12. Choose **Next**.

13. For simplicity in this tutorial, we recommend an IP-based access policy. On the **Set up access** page, in the **Network configuration** section, choose **Public access**.

14. For now, you can ignore **Kibana authentication**. For more information about the feature, see Amazon Cognito Authentication for Kibana.

15. For **Set the domain access policy to**, choose **Allow access to the domain from specific IP(s)** and enter your public IP address, which you can find by searching for "What is my IP?" on most search engines. Then choose **OK**.

    To learn more about public access, VPC access, and access policies in general, see Amazon Elasticsearch Service Access Control and VPC Support for Amazon Elasticsearch Service Domains.

16. Choose **Next**.

17. On the **Review** page, review your domain configuration, and then choose **Confirm**. **Note**
New domains take roughly ten minutes to initialize. After your domain is initialized, you can upload data and make changes to the domain.

To create an Amazon ES domain (AWS CLI)

- Run the following command to create an Amazon ES domain.

  The command creates a domain named *movies* with Elasticsearch version 6.0. It specifies one instance of the `t2.small.elasticsearch` instance type. The instance type requires EBS storage, so it specifies a 10 GB volume. Finally, the command applies an IP-based access policy that restricts access to the domain to a single IP address.

  You need to replace `your_ip_address` in the command with your public IP address, which you can find by searching for "What is my IP?" on Google.

```
1 aws es create-elasticsearch-domain --domain-name movies --elasticsearch-version 6.0 --
      elasticsearch-cluster-config InstanceType=t2.small.elasticsearch,InstanceCount=1 --ebs-
      options EBSEnabled=true,VolumeType=standard,VolumeSize=10 --access-policies '{"Version
      ":"2012-10-17","Statement":[{"Effect":"Allow","Principal":{"AWS":"*"},"Action":["es
      :*"],"Condition":{"IpAddress":{"aws:SourceIp":["your_ip_address"]}}}]}'
```

Note
New domains take roughly ten minutes to initialize. After your domain is initialized, you can upload data and make changes to the domain.

Use the following command to query the status of the new domain:

```
1 aws es describe-elasticsearch-domain --domain movies
```

To create an Amazon ES domain (AWS SDKs)

The AWS SDKs (except the Android and iOS SDKs) support all the actions defined in the Amazon ES Configuration API Reference, including the `CreateElasticsearchDomain` action. For more information about installing and using the AWS SDKs, see AWS Software Development Kits.

Step 2: Upload Data to an Amazon ES Domain for Indexing

Important

This process is a concise tutorial for uploading a small amount of test data. For more information, see Indexing Data in Amazon Elasticsearch Service.

You can upload data to an Amazon Elasticsearch Service domain for indexing using the Elasticsearch index and bulk APIs from the command line.

- Use the index API to add or update a single Elasticsearch document.
- Use the bulk API to add or update multiple Elasticsearch documents that are described in the same JSON file.

The following example requests use curl, a common HTTP client, for brevity and convenience. Clients like curl can't perform the request signing that is required if your access policies specify IAM users or roles. To successfully perform the instructions in this step, you must use an IP address-based access policy that allows unauthenticated access, like you configured in step 1.

You can install curl on Windows and use it from the command prompt, but Windows users might find it more convenient to use a tool like Cygwin or the Windows Subsystem for Linux. macOS and most Linux distributions come with curl pre-installed.

To upload a single document to an Amazon ES domain

- Run the following command to add a single document to the *movies* domain:

```
1 curl -XPUT elasticsearch_domain_endpoint/movies/movie/1 -d '{"director": "Burton, Tim", "
    genre": ["Comedy","Sci-Fi"], "year": 1996, "actor": ["Jack Nicholson","Pierce Brosnan
    ","Sarah Jessica Parker"], "title": "Mars Attacks!"}' -H 'Content-Type: application/
    json'
```

For a detailed explanation of this command and how to make signed requests to Amazon ES, see Indexing Data in Amazon Elasticsearch Service.

To upload a JSON file that contains multiple documents to an Amazon ES domain

1. Create a file called bulk_movies.json. Copy and paste the following content into it, and add a trailing newline:

```
1 { "index" : { "_index": "movies", "_type" : "movie", "_id" : "2" } }
2 {"director": "Frankenheimer, John", "genre": ["Drama", "Mystery", "Thriller"], "year":
    1962, "actor": ["Lansbury, Angela", "Sinatra, Frank", "Leigh, Janet", "Harvey, Laurence
    ", "Silva, Henry", "Frees, Paul", "Gregory, James", "Bissell, Whit", "McGiver, John", "
    Parrish, Leslie", "Edwards, James", "Flowers, Bess", "Dhiegh, Khigh", "Payne, Julie", "
    Kleeb, Helen", "Gray, Joe", "Nalder, Reggie", "Stevens, Bert", "Masters, Michael", "
    Lowell, Tom"], "title": "The Manchurian Candidate"}
3 { "index" : { "_index": "movies", "_type" : "movie", "_id" : "3" } }
4 {"director": "Baird, Stuart", "genre": ["Action", "Crime", "Thriller"], "year": 1998, "
    actor": ["Downey Jr., Robert", "Jones, Tommy Lee", "Snipes, Wesley", "Pantoliano, Joe",
    "Jacob, Ir\u00e8ne", "Nelligan, Kate", "Roebuck, Daniel", "Malahide, Patrick", "
    Richardson, LaTanya", "Wood, Tom", "Kosik, Thomas", "Stellate, Nick", "Minkoff, Robert
    ", "Brown, Spitfire", "Foster, Reese", "Spielbauer, Bruce", "Mukherji, Kevin", "Cray,
    Ed", "Fordham, David", "Jett, Charlie"], "title": "U.S. Marshals"}
5 { "index" : { "_index": "movies", "_type" : "movie", "_id" : "4" } }
6 {"director": "Ray, Nicholas", "genre": ["Drama", "Romance"], "year": 1955, "actor": ["
    Hopper, Dennis", "Wood, Natalie", "Dean, James", "Mineo, Sal", "Backus, Jim", "Platt,
    Edward", "Ray, Nicholas", "Hopper, William", "Allen, Corey", "Birch, Paul", "Hudson,
    Rochelle", "Doran, Ann", "Hicks, Chuck", "Leigh, Nelson", "Williams, Robert", "Wessel,
```

17

```
Dick", "Bryar, Paul", "Sessions, Almira", "McMahon, David", "Peters Jr., House"], "
title": "Rebel Without a Cause"}
```

2. Run the following command to upload the file to the *movies* domain:

```
1 curl -XPOST elasticsearch_domain_endpoint/_bulk --data-binary @bulk_movies.json -H 'Content
  -Type: application/json'
```

For more information about the bulk file format, see Indexing Data in Amazon Elasticsearch Service.

Note

Amazon ES supports migrating data from manual snapshots taken on both Amazon ES and self-managed Elasticsearch clusters. Restoring a snapshot from a self-managed Elasticsearch cluster is a common way to migrate data to Amazon ES. For more information, see Restoring Snapshots.

Step 3: Search Documents in an Amazon ES Domain

To search documents in an Amazon Elasticsearch Service domain, use the Elasticsearch search API. Alternatively, you can use Kibana to search documents in the domain.

To search documents from the command line

- Run the following command to search the *movies* domain for the word *mars*:

```
1 curl -XGET 'elasticsearch_domain_endpoint/movies/_search?q=mars'
```

To search documents from an Amazon ES domain by using Kibana

1. Point your browser to the Kibana plugin for your Amazon ES domain. You can find the Kibana endpoint on your domain dashboard on the Amazon ES console. The URL follows the format of:

```
1 https://domain.region.es.amazonaws.com/_plugin/kibana/
```

2. To use Kibana, you must configure at least one index pattern. Kibana uses these patterns to identity which indices you want to analyze. For this tutorial, enter *movies* and choose **Create**.

3. The **Index Patterns** screen shows your various document fields, fields like `actor` and `director`. For now, choose **Discover** to search your data.

4. In the search bar, type *mars*, and then press **Enter**. Note how the similarity score (`_score`) increases when you search for the phrase *mars attacks*.

Step 4: Delete an Amazon ES Domain

Because the *movies* domain from this tutorial is for test purposes, you should delete it when you are finished experimenting to avoid incurring charges.

To delete an Amazon ES domain (console)

1. Log in to the **Amazon Elasticsearch Service** console.

2. In the navigation pane, under **My domains**, choose the *movies* domain.

3. Choose **Delete Elasticsearch domain.**

4. Choose **Delete domain.**

5. Select the **Delete the domain** check box, and then choose **Delete.**

To delete an Amazon ES domain (AWS CLI)

- Run the following command to delete the *movies* domain:

```
1 aws es delete-elasticsearch-domain --domain-name movies
```

Note

Deleting a domain deletes all billable Amazon ES resources. However, any manual snapshots of the domain that you created are not deleted. Consider saving a snapshot if you might need to recreate the Amazon ES domain in the future. If you don't plan to recreate the domain, you can safely delete any snapshots that you created manually.

To delete an Amazon ES domain (AWS SDKs)

The AWS SDKs (except the Android and iOS SDKs) support all the actions defined in the Amazon ES Configuration API Reference, including the `DeleteElasticsearchDomain` action. For more information about installing and using the AWS SDKs, see AWS Software Development Kits.

Creating and Configuring Amazon Elasticsearch Service Domains

This chapter describes how to create and configure Amazon Elasticsearch Service (Amazon ES) domains. An Amazon ES domain is the hardware, software, and data exposed by Amazon Elasticsearch Service endpoints.

Unlike the brief instructions in the Getting Started tutorial, this chapter describes all options and provides relevant reference information. You can complete each procedure by using instructions for the Amazon ES console, the AWS Command Line Interface (AWS CLI), or the AWS SDKs.

Topics

- Creating Amazon ES Domains
- Configuring Amazon ES Domains
- Configuring EBS-based Storage
- Modifying VPC Access Configuration
- Configuring Amazon Cognito Authentication for Kibana
- Configuring Access Policies
- Configuring Automatic Snapshots
- Configuring Advanced Options
- Configuring Slow Logs

Creating Amazon ES Domains

This section describes how to create Amazon ES domains by using the Amazon ES console or by using the AWS CLI with the `create-elasticsearch-domain` command. The procedures for the AWS CLI include syntax and examples.

Creating Amazon ES Domains (Console)

Use the following procedure to create an Amazon ES domain by using the console.

To create an Amazon ES domain (console)

1. Go to https://aws.amazon.com, and then choose **Sign In to the Console**.

2. Under **Analytics**, choose **Elasticsearch Service**.

3. Choose **Create a new domain**.

   Alternatively, choose **Get Started** if this is the first Amazon ES domain that you will create for your AWS account.

4. On the **Define domain** page, for **Domain name**, type a name for your domain. The domain name must meet the following criteria:

   - Uniquely identifies a domain
   - Starts with a lowercase letter
   - Contains between 3 and 28 characters
   - Contains only lowercase letters a-z, the numbers 0-9, and the hyphen (-)

5. For **Version**, choose an Elasticsearch version for your domain. We recommend that you choose the latest version. For more information, see Supported Elasticsearch Versions.

6. Choose **Next**.

7. For **Instance count**, choose the number of instances that you want.

   The default is one. For maximum values, see Cluster and Instance Limits. We recommend a minimum of three instances to avoid potential Elasticsearch issues, such as the split brain issue. If you have three dedicated master nodes, we still recommend a minimum of two data nodes for replication. Single node clusters are fine for development and testing, but should not be used for production workloads. For more guidance, see Sizing Amazon ES Domains.

8. For **Instance type**, choose an instance type for the data nodes.

   To see a list of the instance types that Amazon ES supports, see Supported Instance Types.

9. (Optional) If you must ensure cluster stability or if you have a domain that has more than 10 instances, enable a dedicated master node. Dedicated master nodes increase cluster stability and are required for a domain that has an instance count greater than 10. For more information, see About Dedicated Master Nodes.

   1. Select the **Enable dedicated master** check box.

   2. For **Dedicated master instance type**, choose an instance type for the dedicated master node.

      For a list of the instance types that Amazon ES supports, see Supported Instance Types. **Note** You can choose an instance type for the dedicated master node that differs from the instance type that you choose for the data nodes. For example, you might select general purpose or storage-optimized instances for your data nodes, but compute-optimized instances for your dedicated master nodes.

   3. For **Dedicated master instance count**, choose the number of instances for the dedicated master node.

      We recommend choosing an odd number of instances to avoid potential Elasticsearch issues, such as the split brain issue. The default and recommended number is three.

10. (Optional) For enhanced data durability, select the **Enable zone awareness** check box.

    Zone awareness distributes Amazon ES data nodes across two Availability Zones in the same region. If you enable zone awareness, you must have an even number of instances in the instance count, and you must use the native Elasticsearch API to create replica shards for your cluster. This process allows for the even distribution of shards across two Availability Zones. For more information, see Enabling Zone Awareness.

11. For **Storage type**, choose either **Instance** (the default) or **EBS**.

    If your Amazon ES domain requires more storage, use an EBS volume for storage rather than the storage that is attached to the selected instance type. Domains with large indices or large numbers of indices often benefit from the increased storage capacity of EBS volumes. For guidance on creating especially large domains, see Petabyte Scale. If you choose **EBS**, the following boxes appear:

    1. For **EBS volume type**, choose an EBS volume type.

       If you choose Provisioned IOPS (SSD) for the EBS volume type, for **Provisioned IOPS**, type the baseline IOPS performance that you want. For more information, see Amazon EBS Volumes in the Amazon EC2 documentation.

    2. For **EBS volume size**, type the size of the EBS volume that you want to attach to each data node.

    EBS volume size is per node. You can calculate the total cluster size for the Amazon ES domain using the following formula: (number of data nodes) * (EBS volume size). The minimum and maximum size of an EBS volume depends on both the specified EBS volume type and the instance type that it's attached to. To learn more, see EBS Volume Size Limits.

12. (Optional) To enable encryption of data at rest, select the **Enable encryption at rest** check box.

    Select **(Default) aws/es** to have Amazon ES create a KMS encryption key on your behalf (or use the one that it already created). Otherwise, choose your own KMS encryption key from the **KMS master key** menu. To learn more, see Encryption of Data at Rest for Amazon Elasticsearch Service.

13. For **Automated snapshot start hour**, choose the hour for automated daily snapshots of domain indices.

    For more information and recommendations, see Configuring Automatic Snapshots.

14. (Optional) Choose **Advanced options**. For a summary of options, see Configuring Advanced Options

15. Choose **Next**.

16. On the **Set up access** page, in the **Network configuration** section, choose either **Public Access** or **VPC access**. If you choose **Public access**, skip to step 17. If you choose **VPC access**, ensure that you have met the prerequisites, and then do the following:

    1. For **VPC**, choose the ID of the VPC that you want to use. **Note**
    The VPC and domain must be in the same AWS Region, and you must select a VPC with tenancy set to **Default**. Amazon ES does not yet support VPCs that use dedicated tenancy.

    2. For **Subnet**, choose a subnet. If you enabled zone awareness in step 10, you must choose two subnets. Amazon ES will place a VPC endpoint and *elastic network interfaces* (ENIs) in the subnet or subnets. **Note**
    You must reserve sufficient IP addresses for the network interfaces in the subnet (or subnets). For more information, see Reserving IP Addresses in a VPC Subnet.

    3. For **Security groups**, choose the VPC security groups that need access to the Amazon ES domain. For more information, see VPC Support for Amazon Elasticsearch Service Domains.

    4. For **IAM role**, keep the default role. Amazon ES uses this predefined role (also known as a *service-linked role*) to access your VPC and to place a VPC endpoint and network interfaces in the subnet of the VPC. For more information, see Service-Linked Role for VPC Access.

17. (Optional) If you want to protect Kibana with a login page, choose **Enable Amazon Cognito for authentication**.

    1. Choose the Amazon Cognito user pool and identity pool that you want to use for Kibana authentication. For guidance on creating these resources, see Amazon Cognito Authentication for Kibana.

18. For **Set the domain access policy to**, choose a preconfigured policy from the **Select a template** dropdown list and edit it to meet the needs of your domain. Alternatively, you can add one or more Identity and Access Management (IAM) policy statements in the **Add or edit the access policy** box. For more information, see Amazon Elasticsearch Service Access Control, Configuring Access Policies, and About Access Policies on VPC Domains. **Note**
If you chose **VPC access** in step 16, the IP-based policy template is not available in the dropdown list, and you can't configure an IP-based policy manually. Instead, you can use security groups to control which IP addresses can access the domain. To learn more, see About Access Policies on VPC Domains.

19. Choose **Next**.

20. On the **Review** page, review your domain configuration, and then choose **Confirm and create**.

21. Choose **OK**.

Note
New domains take up to ten minutes to initialize. After your domain is initialized, you can upload data and make changes to the domain.

Creating Amazon ES Domains (AWS CLI)

Instead of creating an Amazon ES domain by using the console, you can create a domain by using the AWS CLI. Use the following syntax to create an Amazon ES domain.

```
1  aws es create-elasticsearch-domain --domain-name <value>
2
3    [--elasticsearch-version <value>]
4    [--elasticsearch-cluster-config <value>]
5    [--ebs-options <value>]
6    [--access-policies <value>]
```

```
7   [--snapshot-options <value>]
8   [--vpc-options <value>]
9   [--advanced-options <value>]
10  [--log-publishing-options <value>]
11  [--cli-input-json <value>]
12  [--generate-cli-skeleton <value>]
13  [--encryption-at-rest-options <value>]
14  [--cognito-options <value>]
```

The following table provides more information about each of the optional parameters.

Optional Parameter	Description
--elasticsearch-version	Specifies the Elasticsearch version of the domain. If not specified, the default value is 1.5. For more information, see Choosing an Elasticsearch Version.
--elasticsearch-cluster-config	Specifies the instance type and count of the domain, whether zone awareness is enabled, and whether the domain uses a dedicated master node. Dedicated master nodes increase cluster stability and are required for a domain that has an instance count greater than 10. For more information, see Configuring Amazon ES Domains.
--ebs-options	Specifies whether the domain uses an EBS volume for storage. If true, this parameter must also specify the EBS volume type, size, and, if applicable, IOPS value. For more information, see Configuring EBS-based Storage.
--access-policies	Specifies the access policy for the domain. For more information, see Configuring Access Policies.
--snapshot-options	Specifies the hour in UTC during which the service performs a daily automated snapshot of the indices in the domain. The default value is 0, or midnight, which means that the snapshot is taken anytime between midnight and 1:00 AM. For more information, see Configuring Snapshots.
--advanced-options	Specifies whether to allow references to indices in the bodies of HTTP request objects. For more information, see Configuring Advanced Options.
--generate-cli-skeleton	Displays JSON for all specified parameters. Save the output to a file so that you can later read the file with the --cli-input-json parameter rather than typing the parameters at the command line. For more information, see Generate CLI Skeleton and CLI Input JSON Parameters in the AWS Command Line Interface User Guide.

Optional Parameter	Description
--cli-input-json	Specifies the name of a JSON file that contains a set of CLI parameters. For more information, see Generate CLI Skeleton and CLI Input JSON Parameters in the AWS Command Line Interface User Guide.
--log-publishing-options	Specifies whether Amazon ES should publish Elasticsearch slow logs to CloudWatch. For more information, see Configuring Slow Logs.
--vpc-options	Specifies whether to launch the Amazon ES domain within an Amazon VPC (VPC). To learn more, see VPC Support for Amazon Elasticsearch Service Domains.
--encryption-at-rest-options	Specifies whether to enable encryption of data at rest.
--cognito-options	Specifies whether to use Amazon Cognito Authentication for Kibana.

Examples

The first example demonstrates the following Amazon ES domain configuration:

- Creates an Amazon ES domain named *weblogs* with Elasticsearch version 5.5
- Populates the domain with two instances of the m4.large.elasticsearch instance type
- Uses a 100 GB Magnetic disk EBS volume for storage for each data node
- Allows anonymous access, but only from a single IP address: 192.0.2.0/32

```
1 aws es create-elasticsearch-domain --domain-name weblogs --elasticsearch-version 5.5 --
    elasticsearch-cluster-config  InstanceType=m4.large.elasticsearch,InstanceCount=2 --ebs-
    options EBSEnabled=true,VolumeType=standard,VolumeSize=100 --access-policies '{"Version":
    "2012-10-17", "Statement": [{"Action": "es:*", "Principal":"*","Effect": "Allow", "Condition
    ": {"IpAddress":{"aws:SourceIp":["192.0.2.0/32"]}}}]}'
```

The next example demonstrates the following Amazon ES domain configuration:

- Creates an Amazon ES domain named *weblogs* with Elasticsearch version 5.5
- Populates the domain with six instances of the m4.large.elasticsearch instance type
- Uses a 100 GB General Purpose (SSD) EBS volume for storage for each data node
- Restricts access to the service to a single user, identified by the user's AWS account ID: 555555555555
- Enables zone awareness

```
1 aws es create-elasticsearch-domain --domain-name weblogs --elasticsearch-version 5.5 --
    elasticsearch-cluster-config  InstanceType=m4.large.elasticsearch,InstanceCount=6,
    ZoneAwarenessEnabled=true --ebs-options EBSEnabled=true,VolumeType=gp2,VolumeSize=100 --
    access-policies '{"Version": "2012-10-17", "Statement": [ { "Effect": "Allow", "Principal":
    {"AWS": "arn:aws:iam::555555555555:root" }, "Action":"es:*", "Resource": "arn:aws:es:us-east
    -1:555555555555:domain/logs/*" } ] }'
```

The next example demonstrates the following Amazon ES domain configuration:

- Creates an Amazon ES domain named *weblogs* with Elasticsearch version 5.5
- Populates the domain with ten instances of the m4.xlarge.elasticsearch instance type
- Populates the domain with three instances of the m4.large.elasticsearch instance type to serve as dedicated master nodes
- Uses a 100 GB Provisioned IOPS EBS volume for storage, configured with a baseline performance of 1000 IOPS for each data node

- Restricts access to a single user and to a single subresource, the _search API
- Configures automated daily snapshots of the indices for 03:00 UTC

```
1 aws es create-elasticsearch-domain --domain-name weblogs --elasticsearch-version 5.5 --
    elasticsearch-cluster-config  InstanceType=m4.xlarge.elasticsearch,InstanceCount=10,
    DedicatedMasterEnabled=true,DedicatedMasterType=m4.large.elasticsearch,DedicatedMasterCount
    =3 --ebs-options EBSEnabled=true,VolumeType=io1,VolumeSize=100,Iops=1000 --access-policies
    '{"Version": "2012-10-17", "Statement": [ { "Effect": "Allow", "Principal": { "AWS": "arn:
    aws:iam::555555555555:root" }, "Action": "es:*", "Resource": "arn:aws:es:us-east
    -1:555555555555:domain/mylogs/_search" } ] }' --snapshot-options AutomatedSnapshotStartHour
    =3
```

Note

If you attempt to create an Amazon ES domain and a domain with the same name already exists, the CLI does not report an error. Instead, it returns details for the existing domain.

Creating Amazon ES Domains (AWS SDKs)

The AWS SDKs (except the Android and iOS SDKs) support all the actions defined in the Amazon ES Configuration API Reference, including `CreateElasticsearchDomain`. For more information about installing and using the AWS SDKs, see AWS Software Development Kits.

Configuring Amazon ES Domains

To meet the demands of increased traffic and data, you can update your Amazon ES domain configuration with any of the following changes:

- Change the instance count
- Change the instance type
- Enable or disable dedicated master nodes
- Enable or disable Zone Awareness
- Configure storage configuration
- Change the start time for automated snapshots of domain indices
- Change the VPC subnets and security groups
- Configure advanced options

Note

For information about configuring a domain to use an EBS volume for storage, see Configuring EBS-based Storage.

Configuring Amazon ES Domains (Console)

Use the following procedure to update your Amazon ES configuration by using the console.

To configure an Amazon ES domain (console)

1. Go to https://aws.amazon.com, and then choose **Sign In to the Console**.

2. Under **Analytics**, choose **Elasticsearch Service**.

3. In the navigation pane, under **My domains**, choose the domain that you want to update.

4. Choose **Configure cluster**.

5. On the **Configure cluster** page, update the configuration of the domain.

   The cluster is a collection of one or more data nodes, optional dedicated master nodes, and storage required to run Amazon ES and operate your domain.

1. If you want to change the instance type for data nodes, for **Instance type**, choose a new instance type.

   To see a list of the instance types that Amazon ES supports, see Supported Instance Types.

2. If you want to change the instance count, for **Instance count**, choose an integer from one to twenty. To request an increase up to 100 instances per domain, create a case with the AWS Support Center.

3. If you want to improve cluster stability or if your domain has an instance count greater than 10, enable a dedicated master node for your cluster. For more information, see About Dedicated Master Nodes.

   1. Select the **Enable dedicated master** check box.

   2. For **Dedicated master instance type**, choose an instance type for the dedicated master node.

      You can choose an instance type for the dedicated master node that differs from the instance type that you choose for the data nodes.

      To see a list of the instance types that Amazon ES supports, see Supported Instance Types.

   3. For **Dedicated master instance count**, choose the number of instances for the dedicated master node.

      We recommend choosing an odd number of instances to avoid potential Amazon ES issues, such as the split brain issue. The default and recommended number is three.

4. If you want to enable zone awareness, select the **Enable zone awareness** check box. If you enable zone awareness, you must have an even number of instances in your instance count. This allows for the even distribution of shards across two Availability Zones in the same region.

5. If you want to change the hour during which the service takes automated daily snapshots of the primary index shards of your Amazon ES domain, for **Automated snapshot start hour**, choose an integer.

6. If you didn't enable VPC access when you created the domain, skip to step 7. If you enabled VPC access, you can change the subnet that the VPC endpoint is placed in, and you can change the security groups:

   1. For **Subnets**, choose a subnet. The subnet must have a sufficient number of IP addresses reserved for the network interfaces. If you enabled zone awareness, you must choose two subnets. The subnets must be in different Availability Zones in the same region. For more information, see VPC Support for Amazon Elasticsearch Service Domains.

   2. For **Security groups**, add the security groups that need access to the domain.

7. (Optional) Choose **Advanced options**. For a summary of options, see Configuring Advanced Options

8. Choose **Submit**.

Configuring Amazon ES Domains (AWS CLI)

Use the `elasticsearch-cluster-config` option to configure your Amazon ES cluster by using the AWS CLI. The following syntax is used by both the `create-elasticsearch-domain` and `update-elasticsearch-domain -config` commands.

Syntax

```
1  --elasticsearch-cluster-config InstanceType=<value>,InstanceCount=<value>,DedicatedMasterEnabled
     =<value>,DedicatedMasterType=<value>,DedicatedMasterCount=<value>,ZoneAwarenessEnabled=<
     value>
```

Note

Do not include spaces between parameters for the same option.

The following table describes the parameters in more detail.

Parameter	Valid Values	Description
InstanceType	Any supported instance type. See Supported Instance Types.	The hardware configuration of the computer that hosts the instance. The default is m4.large.elasticsearch.
InstanceCount	Integer	The number of instances in the Amazon ES domain. The default is one, and the maximum default limit is twenty. To request an increase up to 100 instances per domain, create a case with the AWS Support Center.
DedicatedMasterEnabled	true or false	Specifies whether to use a dedicated master node for the Amazon ES domain. The default value is false.
DedicatedMasterType	Any supported instance type	The hardware configuration of the computer that hosts the master node. The default is m4.large.elasticsearch.
DedicatedMasterCount	Integer	The number of instances used for the dedicated master node. The default is three.
ZoneAwarenessEnabled	true or false	Specifies whether to enable zone awareness for the Amazon ES domain. The default value is false.

Examples

The following example creates an Amazon ES domain named `mylogs` with Elasticsearch version 5.5 with two instances of the m4.large.elasticsearch instance type and zone awareness enabled:

```
1 aws es create-elasticsearch-domain --domain-name mylogs --elasticsearch-version 5.5 --
      elasticsearch-cluster-config InstanceType=m4.large.elasticsearch,InstanceCount=2,
      DedicatedMasterEnabled=false,ZoneAwarenessEnabled=true
```

However, you likely will want to reconfigure your new Amazon ES domain as network traffic grows and as the quantity and size of documents increase. For example, you might decide to use a larger instance type, use more instances, and enable a dedicated master node. The following example updates the domain configuration with these changes:

```
1 aws es update-elasticsearch-domain-config --domain-name mylogs --elasticsearch-cluster-config
      InstanceType=m4.xlarge.elasticsearch,InstanceCount=3,DedicatedMasterEnabled=true,
      DedicatedMasterType=m4.large.elasticsearch,DedicatedMasterCount=3
```

Configuring Amazon ES Domains (AWS SDKs)

The AWS SDKs (except the Android and iOS SDKs) support all the actions defined in the Amazon ES Configuration API Reference, including `UpdateElasticsearchDomainConfig`. For more information about installing and using the AWS SDKs, see AWS Software Development Kits.

Configuring EBS-based Storage

An Amazon EBS volume is a block-level storage device that you can attach to a single instance. EBS volumes enable you to independently scale the storage resources of your Amazon ES domain from its compute resources. EBS volumes are most useful for domains with large datasets, but without the need for large compute resources. EBS volumes are much larger than the default storage provided by the instance. Amazon Elasticsearch Service supports the following EBS volume types:

- General Purpose (SSD)
- Provisioned IOPS (SSD)
- Magnetic

Note
When changing an EBS volume type from provisioned IOPS to non-provisioned EBS volume types, set the IOPS value to 0.

Warning
Currently, if the data node that is attached to an EBS volume fails, the EBS volume also fails.

Configuring EBS-based Storage (Console)

Use the following procedure to enable EBS-based storage by using the console.

To enable EBS-based storage (console)

1. Go to https://aws.amazon.com, and then choose **Sign In to the Console**.
2. Under **Analytics**, choose **Elasticsearch Service**.
3. In the navigation pane, under **My domains**, choose the domain that you want to configure.
4. Choose **Configure cluster**.
5. For **Storage type**, choose **EBS**.
6. For **EBS volume type**, choose an EBS volume type.

   If you choose **Provisioned IOPS (SSD)** for the EBS volume type, for **Provisioned IOPS**, type the baseline IOPS performance that you want.
7. For **EBS volume size**, type the size that you want for the EBS volume.

   EBS volume size is per node. You can calculate the total cluster size for the Amazon ES domain using the following formula: (number of data nodes) * (EBS volume size). The minimum and maximum size of an EBS volume depends on both the specified EBS volume type and the instance type to which it is attached. To learn more, see EBS Volume Size Limits.
8. Choose **Submit**.

Note
Set the IOPS value for a Provisioned IOPS EBS volume to no more than 30 times the maximum storage of the volume. For example, if your volume has a maximum size of 100 GB, you can't assign an IOPS value for it that is greater than 3000.

For more information, see Amazon EBS Volumes in the Amazon EC2 documentation.

Configuring EBS-based Storage (AWS CLI)

Use the `--ebs-options` option to configure EBS-based storage by using the AWS CLI. The following syntax is used by both the `create-elasticsearch-domain` and `update-elasticsearch-domain-config` commands.

Syntax

```
1 --ebs-options EBSEnabled=<value>,VolumeType=<value>,VolumeSize=<value>,IOPS=<value>
```

Parameter	Valid Values	Description
EBSEnabled	true or false	Specifies whether to use an EBS volume for storage rather than the storage provided by the instance. The default value is false.
VolumeType	Any of the following:[See the AWS documentation website for more details]	The EBS volume type to use with the Amazon ES domain.
VolumeSize	Integer	Specifies the size of the EBS volume for each data node. The minimum and maximum size of an EBS volume depends on both the specified EBS volume type and the instance type to which it is attached. To see a table that shows the minimum and maximum EBS size for each instance type, see Service Limits.
IOPS	Integer	Specifies the baseline I/O performance for the EBS volume. This parameter is used only by Provisioned IOPS (SSD) volumes. The minimum value is 1000. The maximum value is 16000.

Note

We recommend that you do not set the IOPS value for a Provisioned IOPS EBS volume to more than 30 times the maximum storage of the volume. For example, if your volume has a maximum size of 100 GB, you should not assign an IOPS value for it that is greater than 3000. For more information, including use cases for each volume type, see Amazon EBS Volume Types in the Amazon EC2 documentation.

Examples

The following example creates a domain named `mylogs` with Elasticsearch version 5.5 with a 10 GB General Purpose EBS volume:

```
1 aws es create-elasticsearch-domain --domain-name=mylogs --elasticsearch-version 5.5 --ebs-
    options EBSEnabled=true,VolumeType=gp2,VolumeSize=10
```

However, you might need a larger EBS volume as the size of your search indices increases. For example, you might opt for a 100 GB Provisioned IOPS volume with a baseline I/O performance of 3000 IOPS. The following example updates the domain configuration with those changes:

```
1 aws es update-elasticsearch-domain-config --domain-name=mylogs --ebs-options EBSEnabled=true,
     VolumeType=io1,VolumeSize=100,IOPS=3000
```

Configuring EBS-based Storage (AWS SDKs)

The AWS SDKs (except the Android and iOS SDKs) support all the actions defined in the Amazon ES Configuration API Reference, including the `--ebs-options` parameter for `UpdateElasticsearchDomainConfig`. For more information about installing and using the AWS SDKs, see AWS Software Development Kits.

Modifying VPC Access Configuration

If you configured a domain to reside within a VPC, you can modify the configuration using the Amazon ES console. To migrate a public domain to a VPC domain, see Migrating from Public Access to VPC Access.

Configuring VPC Access (Console)

Use the following procedure to configure VPC access by using the console.

To configure VPC access (console)

1. Go to https://aws.amazon.com, and then choose **Sign In to the Console**.
2. Under **Analytics**, choose **Elasticsearch Service**.
3. In the navigation pane, under **My domains**, choose the domain that you want to configure.
4. Choose **Configure cluster**.
5. In the **Network configuration** section, for **Subnets**, choose a subnet. If you enabled zone awareness, you must choose two subnets. The subnets must be in different Availability Zones in the same region. For more information, see VPC Support for Amazon Elasticsearch Service Domains. **Note**
   You must reserve sufficient IP addresses for the network interfaces in the subnet (or subnets). For more information, see Reserving IP Addresses in a VPC Subnet.
6. For **Security groups**, add the security groups that need access to the domain.
7. Choose **Submit**.

Configuring Amazon Cognito Authentication for Kibana

See Amazon Cognito Authentication for Kibana.

Configuring Access Policies

Amazon Elasticsearch Service offers several ways to configure access to your Amazon ES domains. For more information, see Amazon Elasticsearch Service Access Control.

The console provides preconfigured access policies that you can customize for the specific needs of your domain. You also can import access policies from other Amazon ES domains. For information on how these access policies interact with VPC access, see About Access Policies on VPC Domains.

Configuring Access Policies (Console)

Use the following procedure to configure access policies by using the console.

To configure access policies (console)

1. Go to https://aws.amazon.com, and then choose **Sign In to the Console**.

2. Under **Analytics**, choose **Elasticsearch Service**.

3. In the navigation pane, under **My domains**, choose the domain that you want to update.

4. Choose **Modify access policy**.

5. Edit the access policy.

   Alternatively, choose one of the policy templates from the **Select a template** dropdown list, and then edit it as needed for your domain.

[See the AWS documentation website for more details]

1. Choose **Submit**.

Configuring Access Policies (AWS CLI)

Use the `--access-policies` option to configure access policies by using the AWS CLI. The following syntax is used by both the `create-elasticsearch-domain` and `update-elasticsearch-domain-config` commands.

Syntax

```
1 --access-policies=<value>
```

Parameter	Valid Values	Description
--access-policies	JSON	Specifies the access policy for the Amazon ES domain.

Example

The following resource-based policy example restricts access to the service to a single user, identified by the user's AWS account ID, 555555555555, in the `Principal` policy element. This user receives access to `index1`, but can't access other indices in the domain:

```
1 aws es update-elasticsearch-domain-config --domain-name mylogs --access-policies '{"Version":
    "2012-10-17", "Statement": [ { "Effect": "Allow","Principal": {"AWS": "arn:aws:iam
    ::123456789012:root" },"Action":"es:*","Resource":"arn:aws:es:us-east-1:555555555555:domain/
    index1/*" } ] }'
```

Tip

If you configure access policies using the AWS CLI, you can use one of many online tools to minify the JSON policy statement.

Configuring Access Policies (AWS SDKs)

The AWS SDKs (except the Android and iOS SDKs) support all the actions defined in the Amazon ES Configuration API Reference, including the `--access-policies` parameter for `UpdateElasticsearchDomainConfig`.

For more information about installing and using the AWS SDKs, see AWS Software Development Kits.

Configuring Automatic Snapshots

Amazon Elasticsearch Service provides automatic daily snapshots of a domain's primary index shards and the number of replica shards. By default, the service takes automatic snapshots at midnight, but you should choose a time when the service is under minimal load.

For information on working with these snapshots, see Restoring Snapshots.

Warning
The service stops taking snapshots of Amazon ES indices while the health of a cluster is red. Any documents that you add to a red cluster, even to indices with a health status of green, can be lost in the event of a cluster failure due to this lack of backups. To prevent loss of data, return the health of your cluster to green before uploading additional data to any index in the cluster. To learn more, see Red Cluster Status.

Configuring Snapshots (Console)

Use the following procedure to configure daily automatic index snapshots by using the console.

To configure automatic snapshots

1. Go to https://aws.amazon.com, and then choose **Sign In to the Console**.
2. Under **Analytics**, choose **Elasticsearch Service**.
3. In the navigation pane, under **My domains**, choose the domain that you want to update.
4. Choose **Configure cluster**.
5. For **Automated snapshot start hour**, choose the new hour for the service to take automated snapshots.
6. Choose **Submit**.

Configuring Snapshots (AWS CLI)

Use the following syntax for the `--snapshot-options` option. The syntax for the option is the same for both the `create-elasticsearch-domain` and `update-elasticsearch-domain-config` commands.

Syntax

```
1 --snapshot-options AutomatedSnapshotStartHour=<value>
```

Parameter	Valid Values	Description
AutomatedSnapshot-StartHour	Integer between 0 and 23	Specifies the hour in UTC during which the service performs a daily automated snapshot of the indices in the new domain. The default value is 0, or midnight, which means that the snapshot is taken anytime between midnight and 1:00 AM.

Example

The following example configures automatic snapshots at 01:00 UTC:

```
1 aws es update-elasticsearch-domain-config --domain-name mylogs --region us-east-2 --snapshot-
     options AutomatedSnapshotStartHour=1
```

Configuring Snapshots (AWS SDKs)

The AWS SDKs (except the Android and iOS SDKs) support all the actions that are defined in the Amazon ES Configuration API Reference. This includes the `--snapshots-options` parameter for `UpdateElasticsearchDomainConfig`. For more information about installing and using the AWS SDKs, see AWS Software Development Kits.

Configuring Advanced Options

Use advanced options to configure the following:

rest.action.multi.allow_explicit_index
Specifies whether explicit references to indices are allowed inside the body of HTTP requests. Setting this property to false prevents users from bypassing access control for subresources. By default, the value is true. For more information, see Advanced Options and API Considerations.

indices.fielddata.cache.size
Specifies the percentage of Java heap space that is allocated to field data. By default, this setting is unbounded. Many customers query rotating daily indices. We recommend that you begin benchmark testing with `indices.fielddata.cache.size` configured to 40% of the JVM heap for most such use cases. However, if you have very large indices you might need a large field data cache.

indices.query.bool.max_clause_count
Specifies the maximum number of clauses allowed in a Lucene Boolean query. 1024 is the default. Queries with more than the permitted number of clauses result in a `TooManyClauses` error. For more information, see the Lucene documentation.

Configuring Advanced Options (Console)

To configure advanced options (console)

1. Go to https://aws.amazon.com, and then choose **Sign In to the Console**.
2. Under **Analytics**, choose **Elasticsearch Service**.
3. In the navigation pane, under **My domains**, choose the domain that you want to update.
4. Choose **Configure cluster**.
5. Choose **Advanced options**.
6. Specify the options that you want and choose **Submit**.

Configuring Advanced Options (AWS CLI)

Use the following syntax for the `--advanced-options` option. The syntax for the option is the same for both the `create-elasticsearch-domain` and `update-elasticsearch-domain-config` commands.

Syntax

```
1 --advanced-options rest.action.multi.allow_explicit_index=<true|false>, indices.fielddata.cache.
     size=<percentage_heap>, indices.query.bool.max_clause_count=<int>
```

[See the AWS documentation website for more details]

Example

The following example disables explicit references to indices in the HTTP request bodies. It also limits the field data cache to 40 percent of the total Java heap:

```
1 aws es update-elasticsearch-domain-config --domain-name mylogs --region us-east-1 --advanced-
    options rest.action.multi.allow_explicit_index=false, indices.fielddata.cache.size=40
```

Configuring Advanced Options (AWS SDKs)

The AWS SDKs (except the Android and iOS SDKs) support all of the actions defined in the Amazon ES Configuration API Reference, including the `--advanced-options` parameter for `UpdateElasticsearchDomainConfig`. For more information about installing and using the AWS SDKs, see AWS Software Development Kits.

Configuring Slow Logs

Slow logs are an Elasticsearch feature that Amazon ES exposes through Amazon CloudWatch Logs. These logs are useful for troubleshooting performance issues, but are *disabled* by default. If enabled, standard CloudWatch pricing applies.

Amazon ES exposes two slow logs: search and index.

Enabling Slow Logs Publishing (Console)

Use the following procedure to enable the publishing of slow logs to CloudWatch.

To enable slow logs publishing to CloudWatch

1. Go to https://aws.amazon.com, and then choose **Sign In to the Console**.

2. Under **Analytics**, choose **Elasticsearch Service**.

3. In the navigation pane, under **My domains**, choose the domain that you want to update.

4. On the **Logs** tab, choose **Enable** for the log that you want.

5. Create a CloudWatch log group, or choose an existing one. **Note**
   If you plan to enable search *and* index slow logs, we recommend publishing each to its own log group. This separation makes the logs easier to scan.

6. Choose an access policy that contains the appropriate permissions, or create a policy using the JSON that the console provides:

```
1 {
2   "Version": "2012-10-17",
3   "Statement": [
4     {
5       "Effect": "Allow",
6       "Principal": {
7         "Service": "es.amazonaws.com"
8       },
9       "Action": [
10         "logs:PutLogEvents",
11         "logs:CreateLogStream"
```

35

```
12      ],
13          "Resource": "cw_log_group_arn"
14      }
15  ]
16 }
```

Important

CloudWatch Logs supports 10 resource policies per region. If you plan to enable slow logs for several Amazon ES domains, you should create and reuse a broader policy that includes multiple log groups to avoid reaching this limit.

1. Choose **Enable**.

   The status of your domain changes from **Active** to **Processing**. The status must return to **Active** before log publishing is enabled. This process can take up to 30 minutes.

After you enable log publishing, see Setting Elasticsearch Logging Thresholds.

Enabling Slow Logs Publishing (AWS CLI)

Before you can enable log publishing, you need a CloudWatch log group. If you don't already have one, you can create one using the following command:

```
1 aws logs create-log-group --log-group-name my-log-group
```

Type the next command to find the log group's ARN, and then *make a note of it*:

```
1 aws logs describe-log-groups --log-group-name my-log-group
```

Now you can give Amazon ES permissions to write to the log group. You must provide the log group's ARN near the end of the command:

```
1 aws logs put-resource-policy --policy-name my-policy --policy-document '{ "Version":
    "2012-10-17", "Statement": [{ "Sid": "", "Effect": "Allow", "Principal": { "Service": "es.
    amazonaws.com"}, "Action":[ "logs:PutLogEvents"," logs:PutLogEventsBatch","logs:
    CreateLogStream"],"Resource": "cw_log_group_arn"}]}'
```

Important

CloudWatch Logs supports 10 resource policies per region. If you plan to enable slow logs for several Amazon ES domains, you should create and reuse a broader policy that includes multiple log groups to avoid reaching this limit.

Finally, you can use the `--log-publishing-options` option to enable publishing. The syntax for the option is the same for both the `create-elasticsearch-domain` and `update-elasticsearch-domain-config` commands.

[See the AWS documentation website for more details]

Note

If you plan to enable search *and* index slow logs, we recommend publishing each to its own log group. This separation makes the logs easier to scan.

Example

The following example enables the publishing of search and index slow logs for the specified domain:

```
1 aws es update-elasticsearch-domain-config --domain-name my-domain --log-publishing-options "
    SEARCH_SLOW_LOGS={CloudWatchLogsLogGroupArn=arn:aws:logs:us-east-1:123456789012:log-group:my
    -log-group,Enabled=true},INDEX_SLOW_LOGS={CloudWatchLogsLogGroupArn=arn:aws:logs:us-east
    -1:123456789012:log-group:my-other-log-group,Enabled=true}"
```

To disable publishing to CloudWatch, run the same command with `Enabled=false`.

After you enable log publishing, see Setting Elasticsearch Logging Thresholds.

Enabling Slow Logs Publishing (AWS SDKs)

Before you can enable slow logs publishing, you must first create a CloudWatch log group, get its ARN, and give Amazon ES permissions to write to it. The relevant operations are documented in the Amazon CloudWatch Logs API Reference:

- `CreateLogGroup`
- `DescribeLogGroup`
- `PutResourcePolicy`

You can access these operations using the AWS SDKs.

The AWS SDKs (except the Android and iOS SDKs) support all the operations that are defined in the Amazon ES Configuration API Reference, including the `--log-publishing-options` option for `CreateElasticsearchDomain` and `UpdateElasticsearchDomainConfig`.

After you enable log publishing, see Setting Elasticsearch Logging Thresholds.

Setting Elasticsearch Logging Thresholds

Elasticsearch disables slow logs by default. After you enable the *publishing* of slow logs to CloudWatch, you still must specify logging thresholds for each Elasticsearch index. These thresholds define precisely what should be logged and at which log level. Settings vary slightly by Elasticsearch version.

You specify these settings through the Elasticsearch REST API. An example follows:

```
1 curl -XPUT elasticsearch_domain_endpoint/index/_settings --data '{"index.search.slowlog.
    threshold.query.warn": "5s","index.search.slowlog.threshold.query.info": "2s"}' -H 'Content-
    Type: application/json'
```

To test that slow logs are publishing successfully, consider starting with very low values to verify that logs appear in CloudWatch, and then increase the thresholds to more useful levels.

If the logs don't appear, check the following:

- Does the CloudWatch log group exist? Check the CloudWatch console.

- Does Amazon ES have permissions to write to the log group? Check the Amazon ES console.

- Is the Amazon ES domain configured to publish to the log group? Check the Amazon ES console, use the AWS CLI `describe-elasticsearch-domain-config` option, or call `DescribeElasticsearchDomainConfig` using one of the SDKs.

- Are the Elasticsearch logging thresholds low enough that your requests are exceeding them? To review your thresholds for an index, use the following command:

  ```
  1 curl -XGET elasticsearch_domain_endpoint/index/_settings?pretty
  ```

If you want to disable slow logs for an index, return any thresholds that you changed to their default values of `-1`.

Disabling publishing to CloudWatch using the Amazon ES console or AWS CLI does *not* stop Elasticsearch from generating logs; it only stops the *publishing* of those logs. Be sure to check your index settings if you no longer need the slow logs.

Viewing Slow Logs

Viewing the slow logs in CloudWatch is just like viewing any other CloudWatch log. For more information, see View Log Data in the *Amazon CloudWatch Logs User Guide*.

Here are some considerations for viewing the logs:

- Amazon ES publishes only the first 255,000 characters of each line of the slow logs to CloudWatch. Any remaining content is truncated.
- In CloudWatch, the log stream names have suffixes of `-index-slow-logs` or `-search-slow-logs` to help identify their contents.

Amazon Elasticsearch Service Access Control

Amazon Elasticsearch Service offers several ways of controlling access to your domains. This section covers the various policy types, how they interact with each other, and how to create your own, custom policies.

Important
VPC support introduces some additional considerations to Amazon ES access control. For more information, see About Access Policies on VPC Domains.

Types of Policies

Amazon ES supports three types of access policies:

- Resource-based Policies
- Identity-based policies
- IP-based Policies

Resource-based Policies

You attach resource-based policies to domains. These policies specify which actions a principal can perform on the domain's *subresources*. Subresources include Elasticsearch indices and APIs.

The http://docs.aws.amazon.com/IAM/latest/UserGuide/reference_policies_elements_principal.html element specifies the accounts, users, or roles that are allowed access. The http://docs.aws.amazon.com/IAM/latest/UserGuide/reference_policies_elements_resource.html element specifies which subresources these principals can access. The following resource-based policy grants `test-user` full access (`es:*`) to `test-domain`:

```
1  {
2    "Version": "2012-10-17",
3    "Statement": [
4      {
5        "Effect": "Allow",
6        "Principal": {
7          "AWS": [
8            "arn:aws:iam::123456789012:user/test-user"
9          ]
10       },
11       "Action": [
12         "es:*"
13       ],
14       "Resource": "arn:aws:es:us-west-1:987654321098:domain/test-domain/*"
15     }
16   ]
17 }
```

Two important considerations apply to this policy:

- These privileges apply only to this domain. Unless you create additional policies, `test-user` can't access other domains or even view a list of them in the Amazon ES dashboard.

- The trailing `/*` in the `Resource` element is significant. Despite having full access, `test-user` can perform these actions only on the domain's subresources, not on the domain's configuration.

  For example, `test-user` can make requests against an index (GET `https://search-test-domain.us-west-1.es.amazonaws.com/test-index`), but can't update the domain's configuration (POST https

://es.us-west-1.amazonaws.com/2015-01-01/es/domain/test-domain/config). Note the difference between the two endpoints. Accessing the configuration API requires an identity-based policy.

To further restrict `test-user`, you can apply the following policy:

```
1  {
2    "Version": "2012-10-17",
3    "Statement": [
4      {
5        "Effect": "Allow",
6        "Principal": {
7          "AWS": [
8            "arn:aws:iam::123456789012:user/test-user"
9          ]
10       },
11       "Action": [
12         "es:ESHttpGet"
13       ],
14       "Resource": "arn:aws:es:us-west-1:987654321098:domain/test-domain/test-index/_search"
15     }
16   ]
17 }
```

Now `test-user` can perform only one operation: searches against `test-index`. All other indices within the domain are inaccessible, and without permissions to use the `es:ESHttpPut` or `es:ESHttpPost` actions, `test-user` can't add or modify documents.

Next, you might decide to configure a role for power users. This policy allows `power-user-role` access to all HTTP methods, except for the ability to delete a critical index and its documents:

```
1  {
2    "Version": "2012-10-17",
3    "Statement": [
4      {
5        "Effect": "Allow",
6        "Principal": {
7          "AWS": [
8            "arn:aws:iam::123456789012:role/power-user-role"
9          ]
10       },
11       "Action": [
12         "es:ESHttpDelete",
13         "es:ESHttpGet",
14         "es:ESHttpHead",
15         "es:ESHttpPost",
16         "es:ESHttpPut"
17       ],
18       "Resource": "arn:aws:es:us-west-1:987654321098:domain/test-domain/*"
19     },
20     {
21       "Effect": "Deny",
22       "Principal": {
23         "AWS": [
24           "arn:aws:iam::123456789012:role/power-user-role"
25         ]
26       },
27       "Action": [
```

```
28        "es:ESHttpDelete"
29      ],
30      "Resource": "arn:aws:es:us-west-1:987654321098:domain/test-domain/critical-index*"
31    }
32  ]
33 }
```

For information about all available actions, see Policy Element Reference.

Identity-based policies

Unlike resource-based policies, which you attach to domains in Amazon ES, you attach identity-based policies to users or roles using the AWS Identity and Access Management (IAM) service. Just like resource-based policies, identity-based policies specify who can access a service, which actions they can perform, and if applicable, the resources on which they can perform those actions.

While they certainly don't have to be, identify-based policies tend to be more generic. They often govern the basic, service-level actions a user can perform. After you have these policies in place, you can use resource-based policies in Amazon ES to offer users additional permissions.

Because identity-based policies attach to users or roles (principals), the JSON doesn't specify a principal. The following policy grants access to actions that begin with `Describe` and `List` and allows `GET` requests against all domains. This combination of actions provides read-only access:

```
1  {
2    "Version": "2012-10-17",
3    "Statement": [
4      {
5        "Action": [
6          "es:Describe*",
7          "es:List*",
8          "es:ESHttpGet"
9        ],
10       "Effect": "Allow",
11       "Resource": "*"
12     }
13   ]
14 }
```

An administrator might have full access to Amazon ES:

```
1  {
2    "Version": "2012-10-17",
3    "Statement": [
4      {
5        "Action": [
6          "es:*"
7        ],
8        "Effect": "Allow",
9        "Resource": "*"
10     }
11   ]
12 }
```

For more information about the differences between resource-based and identity-based policies, see IAM Policies in the *IAM User Guide.*

Note

Users with the AWS managed `AmazonESReadOnlyAccess` policy can't see cluster health status in the console. To allow them to see cluster health status, add the `"es:ESHttpGet"` action to an access policy and attach it to their accounts or roles.

IP-based Policies

IP-based policies restrict access to a domain to one or more IP addresses or CIDR blocks. Technically, IP-based policies are not a distinct type of policy. Instead, they are just resource-based policies that specify an anonymous principal and include a special http://docs.aws.amazon.com/IAM/latest/UserGuide/reference_policies_elements_condition.html element.

The primary appeal of IP-based policies is that they allow unsigned requests to an Amazon ES domain, which lets you use clients like curl and Kibana or access the domain through a proxy server. To learn more, see Using a Proxy to Access Amazon ES from Kibana.

Note

If you enabled VPC access for your domain, you can't configure an IP-based policy. Instead, you can use security groups to control which IP addresses can access the domain. For more information, see About Access Policies on VPC Domains.

The following IP-based access policy grants all requests that originate from `12.345.678.901` access to `test-domain`:

```
1  {
2    "Version": "2012-10-17",
3    "Statement": [
4      {
5        "Effect": "Allow",
6        "Principal": {
7          "AWS": "*"
8        },
9        "Action": [
10          "es:*"
11        ],
12        "Condition": {
13          "IpAddress": {
14            "aws:SourceIp": [
15              "12.345.678.901"
16            ]
17          }
18        },
19        "Resource": "arn:aws:es:us-west-1:987654321098:domain/test-domain/*"
20      }
21    ]
22  }
```

Signing Amazon ES Requests

Even if you configure a completely open resource-based access policy, *all* requests to the Amazon ES configuration API must be signed. If your policies specify IAM users or roles, requests to the Elasticsearch APIs also must be signed. The signing method differs by API:

- To make calls to the Amazon ES configuration API, we recommend that you use one of the AWS SDKs. The SDKs greatly simplify the process and can save you a significant amount of time compared to creating and signing your own requests.
- To make calls to the Elasticsearch APIs, you must sign your own requests. For sample code, see Programmatic Indexing.

To sign a request, you calculate a digital signature using a cryptographic hash function, which returns a hash value based on the input. The input includes the text of your request and your secret access key. The hash function returns a hash value that you include in the request as your signature. The signature is part of the `Authorization` header of your request.

After receiving your request, Amazon ES recalculates the signature using the same hash function and input that you used to sign the request. If the resulting signature matches the signature in the request, Amazon ES processes the request. Otherwise, Amazon ES rejects the request.

Amazon ES supports authentication using AWS Signature Version 4. For more information, see Signature Version 4 Signing Process.

Note
The service ignores parameters passed in URLs for HTTP POST requests that are signed with Signature Version 4.

When Policies Collide

Complexities arise when policies disagree or make no explicit mention of a user. Understanding How IAM Works in the *IAM User Guide* provides a concise summary of policy evaluation logic:

- By default, all requests are denied.
- An explicit allow overrides this default.
- An explicit deny overrides any allows.

For example, if a resource-based policy grants you access to a domain, but an identify-based policy denies you access, you are denied access. If an identity-based policy grants access and a resource-based policy does not specify whether or not you should have access, you are allowed access. See the following table of intersecting policies for a full summary of outcomes.

	Allowed in Resource-based Policy	Denied in Resource-based Policy	Neither Allowed nor Denied in Resource-based Policy
Allowed in Identity-based Policy	Allow	Deny	Allow
Denied in Identity-based Policy	Deny	Deny	Deny
Neither Allowed nor Denied in Identity-based Policy	Allow	Deny	Deny

Policy Element Reference

Amazon ES supports all the policy elements that are documented in the IAM Policy Elements Reference. The following table shows the most common elements.

JSON Policy Element	Summary
Version	The current version of the policy language is 2012-10-17. All access policies should specify this value.
Effect	This element specifies whether the statement allows or denies access to the specified actions. Valid values are `Allow` or `Deny`.
Principal	This element specifies the AWS account or IAM user or role that is allowed or denied access to a resource and can take several forms: [See the AWS documentation website for more details] Specifying the * wildcard enables anonymous access to the domain, which we don't recommend unless you add an IP-based condition.

JSON Policy Element	Summary
Action	Amazon ES uses the following actions for HTTP methods:[See the AWS documentation website for more details]Amazon ES uses the following actions for the configuration API:[See the AWS documentation website for more details] You can use wildcards to specify a subset of actions, such as `"Action":"es:*"` or `"Action":"es:Describe*"`. Certain `es:` actions support resource-level permissions. For example, you can give a user permissions to delete one particular domain without giving that user permissions to delete *any* domain. Other actions apply only to the service itself. For example, `es:ListDomainNames` makes no sense in the context of a single domain and thus requires a wildcard. Resource-based policies differ from resource-level permissions. Resource-based policies are full JSON policies that attach to domains. Resource-level permissions let you restrict actions to particular domains or subresources. In practice, you can think of resource-level permissions as an optional part of a resource- or identity-based policy. The following identity-based policy lists all `es:` actions and groups them according to whether they apply to the domain subresources (`test-domain/*`), to the domain configuration (`test-domain`), or only to the service (`*`):{ "Version": "2012-10-17", "Statement": [{ "Effect": "Allow", "Action": ["es:ESHttpDelete", "es:ESHttpGet", "es:ESHttpHead", "es:ESHttpPost", "es:ESHttpPut"], "Resource": "arn:awsus-west-1:987654321098:domain/test-domain/" }, { "Effect": "Allow", "Action": ["es:CreateElasticsearchDomain", "es:DeleteElasticsearchDomain", "es:DescribeElasticsearchDomain", "es:DescribeElasticsearchDomainConfig", "es:DescribeElasticsearchDomains", "es:UpdateElasticsearchDomainConfig"], "Resource": "arn:awsus-west-1:987654321098:domain/test-domain" }, { "Effect": "Allow", "Action": ["es:AddTags", "es:DeleteElasticsearchServiceRole", "es:DescribeElasticsearchInstanceTypeLimits", "es:ListDomainNames", "es:ListElasticsearchInstanceTypes", "es:ListElasticsearchVersions", "es:ListTags", "es:RemoveTags"], "Resource": "" }]} While resource-level permissions for `es:CreateElasticsearchDomain` might seem unintuitive—after all, why give a user permissions to create a domain that already exists?—the use of a wildcard lets you enforce a simple naming scheme for your domains, such as `"Resource": "arn: aws:es:us-west-1:987654321098:domain`

45

JSON Policy Element	Summary
Condition	Amazon ES supports all the conditions that are described in Available Global Condition Keys in the *IAM User Guide*. When configuring an IP-based policy, you specify the IP addresses or CIDR block as a condition, such as the following: "Condition": { "IpAddress": { "aws:SourceIp": ["192.0.2.0/32"] }}
Resource	Amazon ES uses `Resource` elements in three basic ways: [See the AWS documentation website for more details] For details about which actions support resource-level permissions, see the `Action` element in this table.

Advanced Options and API Considerations

Amazon ES has several advanced options, one of which has access control implications: `rest.action.multi.allow_explicit_index`. At its default setting of true, it allows users to bypass subresource permissions under certain circumstances.

For example, consider the following resource-based policy:

```
1  {
2    "Version": "2012-10-17",
3    "Statement": [
4      {
5        "Effect": "Allow",
6        "Principal": {
7          "AWS": [
8            "arn:aws:iam::123456789012:user/test-user"
9          ]
10       },
11       "Action": [
12         "es:ESHttp*"
13       ],
14       "Resource": [
15         "arn:aws:es:us-west-1:987654321098:domain/test-domain/test-index/*",
16         "arn:aws:es:us-west-1:987654321098:domain/test-domain/_bulk"
17       ]
18     },
19     {
20       "Effect": "Allow",
21       "Principal": {
22         "AWS": [
23           "arn:aws:iam::123456789012:user/test-user"
24         ]
25       },
26       "Action": [
27         "es:ESHttpGet"
28       ],
29       "Resource": "arn:aws:es:us-west-1:987654321098:domain/test-domain/restricted-index/*"
30     }
31   ]
32 }
```

This policy grants `test-user` full access to `test-index` and the Elasticsearch bulk API. It also allows `GET` requests to `restricted-index`.

The following indexing request, as you might expect, fails due to a permissions error:

```
1  PUT https://search-test-domain.us-west-1.es.amazonaws.com/restricted-index/movie/1
2  {
3    "title": "Your Name",
4    "director": "Makoto Shinkai",
5    "year": "2016"
6  }
```

Unlike the index API, the bulk API lets you create, update, and delete many documents in a single call. You often specify these operations in the request body, however, rather than in the request URL. Because Amazon ES uses URLs to control access to domain subresources, `test-user` can, in fact, use the bulk API to make changes to `restricted-index`. Even though the user lacks `POST` permissions on the index, the following request **succeeds**:

```
1  POST https://search-test-domain.us-west-1.es.amazonaws.com/_bulk
2  { "index" : { "_index": "restricted-index", "_type" : "movie", "_id" : "1" } }
3  { "title": "Your Name", "director": "Makoto Shinkai", "year": "2016" }
```

In this situation, the access policy fails to fulfill its intent. To prevent users from bypassing these kinds of restrictions, you can change `rest.action.multi.allow_explicit_index` to false. If this value is false, all calls to the bulk, mget, and msearch APIs that specify index names in the request body stop working. In other words, calls to `_bulk` no longer work, but calls to `test-index/_bulk` do. This second endpoint contains an index name, so you don't need to specify one in the request body.

Kibana relies heavily on mget and msearch, so it is unlikely to work properly after this change. For partial remediation, you can leave `rest.action.multi.allow_explicit_index` as true and deny certain users access to one or more of these APIs.

For information about changing this setting, see Configuring Advanced Options.

Similarly, the following resource-based policy contains two subtle issues:

```
1  {
2    "Version": "2012-10-17",
3    "Statement": [
4      {
5        "Effect": "Allow",
6        "Principal": {
7          "AWS": "arn:aws:iam::123456789012:user/test-user"
8        },
9        "Action": "es:ESHttp*",
10       "Resource": "arn:aws:es:us-west-1:987654321098:domain/test-domain/*"
11     },
12     {
13       "Effect": "Deny",
14       "Principal": {
15         "AWS": "arn:aws:iam::123456789012:user/test-user"
16       },
17       "Action": "es:*",
18       "Resource": "arn:aws:es:us-west-1:987654321098:domain/test-domain/restricted-index/*"
19     }
20   ]
21 }
```

- Despite the explicit deny, `test-user` can still make calls such as `GET` `https://search-test-domain.us-west-1.es.amazonaws.com/_all/_search` and `GET` `https://search-test-domain.us-west-1.es.amazonaws.com/*/_search` to access the documents in `restricted-index`.
- Because the `Resource` element references `restricted-index/*`, `test-user` doesn't have permissions to directly access the index's documents. The user does, however, have permissions to *delete the entire index*. To prevent access and deletion, the policy instead must specify `restricted-index*`.

Rather than mixing broad allows and focused denies, the safest approach is to follow the principle of least privilege and grant only the permissions that are required to perform a task.

Configuring Access Policies

- For instructions on creating or modifying resource- and IP-based policies in Amazon ES, see Configuring Access Policies.
- For instructions on creating or modifying identity-based policies in IAM, see Creating IAM Policies in the *IAM User Guide*.

Additional Sample Policies

Although this chapter includes many sample policies, AWS access control is a complex subject that is best understood through examples. For more, see Example Policies in the *IAM User Guide*.

Managing Amazon Elasticsearch Service Domains

As the size and number of documents in your Amazon Elasticsearch Service (Amazon ES) domain grow and as network traffic increases, you likely will need to update the configuration of your Elasticsearch cluster. To know when it's time to reconfigure your domain, you need to monitor domain metrics. You might also need to audit data-related API calls to your domain or assign tags to your domain. This section describes how to perform these and other tasks related to managing your domains.

Topics

- About Configuration Changes
- Charges for Configuration Changes
- Enabling Zone Awareness
- Monitoring Cluster Metrics and Statistics with Amazon CloudWatch (Console)
- Auditing Amazon Elasticsearch Service Domains with AWS CloudTrail
- Tagging Amazon Elasticsearch Service Domains

About Configuration Changes

Amazon ES uses a *blue/green* deployment process when updating domains. Blue/green typically refers to the practice of running two production environments, one live and one idle, and switching the two as you make software changes. In the case of Amazon ES, it refers to the practice of creating a new environment for domain updates and routing users to the new environment after those updates are complete. The practice minimizes downtime and maintains the original environment in the event that deployment to the new environment is unsuccessful.

Domain updates occur when you make most configuration changes, but they also occur when the Amazon ES team makes certain software changes to the service. If you make configuration changes, the domain state changes to **Processing**. If the Amazon ES team makes software changes, the state remains **Active**. In both cases, you can review the cluster health and Amazon CloudWatch metrics and see that the number of nodes in the cluster temporarily increases—often doubling—while the domain update occurs. In the following illustration, you can see the number of nodes doubling from 11 to 22 during a configuration change and returning to 11 when the update is complete.

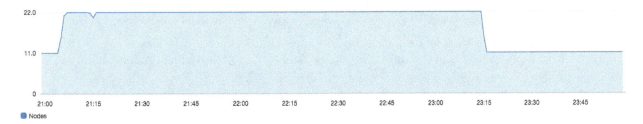

This temporary increase can strain the cluster's dedicated master nodes, which suddenly have many more nodes to manage. It is important to maintain sufficient capacity on dedicated master nodes to handle the overhead that is associated with these blue/green deployments.

Important
You do *not* incur any additional charges during configuration changes and service maintenance. You are billed only for the number of nodes that you request for your cluster. For specifics, see Charges for Configuration Changes.

To prevent overloading dedicated master nodes, you can monitor usage with the Amazon CloudWatch metrics. For recommended maximum values, see Recommended CloudWatch Alarms.

Charges for Configuration Changes

If you change the configuration for a domain, Amazon ES creates a new cluster as described in About Configuration Changes. During the migration of old to new, you incur the following charges:

- If you change the instance type, you are charged for both clusters for the first hour. After the first hour, you are charged only for the new cluster.

    Example: You change the configuration from three `m3.xlarge` instances to four `m4.large` instances. For the first hour, you are charged for both clusters (3 * `m3.xlarge` + 4 * `m4.large`). After the first hour, you are charged only for the new cluster (4 * `m4.large`).

- If you don't change the instance type, you are charged only for the largest cluster for the first hour. After the first hour, you are charged only for the new cluster.

    Example: You change the configuration from six `m3.xlarge` instances to three `m3.xlarge` instances. For the first hour, you are charged for the largest cluster (6 * `m3.xlarge`). After the first hour, you are charged only for the new cluster (3 * `m3.xlarge`).

Enabling Zone Awareness

Each AWS Region is a separate geographic area with multiple, isolated locations known as *Availability Zones*. To prevent data loss and minimize downtime in the event of node and data center failure, you can use the Amazon ES console to allocate an Elasticsearch cluster's nodes and shards across two Availability Zones in the same region. This allocation is known as *zone awareness*. Zone awareness requires an even number of instances and slightly increases network latencies.

If you enable zone awareness, you must have at least one replica for each index in your cluster. Fortunately, the default configuration for any index is a replica count of 1. Amazon ES distributes primary and replica shards across nodes in different Availability Zones, which increases the availability of your cluster.

Important
If you specify a replica count of 0 for an index, enabling zone awareness doesn't provide any additional data durability or availability. Without replicas, Amazon ES can't distribute copies of your data to other Availability Zones.

If you enable zone awareness and use VPC access domains, you must specify Availability Zones for the VPC subnets. For more information about VPCs, see VPC Support for Amazon Elasticsearch Service Domains.

The following illustration shows a four-node cluster with zone awareness enabled. The service distributes the shards so that no replica shard is in the same Availability Zone as its corresponding primary shard.

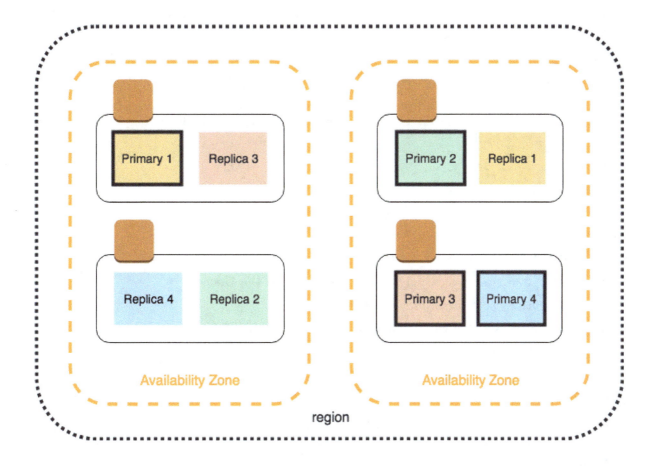

If one Availability Zone (AZ) experiences a service interruption, you have a 50/50 chance of cluster downtime due to how master node election works. For example, if you use the recommended three dedicated master nodes, Amazon ES distributes two dedicated master nodes into one AZ and one dedicated master node into the other. If the AZ with two dedicated master nodes experiences an interruption, your cluster is unavailable until the remaining AZ can automatically replace the now-missing dedicated master nodes, achieve a quorum, and elect a new master.

Further, if one AZ experiences an interruption, the cluster's data nodes might experience a period of extreme load while Amazon ES automatically configures new nodes to replace the now-missing ones. Suddenly, half as many nodes have to process just as many requests to the cluster. As they process these requests, the remaining nodes are also struggling to replicate data onto new nodes as they come online. A cluster with extra resources can alleviate this concern.

To enable zone awareness (console)

1. Go to https://aws.amazon.com, and then choose **Sign In to the Console**.

2. Under **Analytics**, choose **Elasticsearch Service**.

3. In the navigation pane, under **My domains**, choose your Amazon ES domain.

4. Choose **Configure cluster**.

5. In the **Node configuration** pane, choose **Enable zone awareness**.

6. Choose **Submit**.

For more information, see Regions and Availability Zones in the EC2 documentation.

Monitoring Cluster Metrics and Statistics with Amazon CloudWatch (Console)

Amazon ES domains send performance metrics to Amazon CloudWatch every minute. If you use general purpose or magnetic EBS volumes, the EBS volume metrics only update every five minutes. Use the **Monitoring** tab in the Amazon Elasticsearch Service console to view these metrics, provided at no extra charge.

Statistics provide you with broader insight into each metric. For example, view the **Average** statistic for the **CPUUtilization** metric to compute the average CPU utilization for all nodes in the cluster. Each of the metrics falls into one of three categories:

- Cluster metrics
- Dedicated master node metrics
- EBS volume metrics

Note
The service archives the metrics for two weeks before discarding them.

To view configurable statistics for a metric (console)

1. Go to https://aws.amazon.com, and then choose **Sign In to the Console**.

2. Under **Analytics**, choose **Elasticsearch Service**.

3. In the navigation pane, under **My domains**, choose your Amazon ES domain.

4. Choose the **Monitoring** tab.

5. Choose the metric that you want to view.

6. From the **Statistic** list, select a statistic.

   For a list of relevant statistics for each metric, see the tables in Cluster Metrics. Some statistics are not relevant for a given metric. For example, the **Sum** statistic is not meaningful for the **Nodes** metric.

7. Choose **Update graph**.

Cluster Metrics

Note
To check your cluster metrics if metrics are unavailable in the Amazon Elasticsearch Service console, use Amazon CloudWatch.

The **AWS/ES** namespace includes the following metrics for clusters.

Metric	Description
ClusterStatus.green	Indicates that all index shards are allocated to nodes in the cluster. Relevant statistics: Minimum, Maximum

Metric	Description
ClusterStatus.yellow	Indicates that the primary shards for all indices are allocated to nodes in a cluster, but the replica shards for at least one index are not. Single node clusters always initialize with this cluster status because there is no second node to which a replica can be assigned. You can either increase your node count to obtain a green cluster status, or you can use the Elasticsearch API to set the number_of_replicas setting for your index to 0. To learn more, see Configuring Amazon Elasticsearch Service Domains.Relevant statistics: Minimum, Maximum
ClusterStatus.red	Indicates that the primary and replica shards of at least one index are not allocated to nodes in a cluster. To recover, you must delete the indices or restore a snapsnot and then add EBS-based storage, use larger instance types, or add instances. For more information, see Red Cluster Status. Relevant statistics: Minimum, Maximum
Nodes	The number of nodes in the Amazon ES cluster. Relevant Statistics: Minimum, Maximum, Average
SearchableDocuments	The total number of searchable documents across all indices in the cluster. Relevant statistics: Minimum, Maximum, Average
DeletedDocuments	The total number of documents marked for deletion across all indices in the cluster. These documents no longer appear in search results, but Elasticsearch only removes deleted documents from disk during segment merges. This metric increases after delete requests and decreases after segment merges. Relevant statistics: Minimum, Maximum, Average
CPUUtilization	The maximum percentage of CPU resources used for data nodes in the cluster. Relevant statistics: Maximum, Average

Metric	Description
FreeStorageSpace	The free space, in megabytes, for nodes in the cluster. `Sum` shows total free space for the cluster. `Minimum`, `Maximum`, and `Average` show free space for individual nodes. Amazon ES throws a `ClusterBlockException` when this metric reaches 0. To recover, you must either delete indices, add larger instances, or add EBS-based storage to existing instances. To learn more, see Recovering from a Lack of Free Storage Space `FreeStorageSpace` will always be lower than the value that the Elasticsearch `_cluster/stats` API provides. Amazon ES reserves a percentage of the storage space on each instance for internal operations. Relevant statistics: Minimum, Maximum, Average, Sum
ClusterUsedSpace	The total used space, in megabytes, for a cluster. You can view this metric in the Amazon CloudWatch console, but not in the Amazon ES console. Relevant statistics: Minimum, Maximum
ClusterIndexWritesBlocked	Indicates whether your cluster is accepting or blocking incoming write requests. A value of 0 means that the cluster is accepting requests. A value of 1 means that it is blocking requests. Many factors can cause a cluster to begin blocking requests. Some common factors include the following: `FreeStorageSpace` is too low, `JVMMemoryPressure` is too high, or `CPUUtilization` is too high. To alleviate this issue, consider adding more disk space or scaling your cluster. Relevant statistics: Maximum You can view this metric in the Amazon CloudWatch console, but not the Amazon ES console.
JVMMemoryPressure	The maximum percentage of the Java heap used for all data nodes in the cluster. Relevant statistics: Maximum
AutomatedSnapshotFailure	The number of failed automated snapshots for the cluster. A value of 1 indicates that no automated snapshot was taken for the domain in the previous 36 hours. Relevant statistics: Minimum, Maximum
CPUCreditBalance	The remaining CPU credits available for data nodes in the cluster. A CPU credit provides the performance of a full CPU core for one minute. For more information, see CPU Credits in the *Amazon EC2 Developer Guide*. This metric is available only for the t2.micro.elasticsearch, t2.small.elasticsearch, and t2.medium.elasticsearch instance types. Relevant statistics: Minimum

Metric	Description
KibanaHealthyNodes	A health check for Kibana. A value of 1 indicates normal behavior. A value of 0 indicates that Kibana is inaccessible. In most cases, the health of Kibana mirrors the health of the cluster. Relevant statistics: Minimum You can view this metric on the Amazon CloudWatch console, but not the Amazon ES console.
KMSKeyError	A value of 1 indicates that the KMS customer master key used to encrypt data at rest has been disabled. To restore the domain to normal operations, re-enable the key. The console displays this metric only for domains that encrypt data at rest.. Relevant statistics: Minimum, Maximum
KMSKeyInaccessible	A value of 1 indicates that the KMS customer master key used to encrypt data at rest has been deleted or revoked its grants to Amazon ES. You can't recover domains that are in this state. If you have a manual snapshot, though, you can use it to migrate the domain's data to a new domain. The console displays this metric only for domains that encrypt data at rest. Relevant statistics: Minimum, Maximum

The following screenshot shows the cluster metrics that are described in the preceding table.

Dedicated Master Node Metrics

The AWS/ES namespace includes the following metrics for dedicated master nodes.

Metric	Description
MasterCPUUtilization	The maximum percentage of CPU resources used by the dedicated master nodes. We recommend increasing the size of the instance type when this metric reaches 60 percent. Relevant statistics: Average

Metric	Description
MasterFreeStorageSpace	This metric is not relevant and can be ignored. The service does not use master nodes as data nodes.
MasterJVMMemoryPressure	The maximum percentage of the Java heap used for all dedicated master nodes in the cluster. We recommend moving to a larger instance type when this metric reaches 85 percent. Relevant statistics: Maximum
MasterCPUCreditBalance	The remaining CPU credits available for dedicated master nodes in the cluster. A CPU credit provides the performance of a full CPU core for one minute. For more information, see CPU Credits in the *Amazon EC2 User Guide for Linux Instances*. This metric is available only for the t2.micro.elasticsearch, t2.small.elasticsearch, and t2.medium.elasticsearch instance types. Relevant statistics: Minimum
MasterReachableFromNode	A health check for `MasterNotDiscovered` exceptions. A value of 1 indicates normal behavior. A value of 0 indicates that `/_cluster/health/` is failing. Failures mean that the master node stopped or is not reachable. They are usually the result of a network connectivity issue or AWS dependency problem. Relevant statistics: Minimum You can view this metric on the Amazon CloudWatch console, but not the Amazon ES console.

The following screenshot shows the dedicated master nodes metrics that are described in the preceding table.

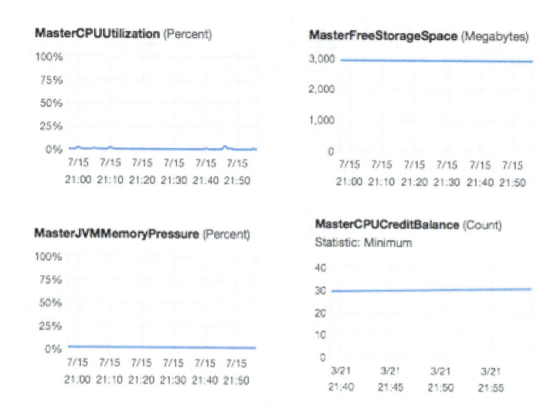

EBS Volume Metrics

The AWS/ES namespace includes the following metrics for EBS volumes.

Metric	Description
ReadLatency	The latency, in seconds, for read operations on EBS volumes. Relevant statistics: Minimum, Maximum, Average
WriteLatency	The latency, in seconds, for write operations on EBS volumes. Relevant statistics: Minimum, Maximum, Average
ReadThroughput	The throughput, in bytes per second, for read operations on EBS volumes. Relevant statistics: Minimum, Maximum, Average
WriteThroughput	The throughput, in bytes per second, for write operations on EBS volumes. Relevant statistics: Minimum, Maximum, Average
DiskQueueDepth	The number of pending input and output (I/O) requests for an EBS volume. Relevant statistics: Minimum, Maximum, Average
ReadIOPS	The number of input and output (I/O) operations per second for read operations on EBS volumes. Relevant statistics: Minimum, Maximum, Average

Metric	Description
WriteIOPS	The number of input and output (I/O) operations per second for write operations on EBS volumes. Relevant statistics: Minimum, Maximum, Average

The following screenshot shows the EBS volume metrics that are described in the preceding table.

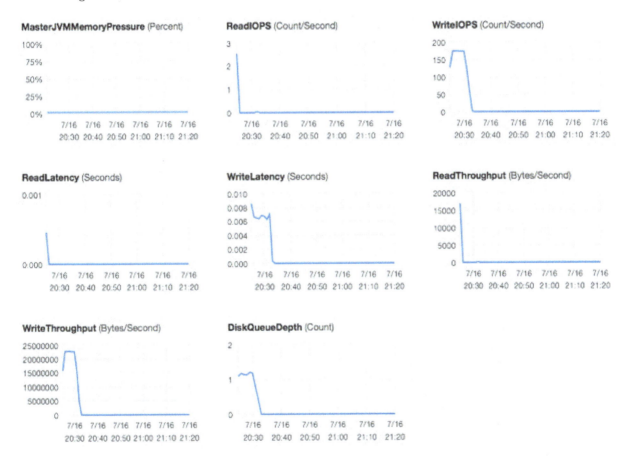

Auditing Amazon Elasticsearch Service Domains with AWS CloudTrail

Amazon Elasticsearch Service (Amazon ES) is integrated with AWS CloudTrail, a service that logs all AWS API calls made by, or on behalf of, your AWS account. The log files are delivered to an Amazon S3 bucket that you create and configure with a bucket policy that grants CloudTrail permissions to write log files to the bucket. CloudTrail captures all Amazon ES configuration service API calls, including those submitted by the Amazon Elasticsearch Service console.

You can use the information collected by CloudTrail to monitor activity for your search domains. You can determine the request that was made to Amazon ES, the source IP address from which the request was made, who made the request, and when it was made. To learn more about CloudTrail, including how to configure and enable it, see the AWS CloudTrail User Guide. To learn more about how to create and configure an S3 bucket for CloudTrail, see Amazon S3 Bucket Policy for CloudTrail.

Note
CloudTrail logs events only for configuration-related API calls to Amazon Elasticsearch Service. Data-related APIs are not logged.

The following example shows a sample CloudTrail log for Amazon ES:

```
1  {
2      "Records": [
3          {
4              "eventVersion": "1.03",
5              "userIdentity": {
6                  "type": "Root",
7                  "principalId": "000000000000",
8                  "arn": "arn:aws:iam::000000000000:root",
9                  "accountId": "000000000000",
10                 "accessKeyId": "A****************A"
11             },
12             "eventTime": "2015-07-31T21:28:06Z",
13             "eventSource": "es.amazonaws.com",
14             "eventName": "CreateElasticsearchDomain",
15             "awsRegion": "us-east-1",
16             "sourceIPAddress": "Your IP",
17             "userAgent": "es/test",
18             "requestParameters": {
19                 "elasticsearchClusterConfig": {},
20                 "snapshotOptions": {
21                     "automatedSnapshotStartHour": "0"
22                 },
23                 "domainName": "your-domain-name",
24                 "eBSOptions": {
25                     "eBSEnabled": false
26                 }
27             },
28             "responseElements": {
29                 "domainStatus": {
30                     "created": true,
31                     "processing": true,
32                     "aRN": "arn:aws:es:us-east-1:000000000000:domain/your-domain-name",
33                     "domainId": "000000000000/your-domain-name",
34                     "elasticsearchClusterConfig": {
35                         "zoneAwarenessEnabled": false,
36                         "instanceType": "m3.medium.elasticsearch",
37                         "dedicatedMasterEnabled": false,
38                         "instanceCount": 1
39                     },
40                     "deleted": false,
41                     "domainName": "your-domain-name",
42                     "domainVersion": "1.5",
43                     "accessPolicies": "",
44                     "advancedOptions": {
45                         "rest.action.multi.allow_explicit_index": "true"
46                     },
47                     "snapshotOptions": {
48                         "automatedSnapshotStartHour": "0"
49                     },
50                     "eBSOptions": {
51                         "eBSEnabled": false
52                     }
53                 }
```

```
54              },
55              "requestID": "05dbfc84-37cb-11e5-a2cd-fbc77a4aae72",
56              "eventID": "c21da94e-f5ed-41a4-8703-9a5f49e2ec85",
57              "eventType": "AwsApiCall",
58              "recipientAccountId": "000000000000"
59          }
60      ]
61  }
```

Amazon Elasticsearch Service Information in CloudTrail

When CloudTrail logging is enabled in your AWS account, API calls made to Amazon Elasticsearch Service (Amazon ES) operations are tracked in log files. Amazon ES records are written together with other AWS service records in a log file. CloudTrail determines when to create and write to a new file based on a time period and file size.

All Amazon ES configuration service operations are logged. For example, calls to CreateElasticsearchDomain, DescribeElasticsearchDomain, and UpdateElasticsearchDomainConfig generate entries in the CloudTrail log files. Every log entry contains information about who generated the request. The user identity information in the log helps you determine whether the request was made with root or IAM user credentials, with temporary security credentials for a role or federated user, or by another AWS service. For more information, see the userIdentity field in the CloudTrail Event Reference.

You can store your log files in your bucket indefinitely, or you can define Amazon S3 lifecycle rules to archive or delete log files automatically. By default, your log files are encrypted using Amazon S3 server-side encryption (SSE). You can choose to have CloudTrail publish Amazon SNS notifications when new log files are delivered if you want to take quick action upon log file delivery. For more information, see Configuring Amazon SNS Notifications for CloudTrail. You also can aggregate Amazon ES log files from multiple AWS Regions and multiple AWS accounts into a single Amazon S3 bucket. For more information, see Receiving CloudTrail Log Files from Multiple Regions.

Understanding Amazon Elasticsearch Service Log File Entries

CloudTrail log files contain one or more log entries where each entry is made up of multiple JSON-formatted events. A log entry represents a single request from any source and includes information about the requested action, any parameters, the date and time of the action, and so on. The log entries are not guaranteed to be in any particular order—they are not an ordered stack trace of the public API calls. CloudTrail log files include events for all AWS API calls for your AWS account, not just calls to the Amazon ES configuration service API. However, you can read the log files and scan for eventSource es.amazonaws.com. The eventName element contains the name of the configuration service action that was called.

Tagging Amazon Elasticsearch Service Domains

You can use Amazon ES tags to add metadata to your Amazon ES domains. AWS does not apply any semantic meaning to your tags. Tags are interpreted strictly as character strings. All tags have the following elements.

Tag Element	Description
Tag key	The tag key is the required name of the tag. Tag keys must be unique for the Amazon ES domain to which they are attached. For a list of basic restrictions on tag keys and values, see User-Defined Tag Restrictions.
Tag value	The tag value is an optional string value of the tag. Tag values can be null and do not have to be unique in a tag set. For example, you can have a key-value pair in a tag set of project/Trinity and cost-center/Trinity. For a list of basic restrictions on tag keys and values, see User-Defined Tag Restrictions.

Each Amazon ES domain has a tag set, which contains all the tags that are assigned to that Amazon ES domain. AWS does not automatically set any tags on Amazon ES domains. A tag set can contain up to 50 tags, or it can be empty. If you add a tag to an Amazon ES domain that has the same key as an existing tag for a resource, the new value overwrites the old value.

You can use these tags to track costs by grouping expenses for similarly tagged resources. An Amazon ES domain tag is a name-value pair that you define and associate with an Amazon ES domain. The name is referred to as the *key*. You can use tags to assign arbitrary information to an Amazon ES domain. A tag key could be used, for example, to define a category, and the tag value could be an item in that category. For example, you could define a tag key of "project" and a tag value of "Salix," indicating that the Amazon ES domain is assigned to the Salix project. You could also use tags to designate Amazon ES domains as being used for test or production by using a key such as environment=test or environment=production. We recommend that you use a consistent set of tag keys to make it easier to track metadata that is associated with Amazon ES domains.

You also can use tags to organize your AWS bill to reflect your own cost structure. To do this, sign up to get your AWS account bill with tag key values included. Then, organize your billing information according to resources with the same tag key values to see the cost of combined resources. For example, you can tag several Amazon ES domains with key-value pairs, and then organize your billing information to see the total cost for each domain across several services. For more information, see Using Cost Allocation Tags in the *AWS Billing and Cost Management* documentation.

Note
Tags are cached for authorization purposes. Because of this, additions and updates to tags on Amazon ES domains might take several minutes before they are available.

Working with Tags (Console)

Use the following procedure to create a resource tag.

To create a tag (console)

1. Go to https://aws.amazon.com, and then choose **Sign In to the Console**.

2. Under **Analytics**, choose **Elasticsearch Service**.

3. In the navigation pane, choose your Amazon ES domain.

4. On the domain dashboard, choose **Manage tags**.

5. In the **Key** column, type a tag key.

6. (Optional) In the **Value** column, type a tag value.

7. Choose **Submit**.

To delete a tag (console)

Use the following procedure to delete a resource tag.

1. Go to https://aws.amazon.com, and then choose **Sign In to the Console**.

2. Under **Analytics**, choose **Elasticsearch Service**.

3. In the navigation pane, choose your Amazon ES domain.

4. On the domain dashboard, choose **Manage tags**.

5. Next to the tag that you want to delete, choose **Remove**.

6. Choose **Submit**.

For more information about using the console to work with tags, see Working with Tag Editor in the *AWS Management Console Getting Started Guide*.

Working with Tags (AWS CLI)

You can create resource tags using the AWS CLI with the --add-tags command.

Syntax

```
add-tags --arn=<domain_arn> --tag-list Key=<key>,Value=<value>
```

Parameter	Description
--arn	Amazon resource name for the Amazon ES domain to which the tag is attached.
--tag-list	Set of space-separated key-value pairs in the following format: Key=,Value=

Example

The following example creates two tags for the *logs* domain:

```
1 aws es add-tags --arn arn:aws:es:us-east-1:379931976431:domain/logs --tag-list Key=service,Value
    =Elasticsearch Key=instances,Value=m3.2xlarge
```

You can remove tags from an Amazon ES domain using the remove-tags command.

** Syntax **

```
remove-tags --arn=<domain_arn> --tag-keys Key=<key>,Value=<value>
```

Parameter	Description
--arn	Amazon Resource Name (ARN) for the Amazon ES domain to which the tag is attached.
--tag-keys	Set of space-separated key-value pairs that you want to remove from the Amazon ES domain.

Example

The following example removes two tags from the *logs* domain that were created in the preceding example:

```
1 aws es remove-tags --arn arn:aws:es:us-east-1:379931976431:domain/logs --tag-keys service
    instances
```

You can view the existing tags for an Amazon ES domain with the list-tags command:

Syntax

```
list-tags --arn=<domain_arn>
```

Parameter	Description
--arn	Amazon Resource Name (ARN) for the Amazon ES domain to which the tags are attached.

Example

The following example lists all resource tags for the *logs* domain:

```
1 aws es list-tags --arn arn:aws:es:us-east-1:379931976431:domain/logs
```

Working with Tags (AWS SDKs)

The AWS SDKs (except the Android and iOS SDKs) support all the actions defined in the Amazon ES Configuration API Reference, including the **AddTags**, **ListTags**, and **RemoveTags** operations. For more information about installing and using the AWS SDKs, see AWS Software Development Kits.

Indexing Data in Amazon Elasticsearch Service

Because Elasticsearch uses a REST API, numerous methods exist for indexing documents. You can use standard clients like curl or any programming language that can send HTTP requests. To further simplify the process of interacting with it, Elasticsearch has clients for many programming languages. Advanced users can skip directly to Programmatic Indexing.

For situations in which new data arrives incrementally (for example, customer orders from a small business), you might use the `_index` API to index documents as they arrive. For situations in which the flow of data is less frequent (for example, weekly updates to a marketing website), you might prefer to generate a file and send it to the `_bulk` API. For large numbers of documents, lumping requests together and using the `_bulk` API offers superior performance. If your documents are enormous, however, you might need to index them individually using the `_index` API.

For information about integrating data from other AWS services, see Loading Streaming Data into Amazon Elasticsearch Service.

Introduction to Indexing

Before you can search data, you must *index* it. Indexing is the method by which search engines organize data for fast retrieval. The resulting structure is called, fittingly, an index.

In Elasticsearch, the basic unit of data is a JSON *document*. Within an index, Elasticsearch organizes documents into *types* (arbitrary data categories that you define) and identifies them using a unique *ID*.

A request to the `_index` API looks like the following:

```
1 PUT elasticsearch_domain/index/type/id
2 { "A JSON": "document" }
```

A request to the `_bulk` API looks a little different, because you specify the index, type, and ID in the bulk data:

```
1 POST elasticsearch_domain/_bulk
2 { "index": { "_index" : "index", "_type" : "type", "_id" : "id" } }
3 { "A JSON": "document" }
```

Bulk data must conform to a specific format, which requires a newline character (\n) at the end of every line, including the last line. This is the basic format:

```
1 action_and_metadata\n
2 optional_document\n
3 action_and_metadata\n
4 optional_document\n
5 ...
```

For a short sample file, see Step 2: Upload Data to an Amazon ES Domain for Indexing.

Elasticsearch features automatic index creation when you add a document to an index that doesn't already exist. It also features automatic ID generation if you don't specify an ID in the request. This simple example automatically creates the `movies` index, establishes the document type of `movie`, indexes the document, and assigns it a unique ID:

```
1 curl -XPOST elasticsearch_domain/movies/movie -d '{"title": "Spirited Away"}' -H 'Content-Type:
    application/json'
```

Important
To use automatic ID generation, you must use the `POST` method instead of `PUT`.

To verify that the document exists, you can perform the following search:

```
1 curl -XGET elasticsearch_domain/movies/_search?pretty
```

The response should contain the following:

```
1  "hits" : {
2    "total" : 1,
3    "max_score" : 1.0,
4    "hits" : [
5      {
6        "_index" : "movies",
7        "_type" : "movie",
8        "_id" : "AV4WaTnYxBoJaZkSFeX9",
9        "_score" : 1.0,
10       "_source" : {
11         "title" : "Spirited Away"
12       }
13     }
14   ]
15 }
```

Automatic ID generation has a clear downside: because the indexing code didn't specify a document ID, you can't easily update the document at a later time. To specify an ID of 7, use the following request:

```
1 curl -XPUT elasticsearch_domain/movies/movie/7 -d '{"title": "Spirited Away"}' -H 'Content-Type:
    application/json'
```

Indices default to five primary shards and one replica. If you want to specify non-default settings, create the index before adding documents:

```
1 curl -XPUT elasticsearch_domain/movies -d '{"settings": {"number_of_shards": 6, "
    number_of_replicas": 2}}' -H 'Content-Type: application/json'
```

Note
Requests using curl are unauthenticated and rely on an IP-based access policy. For examples of signed requests, see Programmatic Indexing.

Elasticsearch indices have the following naming restrictions:

- All letters must be lowercase.
- Index names cannot begin with _ or -.
- Index names cannot contain spaces, commas, ", *, +, /, \, |, ?, >, or <.

Programmatic Indexing

This section includes examples of how to use popular Elasticsearch clients and standard HTTP requests to index documents.

Python

You can install elasticsearch-py, the official Elasticsearch client for Python, using pip. Instead of the client, you might prefer requests. The requests-aws4auth package simplifies the authentication process, but is not strictly required. From the terminal, run the following commands:

```
1 pip install elasticsearch
2 pip install requests
3 pip install requests-aws4auth
```

The following sample code establishes a secure connection to the specified Amazon ES domain and indexes a single document using the _index API. You must provide values for AWS_ACCESS_KEY, AWS_SECRET_KEY, region, and host:

```
1 from elasticsearch import Elasticsearch, RequestsHttpConnection
2 from requests_aws4auth import AWS4Auth
3
4 AWS_ACCESS_KEY = ''
5 AWS_SECRET_KEY = ''
6 region = '' # For example, us-east-1
7 service = 'es'
8
9 awsauth = AWS4Auth(AWS_ACCESS_KEY, AWS_SECRET_KEY, region, service)
10
11 host = '' # For example, my-test-domain.us-east-1.es.amazonaws.com
12
13 es = Elasticsearch(
14     hosts = [{'host': host, 'port': 443}],
15     http_auth = awsauth,
16     use_ssl = True,
17     verify_certs = True,
18     connection_class = RequestsHttpConnection
19 )
20
21 document = {
22     "title": "Moneyball",
23     "director": "Bennett Miller",
24     "year": "2011"
25 }
26
27 es.index(index="movies", doc_type="movie", id="5", body=document)
28
29 print(es.get(index="movies", doc_type="movie", id="5"))
```

Important
These samples are for testing purposes. We do not recommend storing your AWS access key and AWS secret key directly in code.

If you don't want to use the **elasticsearch.py** client, you can just make standard HTTP requests. This sample creates a new index with seven shards and two replicas:

```
1 import requests
2 from requests_aws4auth import AWS4Auth
3
4 AWS_ACCESS_KEY = ''
5 AWS_SECRET_KEY = ''
6 region = '' # For example, us-east-1
7 service = 'es'
8
9 awsauth = AWS4Auth(AWS_ACCESS_KEY, AWS_SECRET_KEY, region, service)
10
11 host = '' # The domain with https:// and trailing slash. For example, https://my-test-domain.us-
      east-1.es.amazonaws.com/
12 path = 'my-index' # the Elasticsearch API endpoint
13
14 url = host + path
15
16 # The JSON body to accompany the request (if necessary)
17 payload = {
18     "settings" : {
19         "number_of_shards" : 7,
20         "number_of_replicas" : 2
21     }
22 }
23
24 r = requests.put(url, auth=awsauth, json=payload) # requests.get, post, and delete have similar
      syntax
25
26 print(r.text)
```

This next example uses the Beautiful Soup library to help build a bulk file from a local directory of HTML files. Using the same client as the first example, you can send the file to the `_bulk` API for indexing. You could use this code as the basis for adding search functionality to a website:

```
1 from bs4 import BeautifulSoup
2 from elasticsearch import Elasticsearch, RequestsHttpConnection
3 from requests_aws4auth import AWS4Auth
4 import glob
5 import json
6
7 bulk_file = ''
8 id = 1
9
10 # This loop iterates through all HTML files in the current directory and
11 # indexes two things: the contents of the first h1 tag and all other text.
12
13 for html_file in glob.glob('*.htm'):
14
15     with open(html_file) as f:
16         soup = BeautifulSoup(f, 'html.parser')
17
18     title = soup.h1.string
19     body = soup.get_text(" ", strip=True)
20     # If get_text() is too noisy, you can do further processing on the string.
21
22     index = { 'title': title, 'body': body, 'link': html_file }
```

```
23    # If running this script on a website, you probably need to prepend the URL and path to
         html_file.
24
25    # The action_and_metadata portion of the bulk file
26    bulk_file += '{ "index" : { "_index" : "site", "_type" : "page", "_id" : "' + str(id) + '" }
         }\n'
27
28    # The optional_document portion of the bulk file
29    bulk_file += json.dumps(index) + '\n'
30
31    id += 1
32
33 AWS_ACCESS_KEY = ''
34 AWS_SECRET_KEY = ''
35 region = '' # For example, us-east-1
36 service = 'es'
37
38 awsauth = AWS4Auth(AWS_ACCESS_KEY, AWS_SECRET_KEY, region, service)
39
40 host = '' # For example, my-test-domain.us-east-1.es.amazonaws.com
41
42 es = Elasticsearch(
43     hosts = [{'host': host, 'port': 443}],
44     http_auth = awsauth,
45     use_ssl = True,
46     verify_certs = True,
47     connection_class = RequestsHttpConnection
48 )
49
50 es.bulk(bulk_file)
51
52 print(es.search(q='some test query'))
```

Java

This first example uses the Elasticsearch low-level Java REST Client, which you must configure as a dependency. The request is unauthenticated and relies on an IP-based access policy. You must provide a value for host:

```
1  import java.io.IOException;
2  import java.util.Collections;
3
4  import org.elasticsearch.client.Response;
5  import org.elasticsearch.client.RestClient;
6  import org.elasticsearch.client.http.entity.ContentType;
7  import org.elasticsearch.client.http.HttpEntity;
8  import org.elasticsearch.client.http.HttpHost;
9  import org.elasticsearch.client.http.nio.entity.NStringEntity;
10
11 public class JavaRestClientExample {
12
13     public static void main(String[] args) throws IOException {
14
15         String host = ""; // For example, my-test-domain.us-east-1.es.amazonaws.com
16         String index = "movies";
```

```
17        String type = "movie";
18        String id = "6";
19
20        String json = "{" + "\"title\":\"Walk the Line\"," + "\"director\":\"James Mangold\"," +
              "\"year\":\"2005\""
21            + "}";
22
23        RestClient client = RestClient.builder(new HttpHost(host, 443, "https")).build();
24
25        HttpEntity entity = new NStringEntity(json, ContentType.APPLICATION_JSON);
26
27        Response response = client.performRequest("PUT", "/" + index + "/" + type + "/" + id,
28            Collections.<String, String>emptyMap(), entity);
29
30        System.out.println(response.toString());
31    }
32 }
```

The easiest way of sending a signed request is to use the AWS Request Signing Interceptor. The repository contains some samples to help you get started. The following example uses the Elasticsearch low-level Java REST client to perform two unrelated actions: registering a snapshot repository and indexing a document.

```
1  import org.apache.http.HttpEntity;
2  import org.apache.http.HttpHost;
3  import org.apache.http.HttpRequestInterceptor;
4  import org.apache.http.entity.ContentType;
5  import org.apache.http.nio.entity.NStringEntity;
6  import org.elasticsearch.client.Response;
7  import org.elasticsearch.client.RestClient;
8  import com.amazonaws.auth.AWS4Signer;
9  import com.amazonaws.auth.AWSCredentialsProvider;
10 import com.amazonaws.auth.DefaultAWSCredentialsProviderChain;
11 import com.amazonaws.http.AWSRequestSigningApacheInterceptor;
12 import java.io.IOException;
13 import java.util.Collections;
14 import java.util.Map;
15
16 public class AmazonElasticsearchServiceSample {
17
18     private static String serviceName = "es";
19     private static String region = "us-west-1";
20     private static String aesEndpoint = "https://domain.us-west-1.es.amazonaws.com";
21
22     private static String payload = "{ \"type\": \"s3\", \"settings\": { \"bucket\": \"your-
            bucket\", \"region\": \"us-west-1\", \"role_arn\": \"arn:aws:iam::123456789012:role/
            TheServiceRole\" } }";
23     private static String snapshotPath = "/_snapshot/my-snapshot-repo";
24
25     private static String sampleDocument = "{" + "\"title\":\"Walk the Line\"," + "\"director
            \":\"James Mangold\"," + "\"year\":\"2005\"}";
26     private static String indexingPath = "/my-index/my-type";
27
28     static final AWSCredentialsProvider credentialsProvider = new
            DefaultAWSCredentialsProviderChain();
29
```

```
30    public static void main(String[] args) throws IOException {
31        RestClient esClient = esClient(serviceName, region);
32
33        // Register a snapshot repository
34        HttpEntity entity = new NStringEntity(payload, ContentType.APPLICATION_JSON);
35        Map<String, String> params = Collections.emptyMap();
36        Response response = esClient.performRequest("PUT", snapshotPath, params, entity);
37        System.out.println(response.toString());
38
39        // Index a document
40        entity = new NStringEntity(sampleDocument, ContentType.APPLICATION_JSON);
41        String id = "1";
42        response = esClient.performRequest("PUT", indexingPath + "/" + id, params, entity);
43        System.out.println(response.toString());
44    }
45
46    // Adds the interceptor to the ES REST client
47    public static RestClient esClient(String serviceName, String region) {
48        AWS4Signer signer = new AWS4Signer();
49        signer.setServiceName(serviceName);
50        signer.setRegionName(region);
51        HttpRequestInterceptor interceptor = new AWSRequestSigningApacheInterceptor(serviceName,
                 signer, credentialsProvider);
52        return RestClient.builder(HttpHost.create(aesEndpoint)).setHttpClientConfigCallback(hacb
                 -> hacb.addInterceptorLast(interceptor)).build();
53    }
54 }
```

Ruby

This first example uses the Elasticsearch Ruby client and Faraday middleware to perform the request signing. From the terminal, run the following commands:

```
1 gem install elasticsearch
2 gem install faraday_middleware-aws-sigv4
```

This sample code creates a new Elasticsearch client, configures Faraday middleware to sign requests, and indexes a single document. You must provide values for host and region.

```
1 require 'elasticsearch'
2 require 'faraday_middleware/aws_sigv4'
3
4 host = '' # e.g. https://my-domain.region.es.com
5 index = 'ruby-index'
6 type = 'ruby-type'
7 id = '1'
8 document = {
9   year: 2007,
10   title: '5 Centimeters per Second',
11   info: {
12     plot: 'Told in three interconnected segments, we follow a young man named Takaki through his
             life.',
13     rating: 7.7
14   }
```

```
15 }
16
17 region = '' # e.g. us-west-1
18 service = 'es'
19
20 client = Elasticsearch::Client.new(url: host) do |f|
21   f.request :aws_sigv4,
22     service: service,
23     region: region,
24     access_key_id: ENV['AWS_ACCESS_KEY_ID'],
25     secret_access_key: ENV['AWS_SECRET_ACCESS_KEY'],
26     session_token: ENV['AWS_SESSION_TOKEN'] # optional
27 end
28
29 puts client.index index: index, type: type, id: id, body: document
```

If your credentials don't work, export them at the terminal using the following commands:

```
1 export AWS_ACCESS_KEY_ID="your-access-key"
2 export AWS_SECRET_ACCESS_KEY="your-secret-key"
3 export AWS_SESSION_TOKEN=""your-session-token"
```

This next example uses the AWS SDK for Ruby and standard Ruby libraries to send a signed HTTP request. Like the first example, it indexes a single document. You must provide values for host and region.

```
1 require 'aws-sdk-elasticsearchservice'
2
3 host = '' # e.g. https://my-domain.region.es.com
4 index = 'ruby-index'
5 type = 'ruby-type'
6 id = '2'
7 document = {
8   year: 2007,
9   title: '5 Centimeters per Second',
10   info: {
11     plot: 'Told in three interconnected segments, we follow a young man named Takaki through his
           life.',
12     rating: 7.7
13   }
14 }
15
16 service = 'es'
17 region = '' # e.g. us-west-1
18
19 signer = Aws::Sigv4::Signer.new(
20   service: service,
21   region: region,
22   access_key_id: ENV['AWS_ACCESS_KEY_ID'],
23   secret_access_key: ENV['AWS_SECRET_ACCESS_KEY'],
24   session_token: ENV['AWS_SESSION_TOKEN']
25 )
26
27 signature = signer.sign_request(
28   http_method: 'PUT',
29   url: host + '/' + index + '/' + type + '/' + id,
30   body: document.to_json
```

```
31 )
32
33 uri = URI(host + '/' + index + '/' + type + '/' + id)
34
35 Net::HTTP.start(uri.host, uri.port, :use_ssl => true) do |http|
36   request = Net::HTTP::Put.new uri
37   request.body = document.to_json
38   request['Host'] = signature.headers['host']
39   request['X-Amz-Date'] = signature.headers['x-amz-date']
40   request['X-Amz-Security-Token'] = signature.headers['x-amz-security-token']
41   request['X-Amz-Content-Sha256']= signature.headers['x-amz-content-sha256']
42   request['Authorization'] = signature.headers['authorization']
43   request['Content-Type'] = 'application/json'
44   response = http.request request
45   puts response.body
46 end
```

Node

This example uses the SDK for JavaScript in Node.js. From the terminal, run the following commands:

```
1 npm install aws-sdk
```

This sample code indexes a single document. You must provide values for **region** and **domain**.

```
1 var AWS = require('aws-sdk');
2
3 var region = ''; // e.g. us-west-1
4 var domain = ''; // e.g. search-domain.region.es.amazonaws.com
5 var index = 'node-test';
6 var type = 'node-type';
7 var id = '1';
8 var json = {
9   "title": "Moneyball",
10   "director": "Bennett Miller",
11   "year": "2011"
12 }
13
14 indexDocument(json);
15
16 function indexDocument(document) {
17   var endpoint = new AWS.Endpoint(domain);
18   var request = new AWS.HttpRequest(endpoint, region);
19
20   request.method = 'PUT';
21   request.path += index + '/' + type + '/' + id;
22   request.body = JSON.stringify(document);
23   request.headers['host'] = domain;
24   request.headers['Content-Type'] = 'application/json';
25
26   var credentials = new AWS.EnvironmentCredentials('AWS');
27   var signer = new AWS.Signers.V4(request, 'es');
28   signer.addAuthorization(credentials, new Date());
29
```

```
30    var client = new AWS.HttpClient();
31    client.handleRequest(request, null, function(response) {
32      console.log(response.statusCode + ' ' + response.statusMessage);
33      var responseBody = '';
34      response.on('data', function (chunk) {
35        responseBody += chunk;
36      });
37      response.on('end', function (chunk) {
38        console.log('Response body: ' + responseBody);
39      });
40    }, function(error) {
41      console.log('Error: ' + error);
42    });
43  }
```

If your credentials don't work, export them at the terminal using the following commands:

```
1  export AWS_ACCESS_KEY_ID="your-access-key"
2  export AWS_SECRET_ACCESS_KEY="your-secret-key"
3  export AWS_SESSION_TOKEN=""your-session-token"
```

Loading Streaming Data into Amazon Elasticsearch Service

You can load streaming data into your Amazon Elasticsearch Service domain from many different sources. Some sources, like Amazon Kinesis Firehose and Amazon CloudWatch Logs, have built-in support for Amazon ES. Others, like Amazon S3, Amazon Kinesis, and Amazon DynamoDB, use AWS Lambda functions as event handlers. The Lambda functions respond to new data by processing it and streaming it to your domain.

Note
Lambda supports several popular programming languages and is available in most AWS Regions. For more information, see Building Lambda Functions in the *AWS Lambda Developer Guide* and AWS Lambda Regions in the *AWS General Reference*.

Topics

- Loading Streaming Data into Amazon ES from Amazon S3
- Loading Streaming Data into Amazon ES from Amazon Kinesis
- Loading Streaming Data into Amazon ES from Amazon DynamoDB
- Loading Streaming Data into Amazon ES from Amazon Kinesis Firehose
- Loading Streaming Data into Amazon ES from Amazon CloudWatch
- Loading Data into Amazon ES from AWS IoT

Loading Streaming Data into Amazon ES from Amazon S3

You can use Lambda to send data to your Amazon ES domain from Amazon S3. New data that arrives in an S3 bucket triggers an event notification to Lambda, which then runs your custom code to perform the indexing.

This method of streaming data is extremely flexible. You can index object metadata, or if the object is plaintext, parse and index some elements of the object body. This section includes some unsophisticated Python sample code that uses regular expressions to parse a log file and index the matches.

Tip
For more robust code in Node.js, see amazon-elasticsearch-lambda-samples on GitHub. Some Lambda blueprints also contain useful parsing examples.

Prerequisites

Before proceeding, you must have the following resources.

Prerequisite	Description
Amazon S3 Bucket	For more information, see Creating a Bucket in the Amazon Simple Storage Service Getting Started Guide. The bucket must reside in the same region as your Amazon ES domain.
Amazon ES Domain	The destination for data after your Lambda function processes it. For more information, see Creating Amazon ES Domains.

Creating the Lambda Deployment Package

Deployment packages are ZIP or JAR files that contain your code and its dependencies. This section includes Python sample code. For other programming languages, see Creating a Deployment Package in the *AWS Lambda Developer Guide*.

1. Create a directory. In this sample, we use the name `s3-to-es`.

2. Create a file in the directory named `sample.py`:

```
1  import boto3
2  import re
3  import requests
4  from requests_aws4auth import AWS4Auth
5
6  region = '' # e.g. us-west-1
7  service = 'es'
8  credentials = boto3.Session().get_credentials()
9  awsauth = AWS4Auth(credentials.access_key, credentials.secret_key, region, service,
       session_token=credentials.token)
10
11 host = '' # the Amazon ES domain, including https://
12 index = 'lambda-s3-index'
13 type = 'lambda-type'
14 url = host + '/' + index + '/' + type
15
16 headers = { "Content-Type": "application/json" }
17
18 s3 = boto3.client('s3')
19
20 # Regular expressions used to parse some simple log lines
21 ip_pattern = re.compile('(\d+\.\d+\.\d+\.\d+)')
22 time_pattern = re.compile('\[(\d+\/\w\w\w\/\d\d\d\d:\d\d:\d\d:\d\d\s-\d\d\d\d)\]')
23 message_pattern = re.compile('\"(.+)\"')
24
25 # Lambda execution starts here
26 def handler(event, context):
27     for record in event['Records']:
28
29         # Get the bucket name and key for the new file
30         bucket = record['s3']['bucket']['name']
31         key = record['s3']['object']['key']
32
33         # Get, read, and split the file into lines
34         obj = s3.get_object(Bucket=bucket, Key=key)
35         body = obj['Body'].read()
36         lines = body.splitlines()
37
38         # Match the regular expressions to each line and index the JSON
39         for line in lines:
40             ip = ip_pattern.search(line).group(1)
41             timestamp = time_pattern.search(line).group(1)
42             message = message_pattern.search(line).group(1)
43
44             document = { "ip": ip, "timestamp": timestamp, "message": message }
45             r = requests.post(url, auth=awsauth, json=document, headers=headers)
```

Edit the variables for `region` and `host`.

3. Install dependencies:

```
1  cd s3-to-es
2  pip install requests -t .
```

```
3 pip install requests_aws4auth -t .
```

All Lambda execution environments have Boto3 installed, so you don't need to include it in your deployment package. **Tip**
If you use macOS, these commands might not work properly. As a workaround, add a file named `setup.cfg` to the `eslambda` directory:

```
1 [install]
2 prefix=
```

4. Package the application code and dependencies:

```
1 zip -r lambda.zip *
```

Creating the Lambda Function

After you create the deployment package, you can create the Lambda function. When you create a function, choose a name, runtime (for example, Python 2.7), and IAM role. The IAM role defines the permissions for your function. For detailed instructions, see Create a Simple Lambda Function in the *AWS Lambda Developer Guide*.

This example assumes that you are using the console. Choose Python 2.7 and a role that has S3 read permissions and Amazon ES write permissions, as shown in the following screenshot.

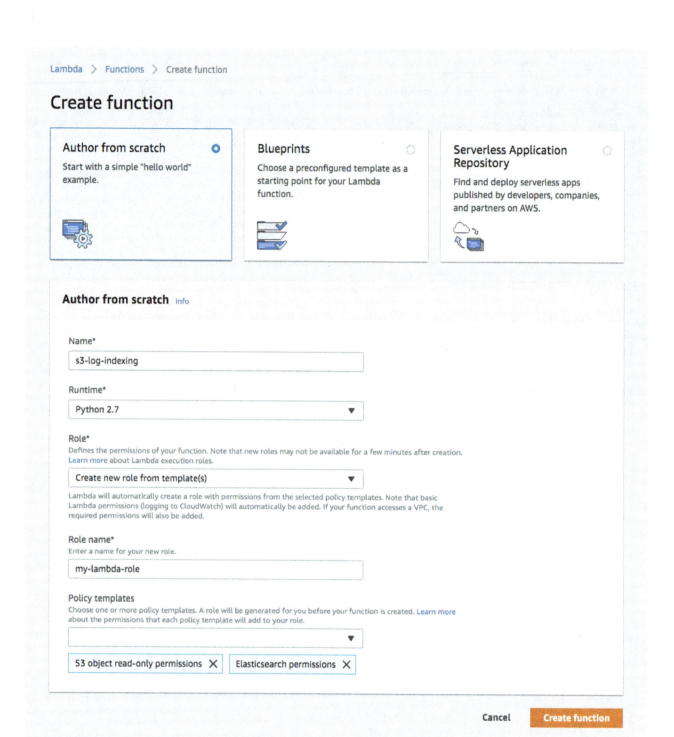

After you create the function, you must add a trigger. For this example, we want the code to execute whenever a log file arrives in an S3 bucket:

1. Choose S3.

2. Choose your bucket.

3. For **Event type**, choose **PUT**.

4. For **Prefix**, type `logs/`.

5. For **Filter pattern**, type `.log`.

6. Select **Enable trigger**.

7. Choose **Add**.

Finally, you can upload your deployment package:

1. For **Handler**, type `sample.handler`. This setting tells Lambda the file (`sample.py`) and method (`handler`) that it should execute after a trigger.

2. For **Code entry type**, choose **Upload a .ZIP file**, and then follow the prompts to upload your deployment package.

3. Choose **Save**.

At this point, you have a complete set of resources: a bucket for log files, a function that executes whenever a log file is added to the bucket, code that performs the parsing and indexing, and an Amazon ES domain for searching and visualization.

Testing the Lambda Function

After you create the function, you can test it by uploading a file to the Amazon S3 bucket. Create a file named `sample.log` using following sample log lines:

```
1  12.345.678.90 - [10/Oct/2000:13:55:36 -0700] "PUT /some-file.jpg"
2  12.345.678.91 - [10/Oct/2000:14:56:14 -0700] "GET /some-file.jpg"
```

Upload the file to the `logs` folder of your S3 bucket. For instructions, see Add an Object to a Bucket in the *Amazon Simple Storage Service Getting Started Guide*.

Then use the Amazon ES console or Kibana to verify that the `lambda-s3-index` index contains two documents. You can also make a standard search request:

```
1  GET https://es-domain/lambda-index/_search?pretty
2  {
3    "hits" : {
4      "total" : 2,
5      "max_score" : 1.0,
6      "hits" : [
7        {
8          "_index" : "lambda-s3-index",
9          "_type" : "lambda-type",
10         "_id" : "vTYXaWIBJWV_TTkEuSDg",
11         "_score" : 1.0,
12         "_source" : {
13           "ip" : "12.345.678.91",
14           "message" : "GET /some-file.jpg",
15           "timestamp" : "10/Oct/2000:14:56:14 -0700"
16         }
17       },
18       {
19         "_index" : "lambda-s3-index",
20         "_type" : "lambda-type",
21         "_id" : "vjYmaWIBJWV_TTkEuCAB",
22         "_score" : 1.0,
23         "_source" : {
24           "ip" : "12.345.678.90",
25           "message" : "PUT /some-file.jpg",
26           "timestamp" : "10/Oct/2000:13:55:36 -0700"
```

```
27        }
28      }
29    ]
30  }
31 }
```

Loading Streaming Data into Amazon ES from Amazon Kinesis

You can load streaming data from Amazon Kinesis to Amazon ES. New data that arrives in the Amazon Kinesis data stream triggers an event notification to Lambda, which then runs your custom code to perform the indexing. This section includes some unsophisticated Python sample code. For more robust code in Node.js, see amazon-elasticsearch-lambda-samples on GitHub.

Prerequisites

Before proceeding, you must have the following resources.

Prerequisite	Description
Amazon Kinesis Data Stream	The event source for your Lambda function. For instructions about creating Amazon Kinesis data streams, see Kinesis Data Streams.
Amazon ES Domain	The destination for data after your Lambda function processes it. For more information, see Creating Amazon ES Domains.
IAM Role	This role must have basic Amazon ES, Kinesis, and Lambda permissions, such as the following: { "Version": "2012-10-17", "Statement": [{ "Effect": "Allow", "Action": ["es:ESHttpPost", "es:ESHttpPut", "logs:CreateLogGroup", "logs:CreateLogStream", "logs:PutLogEvents", "kinesis:GetShardIterator", "kinesis:GetRecords", "kinesis:DescribeStream", "kinesis:ListStreams"], "Resource": "*" }]} The role must have the following trust relationship: { "Version": "2012-10-17", "Statement": [{ "Effect": "Allow", "Principal": { "Service": "lambda.amazonaws.com" }, "Action": "sts:AssumeRole" }]} To learn more, see Creating IAM Roles in the *IAM User Guide*.

Creating the Lambda Function

Follow the instructions in Creating the Lambda Deployment Package, but create a directory named `kinesis-to-es` and use the following code for `sample.py`:

```
1 import base64
2 import boto3
3 import json
4 import requests
```

```
 5 from requests_aws4auth import AWS4Auth
 6
 7 region = '' # e.g. us-west-1
 8 service = 'es'
 9 credentials = boto3.Session().get_credentials()
10 awsauth = AWS4Auth(credentials.access_key, credentials.secret_key, region, service,
       session_token=credentials.token)
11
12 host = '' # the Amazon ES domain, including https://
13 index = 'lambda-kine-index'
14 type = 'lambda-kine-type'
15 url = host + '/' + index + '/' + type + '/'
16
17 headers = { "Content-Type": "application/json" }
18
19 def handler(event, context):
20     count = 0
21     for record in event['Records']:
22         id = record['eventID']
23         timestamp = record['kinesis']['approximateArrivalTimestamp']
24
25         # Kinesis data is base64-encoded, so decode here
26         message = base64.b64decode(record['kinesis']['data'])
27
28         # Create the JSON document
29         document = { "id": id, "timestamp": timestamp, "message": message }
30         # Index the document
31         r = requests.put(url + id, auth=awsauth, json=document, headers=headers)
32         count += 1
33     return 'Processed ' + str(count) + ' items.'
```

Edit the variables for **region** and **host**.

Use the following commands to install your dependencies:

```
1 cd kinesis-to-es
2 pip install requests -t .
3 pip install requests_aws4auth -t .
```

Then follow the instructions in Creating the Lambda Function, but specify the IAM role from Prerequisites and the following settings for the trigger:

- **Kinesis stream**: your Kinesis stream
- **Batch size**: 100
- **Starting position**: Trim horizon

To learn more, see Working with Amazon Kinesis Data Streams in the *Amazon Kinesis Data Streams Developer Guide*.

At this point, you have a complete set of resources: a Kinesis data stream, a function that executes after the stream receives new data and indexes that data, and an Amazon ES domain for searching and visualization.

Testing the Lambda Function

After you create the function, you can test it by adding a new record to the data stream using the AWS CLI:

```
1 aws kinesis put-record --stream-name es-test --data "My test data." --partition-key
    partitionKey1 --region us-west-1
```

Then use the Amazon ES console or Kibana to verify that `lambda-kine-index` contains a document. You can also use the following request:

```
1 GET https://es-domain/lambda-kine-index/_search
2 {
3   "hits" : [
4     {
5       "_index": "lambda-kine-index",
6       "_type": "lambda-kine-type",
7       "_id": "shardId-000000000000:49583511615762699495012960821421456686529436680496087042",
8       "_score": 1,
9       "_source": {
10         "timestamp": 1523648740.051,
11         "message": "My test data.",
12         "id": "shardId-000000000000:49583511615762699495012960821421456686529436680496087042"
13       }
14     }
15   ]
16 }
```

Loading Streaming Data into Amazon ES from Amazon DynamoDB

You can use AWS Lambda to send data to your Amazon ES domain from Amazon DynamoDB. New data that arrives in the database table triggers an event notification to Lambda, which then runs your custom code to perform the indexing.

Prerequisites

Before proceeding, you must have the following resources.

Prerequisite	Description
DynamoDB Table	The table contains your source data. For more information, see Basic Operations for Tables in the *Amazon DynamoDB Developer Guide.*The table must reside in the same region as your Amazon ES domain and have a stream set to **New image**. To learn more, see Enabling a Stream.
Amazon ES Domain	The destination for data after your Lambda function processes it. For more information, see Creating Amazon ES Domains.

Prerequisite	Description
IAM Role	This role must have basic Amazon ES, DynamoDB, and Lambda execution permissions, such as the following:{ "Version": "2012-10-17", "Statement": [{ "Effect": "Allow", "Action": ["es:ESHttpPost", "es:ESHttpPut", "dynamodb:DescribeStream", "dynamodb:GetRecords", "dynamodb:GetShardIterator", "dynamodb:ListStreams", "logs:CreateLogGroup", "logs:CreateLogStream", "logs:PutLogEvents"], "Resource": "*" }]}The role must have the following trust relationship:{ "Version": "2012-10-17", "Statement": [{ "Effect": "Allow", "Principal": { "Service": "lambda.amazonaws.com" }, "Action": "sts:AssumeRole" }]}To learn more, see Creating IAM Roles in the *IAM User Guide*.

Creating the Lambda Function

Follow the instructions in Creating the Lambda Deployment Package, but create a directory named `ddb-to-es` and use the following code for `sample.py`:

```python
import boto3
import requests
from requests_aws4auth import AWS4Auth

region = '' # e.g. us-east-1
service = 'es'
credentials = boto3.Session().get_credentials()
awsauth = AWS4Auth(credentials.access_key, credentials.secret_key, region, service,
    session_token=credentials.token)

host = '' # the Amazon ES domain, with https://
index = 'lambda-index'
type = 'lambda-type'
url = host + '/' + index + '/' + type + '/'

headers = { "Content-Type": "application/json" }

def handler(event, context):
    count = 0
    for record in event['Records']:
        # Get the primary key for use as the Elasticsearch ID
        id = record['dynamodb']['Keys']['id']['S']

        if record['eventName'] == 'REMOVE':
            r = requests.delete(url + id, auth=awsauth)
        else:
            document = record['dynamodb']['NewImage']
            r = requests.put(url + id, auth=awsauth, json=document, headers=headers)
        count += 1
```

```
29    return str(count) + ' records processed.'
```

Edit the variables for `region` and `host`.

Use the following commands to install your dependencies:

```
1 cd ddb-to-es
2 pip install requests -t .
3 pip install requests_aws4auth -t .
```

Then follow the instructions in Creating the Lambda Function, but specify the IAM role from Prerequisites and the following settings for the trigger:

- **Table**: your DynamoDB table
- **Batch size**: 100
- **Starting position**: Trim horizon

To learn more, see Processing New Items in a DynamoDB Table in the *Amazon DynamoDB Developer Guide*.

At this point, you have a complete set of resources: a DynamoDB table for your source data, a DynamoDB stream of changes to the table, a function that executes after your source data changes and indexes those changes, and an Amazon ES domain for searching and visualization.

Testing the Lambda Function

After you create the function, you can test it by adding a new item to the DynamoDB table using the AWS CLI:

```
1 aws dynamodb put-item --table-name es-test --item '{"director": {"S": "Kevin Costner"},"id": {"S
    ": "00001"},"title": {"S": "The Postman"}}' --region us-west-1
```

Then use the Amazon ES console or Kibana to verify that `lambda-index` contains a document. You can also use the following request:

```
1 GET https://es-domain/lambda-index/lambda-type/00001
2 {
3     "_index": "lambda-index",
4     "_type": "lambda-type",
5     "_id": "00001",
6     "_version": 1,
7     "found": true,
8     "_source": {
9         "director": {
10            "S": "Kevin Costner"
11        },
12        "id": {
13            "S": "00001"
14        },
15        "title": {
16            "S": "The Postman"
17        }
18    }
19 }
```

Loading Streaming Data into Amazon ES from Amazon Kinesis Firehose

Amazon Kinesis supports Amazon ES as a delivery destination. For instructions about how to load streaming data into Amazon ES, see Creating an Amazon Kinesis Firehose Delivery Stream and Choose Amazon ES for your destination in the *Amazon Kinesis Firehose Developer Guide*.

Before you load data into Amazon ES, you might need to perform transforms on the data. To learn more about using Lambda functions to perform this task, see Data Transformation in the *Amazon Kinesis Firehose Developer Guide*.

As you configure a delivery stream, Kinesis Firehose features a "one-click" IAM role that gives it the resource access it needs to send data to Amazon ES, back up data on Amazon S3, and transform data using Lambda. Because of the complexity involved in creating such a role manually, we recommend using the provided role.

Loading Streaming Data into Amazon ES from Amazon CloudWatch

You can load streaming data from CloudWatch Logs to your Amazon ES domain by using a CloudWatch Logs subscription. For information about Amazon CloudWatch subscriptions, see Real-time Processing of Log Data with Subscriptions. For configuration information, see Streaming CloudWatch Logs Data to Amazon Elasticsearch Service in the *Amazon CloudWatch Developer Guide*.

Loading Data into Amazon ES from AWS IoT

You can send data from AWS IoT using rules. To learn more, see Amazon ES Action in the *AWS IoT Developer Guide*.

Working with Amazon Elasticsearch Service Index Snapshots

Snapshots are backups of a cluster's data and state. They provide a convenient way to migrate data across Amazon Elasticsearch Service domains and recover from failure. The service supports restoring from snapshots taken on both Amazon ES domains and self-managed Elasticsearch clusters.

Amazon ES takes daily automated snapshots of the primary index shards in a domain, as described in Configuring Automatic Snapshots. The service stores up to 14 of these snapshots for no more than 30 days in a preconfigured Amazon S3 bucket at no additional charge to you. You can use these snapshots to restore the domain.

If the cluster enters red status and you don't correct the problem, you start to lose automated snapshots after 16 days. For troubleshooting steps, see Red Cluster Status.

You cannot use automated snapshots to migrate to new domains. Automated snapshots are read-only from within a given domain. For migrations, you must use manual snapshots stored in your own repository (an S3 bucket). Standard S3 charges apply to manual snapshots.

Tip
Some users find tools like Curator convenient for index and snapshot management. Curator offers advanced filtering functionality that can help simplify tasks on complex clusters.

Topics

- Manual Snapshot Prerequisites
- Registering a Manual Snapshot Repository
- Taking Manual Snapshots
- Restoring Snapshots

Manual Snapshot Prerequisites

To create index snapshots manually, you must work with IAM and Amazon S3. Verify that you have met the following prerequisites before you attempt to take a snapshot.

Prerequisite	Description
S3 bucket	Stores manual snapshots for your Amazon ES domain. Make a note of the bucket's Amazon Resource Name (ARN), which takes the form of `arn:aws:s3:::s3-bucket-name`. You need it in two places:[See the AWS documentation website for more details]For more information, see Create a Bucket in the *Amazon Simple Storage Service Getting Started Guide*.

Prerequisite	Description
IAM role	Delegates permissions to Amazon Elasticsearch Service. The rest of this document refers to this role as `TheServiceRole`. The trust relationship for the role must specify Amazon Elasticsearch Service in the `Principal` statement, as shown in the following example:{ "Version": "2012-10-17", "Statement": [{ "Sid": "", "Effect": "Allow", "Principal": { "Service": "es.amazonaws.com" }, "Action": "sts:AssumeRole" }]}The role must have the following policy attached to it: { "Version": "2012-10-17", "Statement": [{ "Action": ["s3:ListBucket"], "Effect": "Allow", "Resource": ["arn:aws:s3:::s3-bucket-name"] }, { "Action": ["s3:GetObject", "s3:PutObject", "s3:DeleteObject"], "Effect": "Allow", "Resource": ["arn:aws:s3:::s3-bucket-name/*"] }]} For more information, see Creating Customer Managed Policies and Attaching Managed Policies in the *IAM User Guide*.
Permissions	You must be able to assume the IAM role in order to register the snapshot repository. You also need access to the `es:ESHttpPut` action. A common way to provide access is to attach the following policy to your account: { "Version": "2012-10-17", "Statement": [{ "Effect": "Allow", "Action": "iam:PassRole", "Resource": "arn:aws:iam::123456789012:role/TheServiceRole" }, { "Effect": "Allow", "Action": "es:ESHttpPut", "Resource": "arn:awsregion:123456789012:domain/mydomain/*" }]} If your account does not have `iam:PassRole` permissions to assume `TheServiceRole`, you might encounter the following common error: $ python register-repo.py{"Message":"User: arn:aws:iam::123456789012:user/MyUserAccountis not authorized to perform: iam:PassRole on resource:arn:aws:iam::123456789012:role/TheServiceRole"}

Registering a Manual Snapshot Repository

You must register a snapshot repository with Amazon Elasticsearch Service before you can take manual index snapshots. This one-time operation requires that you sign your AWS request with credentials that are allowed to access `TheServiceRole`, as described in Manual Snapshot Prerequisites.

You can't use `curl` to perform this operation, because it doesn't support AWS request signing. Instead, use the sample Python client, Postman, or some other method to send a signed request to register the snapshot repository. The request takes the following form:

```
1  PUT https://elasticsearch-domain.region.es.amazonaws.com/_snapshot/my-snapshot-repo
2  {
3    "type": "s3",
4    "settings": {
5      "bucket": "s3-bucket-name",
6      "region": "region",
7      "role_arn": "arn:aws:iam::123456789012:role/TheServiceRole"
8    }
9  }
```

Registering a snapshot directory is a one-time operation, but to migrate from one domain to another, you must register the same snapshot repository on the old domain and the new domain. To enable server-side encryption with S3-managed keys for the snapshot repository, add `"server_side_encryption": true` to the `"settings"` JSON.

Important
If the S3 bucket is in the us-east-1 region, you need to use `"endpoint": "s3.amazonaws.com"` instead of `"region": "us-east-1"`.

If your domain resides within a VPC, your computer must be connected to the VPC in order for the request to successfully register the snapshot repository. Accessing a VPC varies by network configuration, but likely involves connecting to a VPN or corporate network. To check that you can reach the Amazon ES domain, navigate to `https://your-vpc-domain.region.es.amazonaws.com` in a web browser and verify that you receive the default JSON response.

Sample Python Client

Save the following sample Python code as a Python file, such as `register-repo.py`. The client requires the AWS SDK for Python (Boto 3), requests and requests-aws4auth packages. The client contains commented-out examples for other snapshot operations.

Tip
A Java-based code sample is available in Programmatic Indexing.

You must update the following variables in your code:

`region`
AWS region where you created the snapshot repository

`host`
Endpoint for your Amazon ES domain

`path`
Name of the snapshot repository

`payload`
Must include the name of the S3 bucket, region, and the ARN for the IAM role that you created in Manual Snapshot Prerequisites.

```
1  import boto3
2  import requests
3  from requests_aws4auth import AWS4Auth
4
5  host = '' # include https:// and trailing /
6  region = '' # e.g. us-west-1
7  service = 'es'
8  credentials = boto3.Session().get_credentials()
```

```
 9 awsauth = AWS4Auth(credentials.access_key, credentials.secret_key, region, service,
       session_token=credentials.token)
10
11 # Register repository
12
13 path = '_snapshot/my-snapshot-repo' # the Elasticsearch API endpoint
14 url = host + path
15
16 payload = {
17   "type": "s3",
18   "settings": {
19     "bucket": "s3-bucket-name",
20     "region": "us-west-1",
21     "role_arn": "arn:aws:iam::123456789012:role/TheServiceRole"
22   }
23 }
24
25 headers = {"Content-Type": "application/json"}
26
27 r = requests.put(url, auth=awsauth, json=payload, headers=headers)
28
29 print(r.status_code)
30 print(r.text)
31
32 # # Take snapshot
33 #
34 # path = '_snapshot/my-snapshot-repo/my-snapshot'
35 # url = host + path
36 #
37 # r = requests.put(url, auth=awsauth)
38 #
39 # print(r.text)
40 #
41 # # Delete index
42 #
43 # path = 'my-index'
44 # url = host + path
45 #
46 # r = requests.delete(url, auth=awsauth)
47 #
48 # print(r.text)
49 #
50 # # Restore snapshots (all indices)
51 #
52 # path = '_snapshot/my-snapshot-repo/my-snapshot/_restore'
53 # url = host + path
54 #
55 # r = requests.post(url, auth=awsauth)
56 #
57 # print(r.text)
58 #
59 # # Restore snapshot (one index)
60 #
61 # path = '_snapshot/my-snapshot-repo/my-snapshot/_restore'
```

```
62 # url = host + path
63 #
64 # payload = {"indices": "my-index"}
65 #
66 # headers = {"Content-Type": "application/json"}
67 #
68 # r = requests.post(url, auth=awsauth, json=payload, headers=headers)
69 #
70 # print(r.text)
```

Taking Manual Snapshots

You specify two pieces of information when you create a snapshot:

- Name of your snapshot repository
- Name for the snapshot

The examples in this chapter use curl, a common HTTP client, for convenience and brevity. If your access policies specify IAM users or roles, however, you must sign your snapshot requests. You can use the commented-out examples in the sample Python client to make signed HTTP requests to the same endpoints that the curl commands use.

To manually take a snapshot

- Run the following command to manually take a snapshot:

```
1 curl -XPUT 'elasticsearch-domain-endpoint/_snapshot/repository/snapshot-name'
```

Note
The time required to take a snapshot increases with the size of the Amazon ES domain. Long-running snapshot operations commonly encounter the following error: 504 GATEWAY_TIMEOUT. Typically, you can ignore these errors and wait for the operation to complete successfully. Use the following command to verify the state of all snapshots of your domain:

```
1 curl -XGET 'elasticsearch-domain-endpoint/_snapshot/repository/_all?pretty'
```

Restoring Snapshots

Warning
If you use index aliases, cease write requests to an alias (or switch the alias to another index) prior to deleting its index. Halting write requests helps avoid the following scenario:
You delete an index, which also deletes its alias. An errant write request to the now-deleted alias creates a new index with the same name as the alias. You can no longer use the alias due to a naming conflict with the new index. If you switched the alias to another index, specify "include_aliases": false when you restore from a snapshot.

To restore a snapshot

1. Identify the snapshot that you want to restore. To see all snapshot repositories, run the following command:

```
1 curl -XGET 'elasticsearch-domain-endpoint/_snapshot?pretty'
```

   After you identify the repository, run the following command to see all snapshots:

```
1 curl -XGET 'elasticsearch-domain-endpoint/_snapshot/repository/_all?pretty'
```

Note

Most automated snapshots are stored in the `cs-automated` repository. If your domain encrypts data at rest, they are stored in the `cs-automated-enc` repository. If you don't see the manual snapshot repository that you're looking for, make sure that you registered it to the domain.

1. Delete or rename all open indices in the Amazon ES domain.

   You can't restore a snapshot of your indices to an Elasticsearch cluster that already contains indices with the same names. Currently, Amazon ES does not support the Elasticsearch `_close` API, so you must use one of the following alternatives:

   - Delete the indices on the same Amazon ES domain, and then restore the snapshot.
   - Restore the snapshot to a different Amazon ES domain (only possible with manual snapshots).

   The following example shows how to delete *all* existing indices for a domain:

   ```
   1 curl -XDELETE 'elasticsearch-domain-endpoint/_all'
   ```

   If you don't plan to restore all indices, though, you might want to delete only one:

   ```
   1 curl -XDELETE 'elasticsearch-domain-endpoint/index-name'
   ```

2. To restore a snapshot, run the following command:

   ```
   1 curl -XPOST 'elasticsearch-domain-endpoint/_snapshot/repository/snapshot/_restore'
   ```

   Due to special permissions on the `.kibana` index, attempts to restore all indices might fail, especially if you try to restore from an automated snapshot. The following example restores just one index, `my-index`, from `2017-snapshot` in the `cs-automated` snapshot repository:

   ```
   1 curl -XPOST 'elasticsearch-domain-endpoint/_snapshot/cs-automated/2017-snapshot/_restore' -
       d '{"indices": "my-index"}' -H 'Content-Type: application/json'
   ```

Note

If not all primary shards were available for the indices involved, a snapshot might have a `state` of `PARTIAL`. This value indicates that data from at least one shard was not stored successfully. You can still restore from a partial snapshot, but you might need to use older snapshots to restore any missing indices.

Migrating to a Different Elasticsearch Version

The following table shows how to migrate your data to a newer Elasticsearch version. Most of the steps require you to create and restore manual index snapshots. To learn more about this process, see Working with Amazon Elasticsearch Service Index Snapshots.

Migrating to a newer Elasticsearch version also requires creating a new domain. To learn more, see Creating and Configuring Amazon Elasticsearch Service Domains.

From Version	To Version	Migration Process
6.0	6.2	[See the AWS documentation website for more details]
5.x	6.x	[See the AWS documentation website for more details]
5.1 or 5.3	5.5	[See the AWS documentation website for more details]
2.3	6.x	Elasticsearch 2.3 snapshots are not compatible with 6.x. To migrate your data directly from 2.3 to 6.x, you must manually recreate your indices in the new domain. Alternately, you can follow the 2.3 to 5.x steps in this table, perform _reindex operations in the new 5.x domain to convert your 2.3 indices to 5.x indices, and then follow the 5.x to 6.x steps.
2.3	5.x	[See the AWS documentation website for more details]
1.5	5.x	Elasticsearch 1.5 snapshots are not compatible with 5.x. To migrate your data from 1.5 to 5.x, you must manually recreate your indices in the new domain. 1.5 snapshots *are* compatible with 2.3, but Amazon ES 2.3 domains do not support the _reindex operation. Because you cannot reindex them, indices that originated in a 1.5 domain still fail to restore from 2.3 snapshots to 5.x domains.
1.5	2.3	[See the AWS documentation website for more details]

Kibana and Logstash

This chapter describes some considerations for using Kibana and Logstash with Amazon Elasticsearch Service.

Topics

- Kibana
- Loading Bulk Data with the Logstash Plugin

Kibana

Kibana is a popular open source visualization tool designed to work with Elasticsearch. Amazon ES provides an installation of Kibana with every Amazon ES domain. You can find a link to Kibana on your domain dashboard on the Amazon ES console. The URL is `https://domain.region.es.amazonaws.com/_plugin/kibana/`. Queries using this default Kibana installation have a 60-second timeout.

The following sections address some common Kibana use cases:

- Controlling Access to Kibana
- Configuring Kibana to Use a WMS Map Server
- Connecting a Local Kibana Server to Amazon ES

Controlling Access to Kibana

Kibana does not natively support IAM users and roles, but Amazon ES offers several solutions for controlling access to Kibana:

Domain Configuration	Access Control Options
Public access	[See the AWS documentation website for more details]
VPC access	[See the AWS documentation website for more details]

Using a Proxy to Access Amazon ES from Kibana

Note
This process is only applicable if your domain uses public access and you don't want to use Amazon Cognito Authentication for Kibana. See Controlling Access to Kibana.

Because Kibana is a JavaScript application, requests originate from the user's IP address. IP-based access control might be impractical due to the sheer number of IP addresses you would need to whitelist in order for each user to have access to Kibana. One workaround is to place a proxy server between Kibana and Amazon ES. Then you can add an IP-based access policy that allows requests from only one IP address, the proxy's. The following diagram shows this configuration.

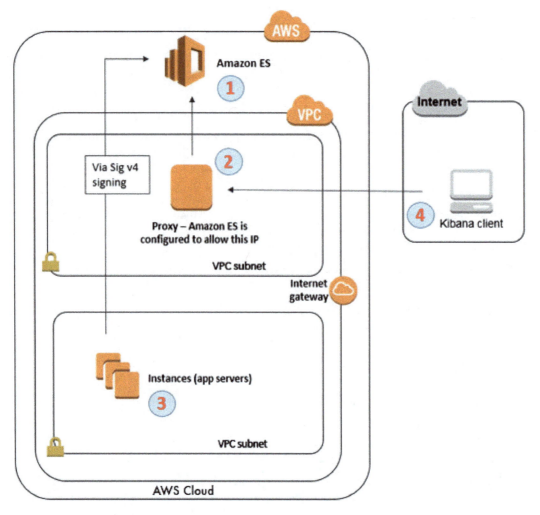

1. This is your Amazon ES domain. IAM provides authorized access to this domain. An additional, IP-based access policy provides access to the proxy server.

2. This is the proxy server, running on an Amazon EC2 instance.

3. Other applications can use the Signature Version 4 signing process to send authenticated requests to Amazon ES.

4. Kibana clients connect to your Amazon ES domain through the proxy.

To enable this sort of configuration, you need a resource-based policy that specifies roles and IP addresses. Here's a sample policy:

```
1  {
2    "Version": "2012-10-17",
3    "Statement": [{
4        "Resource": "arn:aws:es:us-west-2:111111111111:domain/my-domain/*",
5        "Principal": {
6          "AWS": "arn:aws:iam::111111111111:role/allowedrole1"
7        },
8        "Action": [
9          "es:ESHttpGet"
10       ],
11       "Effect": "Allow"
12     },
```

```
13   {
14      "Effect": "Allow",
15      "Principal": {
16        "AWS": "*"
17      },
18      "Action": "es:*",
19      "Condition": {
20        "IpAddress": {
21          "aws:SourceIp": [
22            "123.456.789.123"
23          ]
24        }
25      },
26      "Resource": "arn:aws:es:us-west-2:111111111111:domain/my-domain/*"
27   }
28  ]
29 }
```

We recommend that you configure the EC2 instance running the proxy server with an Elastic IP address. This way, you can replace the instance when necessary and still attach the same public IP address to it. To learn more, see Elastic IP Addresses in the *Amazon EC2 User Guide for Linux Instances.*

If you use a proxy server *and* Amazon Cognito Authentication for Kibana, you might need to add settings for Kibana and Amazon Cognito to avoid `redirect_mismatch` errors. See the following `nginx.conf` example:

```
1  server {
2    listen 443;
3
4    location /login {
5      proxy_pass              https://$cognito_host/login;
6      proxy_cookie_domain  $cognito_host                    $proxy_host;
7      proxy_redirect          https://$kibana_host          https://$proxy_host;
8    }
9
10   location / {
11     proxy_pass              https://$kibana_host;
12     proxy_redirect          https://$cognito_host  https://proxy_host;
13     proxy_cookie_domain  $kibana_host                    $proxy_host;
14     proxy_buffer_size       128k;
15     proxy_buffers           4                              256k;
16     proxy_busy_buffers_size 256k;
17   }
18 }
19
20 $cognito_host=your-cognito-domain-name.auth.us-west-2.amazoncognito.com
21 $kibana_host=search-your-es-domain.us-west-2.es.amazonaws.com
22 $proxy_host=your-proxy-server.us-west-2.compute.amazonaws.com
```

Configuring Kibana to Use a WMS Map Server

Due to licensing restrictions, the default installation of Kibana on Amazon ES domains that use Elasticsearch 5.*x* or greater does *not* include a map server for tile map visualizations. Use the following procedure to configure Kibana to use a Web Map Service (WMS) map server.

To configure Kibana to use a WMS map server:

1. Open Kibana. You can find a link to Kibana in the domain summary at https://console.aws.amazon.com/es/.

2. Choose **Management**.

3. Choose **Advanced Settings**.

4. Locate **visualization:tileMap:WMSdefaults**, and then choose the **edit** button to modify the default value.

5. Change `enabled` to `true` and `url` to the URL of a valid WMS map server.

6. (Optional) Locate **visualization:tileMap:WMSdefaults**, and then choose the **edit** button to modify the default value.

7. (Optional) Change `"layers": "0"` to a comma-separated list of map layers that you want to display. Layers vary by map service. The default value of 0 is often appropriate.

8. Choose the **save** button.

To apply the new default value to visualizations, you might need to reload Kibana.

Note
Map services often have licensing fees or restrictions. You are responsible for all such considerations on any map server that you specify. You might find the map services from the U.S. Geological Survey useful for testing.

Connecting a Local Kibana Server to Amazon ES

If you have invested significant time into configuring your own Kibana instance, you can use it instead of (or in addition to) the default Kibana instance that Amazon ES provides.

To connect a local Kibana server to Amazon ES:

- Make the following changes to `config/kibana.yml`:

```
1 kibana_index: ".kibana-5"
2 elasticsearch_url: "http://elasticsearch_domain_endpoint:80"
```

You must use the `http` prefix and explicitly specify port 80.

Loading Bulk Data with the Logstash Plugin

Logstash provides a convenient way to use the bulk API to upload data into your Amazon ES domain with the S3 plugin. The service also supports all other standard Logstash input plugins that are provided by Elasticsearch. Amazon ES also supports two Logstash output plugins: the standard Elasticsearch plugin and the logstash-output-amazon-es plugin, which signs and exports Logstash events to Amazon ES.

You must install your own local instance of Logstash and make the following changes in the Logstash configuration file to enable interaction with Amazon ES.

Configuration Field	Input | Output Plugin	Description
bucket	Input	Specifies the Amazon S3 bucket containing the data that you want to load into an Amazon ES domain.
region	Input	Specifies the AWS Region where the Amazon S3 bucket resides.

Configuration Field	Input | Output Plugin	Description
hosts	Output	Specifies the service endpoint for the target Amazon ES domain.
ssl	Output	Specifies whether to use SSL to connect to Amazon ES.

This example configures Logstash to do the following:

- Point the output plugin to an Amazon ES endpoint
- Point to the input plugin to the `wikipedia-stats-log` bucket in S3
- Use SSL to connect to Amazon ES

```
1  input{
2      s3 {
3          bucket => "wikipedia-stats-log"
4          access_key_id => "lizards"
5          secret_access_key => "lollipops"
6          region => "us-east-1"
7      }
8  }
9  output{
10     elasticsearch {
11         hosts => "search-logs-demo0-cpxczkdpi4bkb4c44g3csyln5a.us-east-1.es.example.com"
12         ssl => true
13     }
14 }
```

Note

The service request in the preceding example must be signed. For more information about signing requests, see Signing Amazon ES Requests. Use the logstash-output-amazon-es output plugin to sign and export Logstash events to Amazon ES. For instructions, see the plugin https://github.com/awslabs/logstash-output-amazon_es/blob/master/README.md.

Amazon Cognito Authentication for Kibana

Amazon Elasticsearch Service uses Amazon Cognito to offer user name and password protection for Kibana. This authentication feature is optional and available only for domains using Elasticsearch 5.1 or later. If you don't configure Amazon Cognito authentication, you can still protect Kibana using an IP-based access policy and a proxy server.

Much of the authentication process occurs in Amazon Cognito, but this chapter offers guidelines and requirements for configuring Amazon Cognito resources to work with Amazon ES domains. Standard pricing applies to all Amazon Cognito resources.

Tip
The first time that you configure a domain to use Amazon Cognito authentication for Kibana, we recommend using the console. Amazon Cognito resources are extremely customizable, and the console can help you identity and understand the features that matter to you.

Topics

- Prerequisites
- Configuring an Amazon ES Domain
- Allowing the Authenticated Role
- Configuring Identity Providers
- (Optional) Configuring Granular Access
- (Optional) Customizing the Login Page
- Testing
- Limits
- Common Configuration Issues
- Disabling Amazon Cognito Authentication for Kibana
- Deleting Domains that Use Amazon Cognito Authentication for Kibana

Prerequisites

Before you can configure Amazon Cognito authentication for Kibana, you must fulfill several prerequisites. The Amazon ES console helps streamline the creation of these resources, but understanding the purpose of each resource helps with configuration and troubleshooting. Amazon Cognito authentication for Kibana requires the following resources:

- Amazon Cognito user pool
- Amazon Cognito identity pool
- IAM role that has the `AmazonESCognitoAccess` policy attached

Note
The user pool and identity pool must be in the same AWS Region. You can use the same user pool, identity pool, and IAM role to add Amazon Cognito authentication for Kibana to multiple Amazon ES domains. To learn more, see Limits.

About the User Pool

User pools have two main features: create and manage a directory of users, and let users sign up and log in. For instructions about creating a user pool, see Create a User Pool in the *Amazon Cognito Developer Guide*.

When you create a user pool to use with Amazon ES, consider the following:

- Your Amazon Cognito user pool must have a domain name. Amazon ES uses this domain name to redirect users to a login page for accessing Kibana. Other than a domain name, the user pool doesn't require any non-default configuration.

- You must specify the pool's required standard attributes—attributes like name, birth date, email address, and phone number. You can't change these attributes after you create the user pool, so choose the ones that matter to you at this time.
- While creating your user pool, choose whether users can create their own accounts, the minimum password strength for accounts, and whether to enable multi-factor authentication. If you plan to use an external identity provider, these settings are inconsequential. Technically, you can enable the user pool as an identity provider *and* enable an external identity provider, but most people prefer one or the other.

User pool IDs take the form of `region_ID`. If you plan to use the AWS CLI or an AWS SDK to configure Amazon ES, make note of the ID.

About the Identity Pool

Identity pools let you assign temporary, limited-privilege roles to users after they log in. For instructions about creating an identity pool, see Identity Pools in the *Amazon Cognito Developer Guide*. When you create an identity pool to use with Amazon ES, consider the following:

- If you use the Amazon Cognito console, you must select the **Enable access to unauthenticated identities** check box to create the identity pool. After you create the identity pool and configure the Amazon ES domain, Amazon Cognito disables this setting.
- You don't need to add external identity providers to the identity pool. When you configure Amazon ES to use Amazon Cognito authentication, it configures the identity pool to use the user pool that you just created.
- After you create the identity pool, you must choose unauthenticated and authenticated IAM roles. These roles specify the access policies that users have before and after they log in. If you use the Amazon Cognito console, it can create these roles for you. After you create the authenticated role, make note of the ARN, which takes the form of `arn:aws:iam::123456789012:role/Cognito_identitypoolAuth_Role`.

Identity pool IDs take the form of `region:ID-ID-ID-ID-ID`. If you plan to use the AWS CLI or an AWS SDK to configure Amazon ES, make note of the ID.

About the IAM Role

Amazon ES needs permissions to configure the Amazon Cognito user and identity pools and use them for authentication. You can use `AmazonESCognitoAccess`, which is an AWS managed policy, for this purpose. If you use the console to create or configure your Amazon ES domain, it creates an IAM role for you and attaches this policy to the role.

If you use the AWS CLI or one of the AWS SDKs, you must create your own role, attach the policy, and specify the ARN for this role when you configure your Amazon ES domain. The role must have the following trust relationship:

```
1  {
2    "Version": "2012-10-17",
3    "Statement": [
4      {
5        "Effect": "Allow",
6        "Principal": {
7          "Service": "es.amazonaws.com"
8        },
9        "Action": "sts:AssumeRole"
10     }
11   ]
12 }
```

For instructions, see Creating a Role to Delegate Permissions to an AWS Service and Attaching and Detaching IAM Policies in the *IAM User Guide*.

Configuring an Amazon ES Domain

After you complete the prerequisites, you can configure an Amazon ES domain to use Amazon Cognito for Kibana.

Note
Amazon Cognito is not available in all AWS Regions. For a list of supported regions, see AWS Regions and Endpoints. You don't need to use the same region for Amazon Cognito that you use for Amazon ES.

Configuring Amazon Cognito Authentication (Console)

Because it creates the IAM role for you, the console offers the simplest configuration experience. In addition to the standard Amazon ES permissions, you need the following minimal set of permissions to use the console to create a domain that uses Amazon Cognito authentication for Kibana:

```
1  {
2    "Version": "2012-10-17",
3    "Statement": [
4      {
5        "Effect": "Allow",
6        "Action": [
7          "iam:GetRole",
8          "iam:PassRole",
9          "iam:CreateRole",
10         "iam:AttachRolePolicy",
11         "ec2:DescribeVpcs",
12         "cognito-identity:ListIdentityPools",
13         "cognito-idp:ListUserPools"
14       ],
15       "Resource": "*"
16     }
17   ]
18 }
```

To configure Amazon Cognito authentication for Kibana (console)

1. Go to https://aws.amazon.com, and then choose **Sign In to the Console**.

2. Under **Analytics**, choose **Elasticsearch Service**.

3. In the navigation pane, under **My domains**, choose the domain that you want to configure.

4. Choose **Configure cluster**.

5. For **Kibana authentication**, choose **Enable Amazon Cognito for authentication**.

6. For **Region**, select the region that contains your Amazon Cognito user pool and identity pool.

7. For **Cognito User Pool**, select a user pool or create one. For guidance, see About the User Pool.

8. For **Cognito Identity Pool**, select an identity pool or create one. For guidance, see About the Identity Pool. **Note**
The **Create new user pool** and **Create new identity pool** links direct you to the Amazon Cognito console and require you to create these resources manually. The process is not automatic. To learn more, see Prerequisites.

9. For **IAM Role**, use the default value (recommended) or type a new name. To learn more about the purpose of this role, see About the IAM Role.

10. Choose **Submit**.

After your domain finishes processing, see Allowing the Authenticated Role and Configuring Identity Providers for additional configuration steps.

Configuring Amazon Cognito Authentication (AWS CLI)

Use the `--cognito-options` parameter to configure your Amazon ES domain. The following syntax is used by both the `create-elasticsearch-domain` and `update-elasticsearch-domain-config` commands:

```
1  --cognito-options Enabled=true,UserPoolId="user-pool-id",IdentityPoolId="identity-pool-id",
       RoleArn="arn:aws:iam::123456789012:role/CognitoAccessForAmazonES"
```

Example

The following example creates a domain in the `us-east-1` Region that enables Amazon Cognito authentication for Kibana using the `CognitoAccessForAmazonES` role and provides domain access to `Cognito_Auth_Role`:

```
1  aws es create-elasticsearch-domain --domain-name my-domain --region us-east-1 --access-policies
       '{ "Version":"2012-10-17", "Statement":[{"Effect":"Allow","Principal":{"AWS": ["arn:aws:iam
       ::123456789012:role/Cognito_Auth_Role"]},"Action":"es:ESHttp*","Resource":"arn:aws:es:us-
       east-1:123456789012:domain/*" }]}' --elasticsearch-version "6.0" --elasticsearch-cluster-
       config InstanceType=m4.xlarge.elasticsearch,InstanceCount=1 --ebs-options EBSEnabled=true,
       VolumeSize=10 --cognito-options Enabled=true,UserPoolId="us-east-1_123456789",IdentityPoolId
       ="us-east-1:12345678-1234-1234-1234-123456789012",RoleArn="arn:aws:iam::123456789012:role/
       CognitoAccessForAmazonES"
```

After your domain finishes processing, see Allowing the Authenticated Role and Configuring Identity Providers for additional configuration steps.

Configuring Amazon Cognito Authentication (AWS SDKs)

The AWS SDKs (except the Android and iOS SDKs) support all the operations that are defined in the Amazon Elasticsearch Service Configuration API Reference, including the `CognitoOptions` parameter for the `CreateElasticsearchDomain` and `UpdateElasticsearchDomainConfig` operations. For more information about installing and using the AWS SDKs, see AWS Software Development Kits.

After your domain finishes processing, see Allowing the Authenticated Role and Configuring Identity Providers for additional configuration steps.

Allowing the Authenticated Role

By default, the authenticated IAM role that you configured by following the guidelines in About the Identity Pool does not have the necessary privileges to access Kibana. You must provide the role with additional permissions.

You can include these permissions in an identity-based policy, but unless you want authenticated users to have access to all Amazon ES domains, a resource-based policy attached to a single domain is the more common approach:

```
1  {
2    "Version": "2012-10-17",
3    "Statement": [
4      {
```

```
 5        "Effect": "Allow",
 6        "Principal": {
 7          "AWS": [
 8            "arn:aws:iam::123456789012:role/Cognito_identitypoolAuth_Role"
 9          ]
10        },
11        "Action": [
12          "es:ESHttp*"
13        ],
14        "Resource": "arn:aws:es:region:123456789012:domain/domain-name/*"
15      }
16    ]
17 }
```

For instructions about adding a resource-based policy to an Amazon ES domain, see Configuring Access Policies.

Configuring Identity Providers

When you configure a domain to use Amazon Cognito authentication for Kibana, Amazon ES adds an app client to the user pool and adds the user pool to the identity pool as an authentication provider. The following screenshot shows the **App client settings** page in the Amazon Cognito console.

App client AWSElasticsearch-sample-domain

ID 1a2a3a4a5a6a7a8a9a0a

Enabled Identity Providers ☐ Select all

☐ Facebook   ☐ Google   ☐ LoginWithAmazon   ☑ Cognito User Pool

Sign in and sign out URLs

Enter your callback URLs below that you will include in your sign in and sign out requests. Each field can contain multiple URLs by entering a comma after each URL.

Callback URL(s)

```
https://search-sample-domain-1a2a3a4a5a6a7a8a9a0a.us-east-1.es.amazonaws.com/_plugin/kibana/app/kibana
```

Sign out URL(s)

```
https://search-sample-domain-1a2a3a4a5a6a7a8a9a0a.us-east-1.es.amazonaws.com/_plugin/kibana/app/kibana
```

Warning

Don't rename or delete the app client.

Depending on how you configured your user pool, you might need to create user accounts manually, or users might be able to create their own. If these settings are acceptable, you don't need to take further action. Many people, however, prefer to use external identity providers.

To enable a SAML 2.0 identity provider, you must provide a SAML metadata document. To enable social identity providers like Login with Amazon, Facebook, and Google, you must have an app ID and app secret from those providers. You can enable any combination of identity providers. The login page adds options as you add providers, as shown in the following screenshot.

Sign In with your social account

Continue with Google

Continue with Login with Amazon

Continue with Facebook

We won't post to any of your accounts without asking first

or

Sign in with your username and password

Username

> Username

Password

> Password

Forgot your password?

Sign In

Need an account? Sign up

The easiest way to configure your user pool is to use the Amazon Cognito console. Use the **Identity Providers** page to add external identity providers and the **App client settings** page to enable and disable identity providers for the Amazon ES domain's app client. For example, you might want to enable your own SAML identity provider and disable **Cognito User Pool** as an identity provider.

For instructions, see Using Federation from a User Pool and Specifying Identity Provider Settings for Your User Pool App in the *Amazon Cognito Developer Guide*.

(Optional) Configuring Granular Access

You might have noticed that the default identity pool settings assign every user who logs in the same IAM role (`Cognito_identitypoolAuth_Role`), which means that every user can access the same AWS resources. If you want more granular access control—for example, if you want your organization's analysts to have access to all eight of your Amazon ES domains, but everyone else to have access to only five of them—you have two options:

- Create user groups and configure your identity provider to choose the IAM role based on the user's authentication token.
- Configure your identity provider to choose the IAM role based on one or more rules.

You configure these options using the **Edit identity pool** page of the Amazon Cognito console, as shown in the following screenshot.

▼ Authentication providers ⓘ

Amazon Cognito supports the following authentication methods with Amazon Cognito Sign-In or any public provider. If you allow your users to authenticate using any of these public providers, you can specify your application identifiers here. Warning: Changing the application ID that your identity pool is linked to will prevent existing users from authenticating using Amazon Cognito. Learn more about public identity providers.

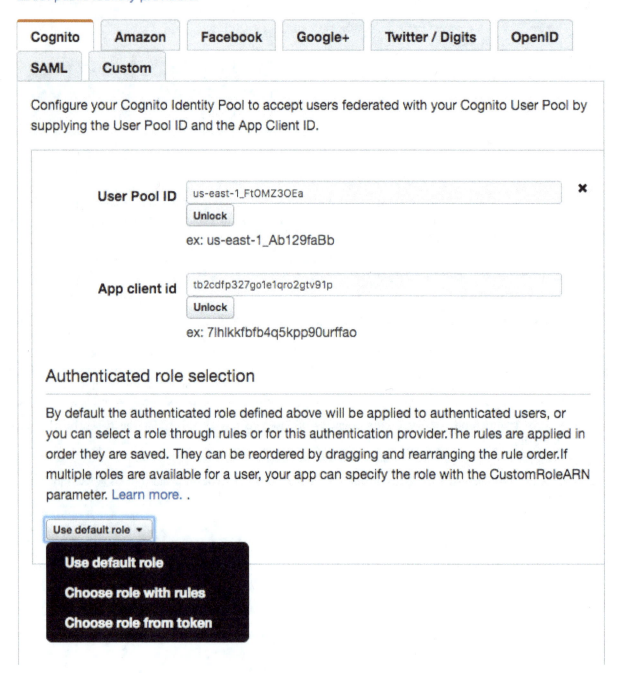

| Cognito | Amazon | Facebook | Google+ | Twitter / Digits | OpenID |

| SAML | Custom |

Configure your Cognito Identity Pool to accept users federated with your Cognito User Pool by supplying the User Pool ID and the App Client ID.

User Pool ID   us-east-1_FtOMZ3OEa   ✖

Unlock

ex: us-east-1_Ab129faBb

App client id   tb2cdfp327go1e1qro2gtv91p

Unlock

ex: 7lhlkkfbfb4q5kpp90urffao

Authenticated role selection

By default the authenticated role defined above will be applied to authenticated users, or you can select a role through rules or for this authentication provider.The rules are applied in order they are saved. They can be reordered by dragging and rearranging the rule order.If multiple roles are available for a user, your app can specify the role with the CustomRoleARN parameter. Learn more. .

Use default role ▼

Use default role

Choose role with rules

Choose role from token

User Groups and Tokens

When you create a user group, you choose an IAM role for members of the group. For information about creating groups, see User Groups in the *Amazon Cognito Developer Guide*.

After you create one or more user groups, you can configure your authentication provider to assign users their groups' roles rather than the identity pool's default role. Choose the **Choose role from token** option. Then choose either **Use default Authenticated role** or **DENY** to specify how the identity pool should handle users who are not part of a group.

Rules

Rules are essentially a series of `if` statements that Amazon Cognito evaluates sequentially. For example, if a user's email address contains `@corporate`, Amazon Cognito assigns that user `Role_A`. If a user's email address contains `@subsidiary`, it assigns that user `Role_B`. Otherwise, it assigns the user the default authenticated role.

To learn more, see Using Rule-Based Mapping to Assign Roles to Users in the *Amazon Cognito Developer Guide*.

(Optional) Customizing the Login Page

The **UI customization** page of the Amazon Cognito console lets you upload a custom logo and make CSS changes to the login page. For instructions and a full list of CSS properties, see Specifying App UI Customization Settings for Your User Pool in the *Amazon Cognito Developer Guide*.

Testing

After you are satisfied with your configuration, verify that the user experience meets your expectations.

To access Kibana

1. Navigate to `https://elasticsearch-domain/_plugin/kibana/` in a web browser.

2. Log in using your preferred credentials.

3. After Kibana loads, configure at least one index pattern. Kibana uses these patterns to identity which indices that you want to analyze. Enter `*`, choose **Next step**, and then choose **Create index pattern**.

4. To search or explore your data, choose **Discover**.

If any step of this process fails, see Common Configuration Issues for troubleshooting information.

Limits

Amazon Cognito has soft limits on many of its resources. If you want to enable Kibana authentication for a large number of Amazon ES domains, review Limits in Amazon Cognito and request limit increases as necessary.

Each Amazon ES domain adds an app client to the user pool, which adds an authentication provider to the identity pool. If you enable Kibana authentication for more than 10 domains, you might encounter the "maximum Amazon Cognito user pool providers per identity pool" limit. If you exceed a limit, any Amazon ES domains that you try to configure to use Amazon Cognito authentication for Kibana can get stuck in a configuration state of **Processing**.

Common Configuration Issues

The following tables list common configuration issues and solutions.

Configuring Amazon ES

Issue	Solution
`Amazon ES can't create the role` (console)	You don't have the correct IAM permissions. Add the permissions specified in Configuring Amazon Cognito Authentication (Console).
`User is not authorized to perform : iam:PassRole on resource CognitoAccessForAmazonES` (console)	You don't have iam:PassRole permissions for the IAM role. Attach the following policy to your account:{ "Version": "2012-10-17", "Statement": [{ "Effect": "Allow", "Action": ["iam:PassRole"], "Resource": "arn:aws:iam::123456789012:role/service-role/CognitoAccessForAmazonES" }]}Alternately, you can attach the `IAMFullAccess` policy.
`User is not authorized to perform: cognito-identity:ListIdentityPools on resource`	You don't have read permissions for Amazon Cognito. Attach the `AmazonCognitoReadOnly` policy to your account.
`An error occurred ( ValidationException)when calling the CreateElasticsearchDomain operation: Amazon Elasticsearch must be allowed to use the passed role`	Amazon ES isn't specified in the trust relationship of the IAM role. Check that your role uses the trust relationship that is specified in About the IAM Role. Alternately, use the console to configure Amazon Cognito authentication. The console creates a role for you.
`An error occurred ( ValidationException)when calling the CreateElasticsearchDomain operation : User is not authorized to perform : cognito-idp:action on resource: user pool`	The role specified in --cognito-options does not have permissions to access Amazon Cognito. Check that the role has the AWS managed AmazonESCognitoAccess policy attached. Alternately, use the console to configure Amazon Cognito authentication. The console creates a role for you.
`An error occurred (ValidationException) when calling the CreateElasticsearchDomain operation: User pool does not exist`	Amazon ES can't find the user pool. Confirm that you created one and have the correct ID. To find the ID, you can use the Amazon Cognito console or the following AWS CLI command: aws cognito-idp list-user-pools --max-results 60 --region region
`An error occurred ( ValidationException)when calling the CreateElasticsearchDomain operation : IdentityPool not found`	Amazon ES can't find the identity pool. Confirm that you created one and have the correct ID. To find the ID, you can use the Amazon Cognito console or the following AWS CLI command: aws cognito-identity list-identity-pools --max-results 60 --region region
`An error occurred ( ValidationException)when calling the CreateElasticsearchDomain operation : Domain needs to be specified for user pool`	The user pool does not have a domain name. You can configure one using the Amazon Cognito console or the following AWS CLI command:aws cognito-idp create-user-pool-domain --domain name --user-pool-id id

Issue	Solution
The login page doesn't show my preferred identity providers.	Check that you enabled the identity provider for the Amazon ES app client as specified in Configuring Identity Providers.
The login page doesn't look as if it's associated with my organization.	See (Optional) Customizing the Login Page.
My login credentials don't work.	Check that you have configured the identity provider as specified in Configuring Identity Providers. If you use the user pool as your identity provider, check that the account exists and is confirmed on the **User and groups** page of the Amazon Cognito console.
Kibana either doesn't load at all or doesn't work properly.	The Amazon Cognito authenticated role needs `es:ESHttp*` permissions for the domain (`/*`) to access and use Kibana. Check that you added an access policy as specified in Allowing the Authenticated Role.
Invalid identity pool configuration. Check assigned IAM roles for this pool.	Amazon Cognito can't assume the authenticated role. If you used a preexisting role rather than creating a new one for the identity pool, modify the trust relationship for the authenticated role:{ "Version": "2012-10-17", "Statement": [{ "Effect": "Allow", "Principal": { "Federated": "cognito-identity.amazonaws.com" }, "Action": "sts:AssumeRoleWithWebIdentity" }]}Alternately, you can create a new role using the Amazon Cognito console.
Token is not from a supported provider of this identity pool.	This uncommon error can occur when you remove the app client from the user pool. Try opening Kibana in a new browser session.

Disabling Amazon Cognito Authentication for Kibana

Use the following procedure to disable Amazon Cognito authentication for Kibana.

To disable Amazon Cognito authentication for Kibana (console)

1. Go to https://aws.amazon.com, and then choose **Sign In to the Console**.

2. Under **Analytics**, choose **Elasticsearch Service**.

3. In the navigation pane, under **My domains**, choose the domain that you want to configure.

4. Choose **Configure cluster**.

5. For **Kibana authentication**, clear the **Enable Amazon Cognito for authentication** check box.

6. Choose **Submit**.

Important
If you no longer need the Amazon Cognito user pool and identity pool, delete them. Otherwise, you can continue to incur charges.

Deleting Domains that Use Amazon Cognito Authentication for Kibana

To prevent domains that use Amazon Cognito authentication for Kibana from becoming stuck in a configuration state of **Processing**, delete Amazon ES domains *before* deleting their associated Amazon Cognito user pools and identity pools.

Tutorial: Visualizing Customer Support Calls with Amazon Elasticsearch Service and Kibana

This chapter is a full walkthrough of the following situation: a business receives some number of customer support calls and wants to analyze them. What is the subject of each call? How many were positive? How many were negative? How can managers search or review the the transcripts of these calls?

A manual workflow might involve employees listening to recordings, noting the subject of each call, and deciding whether or not the customer interaction was positive.

Such a process would be extremely labor-intensive. Assuming an average time of 10 minutes per call, each employee could listen to only 48 calls per day. Barring human bias, the data they generate would be highly accurate, but the *amount* of data would be minimal: just the subject of the call and a Boolean for whether or not the customer was satisfied. Anything more involved, such as a full transcript, would take a huge amount of time.

Using Amazon S3, Amazon Transcribe, Amazon Comprehend, and Amazon Elasticsearch Service (Amazon ES), you can automate a similar process with very little code and end up with much more data. For example, you can get a full transcript of the call, keywords from the transcript, and an overall "sentiment" of the call (positive, negative, neutral, or mixed). Then you can use Elasticsearch and Kibana to search and visualize the data.

While you can use this walkthrough as-is, the intent is to spark ideas about how to enrich your JSON documents before you index them in Amazon ES.

Estimated Costs

In general, performing the steps in this walkthrough should cost less than $2. The walkthrough uses the following resources:

- S3 bucket with less than 100 MB transferred and stored

  To learn more, see Amazon S3 Pricing.

- Amazon ES domain with one `t2.medium` instance and 10 GB of EBS storage for several hours

  To learn more, see Amazon Elasticsearch Service Pricing.

- Several calls to Amazon Transcribe

  To learn more, see Amazon Transcribe Pricing.

- Several natural language processing calls to Amazon Comprehend

  To learn more, see Amazon Comprehend Pricing.

Topics

- Step 1: Configure Prerequisites
- Step 2: Copy Sample Code
- (Optional) Step 3: Add Sample Data
- Step 4: Analyze and Visualize Your Data
- Step 5: Clean Up Resources and Next Steps

Step 1: Configure Prerequisites

Before proceeding, you must have the following resources.

Prerequisite	Description
Amazon S3 Bucket	For more information, see Creating a Bucket in the Amazon Simple Storage Service Getting Started Guide.
Amazon ES Domain	The destination for data. For more information, see Creating Amazon ES Domains.

If you don't already have these resources, you can create them using the following AWS CLI commands:

```
aws s3 mb s3://my-transcribe-test --region us-west-2
```

```
aws es create-elasticsearch-domain --domain-name my-transcribe-test --elasticsearch-version 6.2
    --elasticsearch-cluster-config  InstanceType=t2.medium.elasticsearch,InstanceCount=1 --ebs-
    options EBSEnabled=true,VolumeType=standard,VolumeSize=10 --access-policies '{"Version
    ":"2012-10-17","Statement":[{"Effect":"Allow","Principal":{"AWS":"arn:aws:iam::123456789012:
    root"},"Action":"es:*","Resource":"arn:aws:es:us-west-2:123456789012:domain/my-transcribe-
    test/*"}]}' --region us-west-2
```

Note

These commands use the us-west-2 region, but you can use any region that Amazon Comprehend supports. To learn more, see the AWS General Reference.

Step 2: Copy Sample Code

1. Copy and paste the following sample code into a new file named call-center.py:

```
1  import boto3
2  import datetime
3  import json
4  import requests
5  from requests_aws4auth import AWS4Auth
6  import time
7  import urllib2
8
9  # Variables to update
10 audio_file_name = '' # For example, 000001.mp3
11 bucket_name = '' # For example, my-transcribe-test
12 domain = '' # For example, https://search-my-transcribe-test-12345.us-west-2.es.amazonaws.
      com
13 index = 'support-calls'
14 type = 'call'
15 es_region = 'us-west-2'
16
17 # Upload audio file to S3.
18 s3_client = boto3.client('s3')
19
20 audio_file = open(audio_file_name, 'r')
21
22 print('Uploading ' + audio_file_name + '...')
23 response = s3_client.put_object(
24     Body=audio_file,
25     Bucket=bucket_name,
26     Key=audio_file_name,
```

```python
27 )
28
29 response = s3_client.get_bucket_location(
30     Bucket=bucket_name
31 )
32
33 bucket_region = response['LocationConstraint']
34
35 # Build the URL to the audio file on S3.
36 mp3_uri = 'https://s3-' + bucket_region + '.amazonaws.com/' + bucket_name + '/' +
       audio_file_name
37
38 # Start transcription job.
39 transcribe_client = boto3.client('transcribe')
40
41 print('Starting transcription job...')
42 response = transcribe_client.start_transcription_job(
43     TranscriptionJobName=audio_file_name,
44     LanguageCode='en-US',
45     MediaFormat='mp3',
46     Media={
47         'MediaFileUri': mp3_uri
48     },
49     Settings={
50         'ShowSpeakerLabels': True,
51         'MaxSpeakerLabels': 2 # assumes two people on a phone call
52     }
53 )
54
55 # Wait for the transcription job to finish.
56 print('Waiting for job to complete...')
57 while True:
58     response = transcribe_client.get_transcription_job(TranscriptionJobName=audio_file_name
           )
59     if response['TranscriptionJob']['TranscriptionJobStatus'] in ['COMPLETED', 'FAILED']:
60         break
61     else:
62         print('Still waiting...')
63     time.sleep(10)
64
65 transcript_uri = response['TranscriptionJob']['Transcript']['TranscriptFileUri']
66
67 # Open the JSON file, read it, and get the transcript.
68 response = urllib2.urlopen(transcript_uri)
69 raw_json = response.read()
70 loaded_json = json.loads(raw_json)
71 transcript = loaded_json['results']['transcripts'][0]['transcript']
72
73 # Send transcript to Comprehend for key phrases and sentiment.
74 comprehend_client = boto3.client('comprehend')
75
76 # If necessary, trim the transcript.
77 # If the transcript is more than 5 KB, the Comprehend calls fail.
78 if len(transcript) > 5000:
```

```
79        trimmed_transcript = transcript[:5000]
80 else:
81        trimmed_transcript = transcript
82
83 print('Detecting key phrases...')
84 response = comprehend_client.detect_key_phrases(
85        Text=trimmed_transcript,
86        LanguageCode='en'
87 )
88
89 keywords = []
90 for keyword in response['KeyPhrases']:
91        keywords.append(keyword['Text'])
92
93 print('Detecting sentiment...')
94 response = comprehend_client.detect_sentiment(
95        Text=trimmed_transcript,
96        LanguageCode='en'
97 )
98
99 sentiment = response['Sentiment']
100
101 # Build the Amazon Elasticsearch Service URL.
102 id = audio_file_name.strip('.mp3')
103 url = domain + '/' + index + '/' + type + '/' + id
104
105 # Create the JSON document.
106 json_document = {'transcript': transcript, 'keywords': keywords, 'sentiment': sentiment, '
       timestamp': datetime.datetime.now().isoformat()}
107
108 # Provide all details necessary to sign the indexing request.
109 credentials = boto3.Session().get_credentials()
110 awsauth = AWS4Auth(credentials.access_key, credentials.secret_key, es_region, 'es',
       session_token=credentials.token)
111
112 # Add explicit header for Elasticsearch 6.x.
113 headers = {'Content-Type': 'application/json'}
114
115 # Index the document.
116 print('Indexing document...')
117 response = requests.put(url, auth=awsauth, json=json_document, headers=headers)
118
119 print(response)
120 print(response.json())
```

2. Update the initial six variables.

3. Install the required packages using the following commands:

```
1 pip install boto3
2 pip install requests
3 pip install requests_aws4auth
```

4. Place your MP3 in the same directory as `call-center.py` and run the script. A sample output follows:

```
1 $ python call-center.py
```

```
2 Uploading 000001.mp3...
3 Starting transcription job...
4 Waiting for job to complete...
5 Still waiting...
6 Still waiting...
7 Still waiting...
8 Still waiting...
9 Still waiting...
10 Still waiting...
11 Still waiting...
12 Detecting key phrases...
13 Detecting sentiment...
14 Indexing document...
15 <Response [201]>
16 {u'_type': u'call', u'_seq_no': 0, u'_shards': {u'successful': 1, u'failed': 0, u'total':
       2}, u'_index': u'support-calls4', u'_version': 1, u'_primary_term': 1, u'result': u'
       created', u'_id': u'000001'}
```

`call-center.py` performs a number of operations:

1. The script uploads an audio file (in this case, an MP3, but Amazon Transcribe supports several formats) to your S3 bucket.

2. It sends the audio file's URL to Amazon Transcribe and waits for the transcription job to finish.

   The time to finish the transcription job depends on the length of the audio file. Assume minutes, not seconds. **Tip**
   To improve the quality of the transcription, you can configure a custom vocabulary for Amazon Transcribe.

3. After the transcription job finishes, the script extracts the transcript, trims it to 5,000 characters, and sends it to Amazon Comprehend for keyword and sentiment analysis.

4. Finally, the script adds the full transcript, keywords, sentiment, and current time stamp to a JSON document and indexes it in Amazon ES.

Tip
LibriVox has public domain audiobooks that you can use for testing.

(Optional) Step 3: Add Sample Data

If you don't have a bunch of call recordings handy—and who does?—you can index the sample documents in sample-calls.zip, which are comparable to what `call-center.py` produces.

1. Create a file named `bulk-helper.py`:

```
1 import boto3
2 from elasticsearch import Elasticsearch, RequestsHttpConnection
3 import json
4 from requests_aws4auth import AWS4Auth
5
6 host = '' # For example, my-test-domain.us-west-2.es.amazonaws.com
7 region = '' # For example, us-west-2
8 service = 'es'
9
10 bulk_file = open('sample-calls.bulk', 'r').read()
11
12 credentials = boto3.Session().get_credentials()
```

```
13 awsauth = AWS4Auth(credentials.access_key, credentials.secret_key, region, service,
       session_token=credentials.token)
14
15 es = Elasticsearch(
16     hosts = [{'host': host, 'port': 443}],
17     http_auth = awsauth,
18     use_ssl = True,
19     verify_certs = True,
20     connection_class = RequestsHttpConnection
21 )
22
23 response = es.bulk(bulk_file)
24 print(json.dumps(response, indent=2, sort_keys=True))
```

2. Update the initial two variables for `host` and `region`.

3. Install the required package using the following command:

```
1 pip install elasticsearch
```

4. Download and unzip sample-calls.zip.

5. Place `sample-calls.bulk` in the same directory as `bulk-helper.py` and run the helper. A sample output follows:

```
1 $ python bulk-helper.py
2 {
3   "errors": false,
4   "items": [
5     {
6       "index": {
7         "_id": "1",
8         "_index": "test-data",
9         "_primary_term": 1,
10        "_seq_no": 42,
11        "_shards": {
12          "failed": 0,
13          "successful": 1,
14          "total": 2
15        },
16        "_type": "call",
17        "_version": 9,
18        "result": "updated",
19        "status": 200
20      }
21    },
22    ...
23  ],
24  "took": 27
25 }
```

Step 4: Analyze and Visualize Your Data

Now that you have some data in Amazon ES, you can visualize it using Kibana.

1. Navigate to `https://search-domain.region.es.amazonaws.com/_plugin/kibana`.

2. Before you can use Kibana, you need an index pattern. Kibana uses index patterns to narrow your analysis to one or more indices. To match the `support-calls` index that `call-center.py`created, define an index pattern of `support*`, and then choose **Next step**.

3. For **Time Filter field name**, choose **timestamp**.

4. Now you can start creating visualizations. Choose **Visualize**, and then add a new visualization.

5. Choose the pie chart and the `support*` index pattern.

6. The default visualization is basic, so choose **Split Slices** to create a more interesting visualization.

   For **Aggregation**, choose **Terms**. For **Field**, choose **sentiment.keyword**. Then choose **Apply changes** and **Save**.

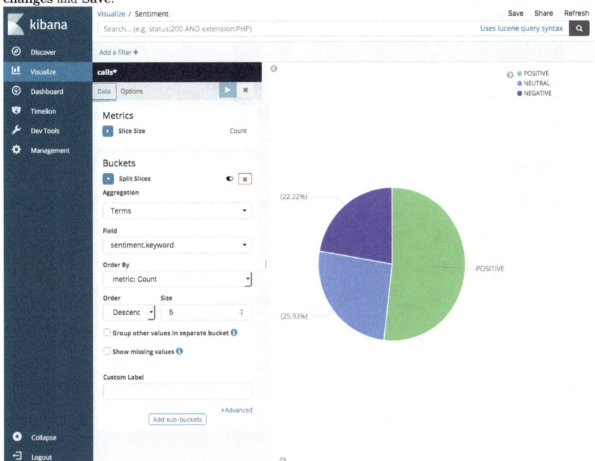

7. Return to the **Visualize** page, and add another visualization. This time, choose the horizontal bar chart.

8. Choose **Split Series**.

   For **Aggregation**, choose **Terms**. For **Field**, choose **keywords.keyword** and change **Size** to 20. Then choose **Apply Changes** and **Save**.

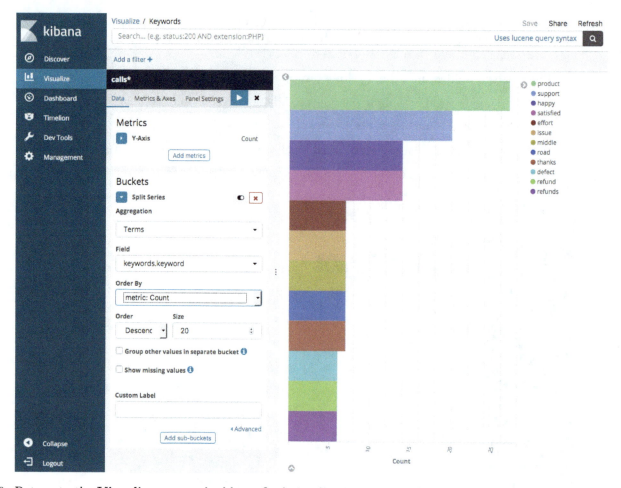

9. Return to the **Visualize** page and add one final visualization, a vertical bar chart.

10. Choose **Split Series**. For **Aggregation**, choose **Date Histogram**. For **Field**, choose **timestamp** and change **Interval** to **Daily**.

11. Choose **Metrics & Axes** and change **Mode** to **normal**.

12. Choose **Apply Changes** and **Save**.

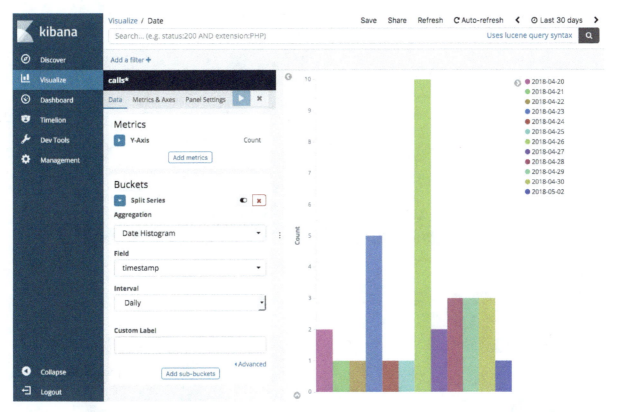

13. Now that you have three visualizations, you can add them to a Kibana dashboard. Choose **Dashboard**, create a dashboard, and add your visualizations.

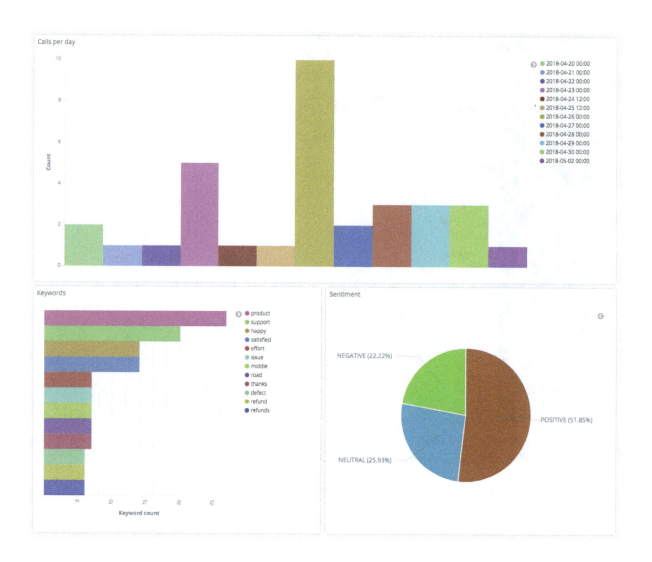

Step 5: Clean Up Resources and Next Steps

To avoid unnecessary charges, delete the S3 bucket and Amazon ES domain. To learn more, see Delete a Bucket in the *Amazon Simple Storage Service Developer Guide* and Delete an Amazon ES Domain in this guide.

Transcripts require much less disk space than MP3 files. You might be able to shorten your MP3 retention window—for example, from three months of call recordings to one month—retain years of transcripts, and still save on storage costs.

You could also automate the transcription process using AWS Step Functions and Lambda, add additional metadata before indexing, or craft more complex visualizations to fit your exact use case.

Amazon Elasticsearch Service Best Practices

These topics address some considerations for operating Amazon Elasticsearch Service domains and provide general guidelines that apply to many use cases.

Topics

- Sizing Amazon ES Domains
- Dedicated Master Nodes
- Recommended CloudWatch Alarms

Sizing Amazon ES Domains

No surefire method of sizing Amazon ES domains exists, but by starting with an understanding of your storage needs, the service, and Elasticsearch itself, you can make an educated initial estimate on your hardware needs. This estimate can serve as a useful starting point for the most critical aspect of sizing domains: testing them with representative workloads and monitoring their performance.

Topics

- Calculating Storage Requirements
- Choosing the Number of Shards
- Choosing Instance Types and Testing

Calculating Storage Requirements

Most Elasticsearch workloads fall into one of two broad categories:

- Long-lived index: You write code that processes data into one or more Elasticsearch indices and then updates those indices periodically as the source data changes. Some common examples are website, document, and e-commerce search.
- Rolling indices: Data continuously flows into a set of temporary indices, with an indexing period and retention window, such as a set of daily indices that is retained for two weeks. Some common examples are log analytics, time-series processing, and clickstream analytics.

For long-lived index workloads, you can examine the source data on disk and easily determine how much storage space it consumes. If the data comes from multiple sources, just add those sources together.

For rolling indices, you can multiply the amount of data generated during a representative time period by the retention period. For example, if you generate 200 MB of log data per hour, that's 4.8 GB per day, which is 67 GB of data at any given time if you have a two-week retention period.

The size of your source data, however, is just one aspect of your storage requirements. You also have to consider the following:

1. Number of replicas: Each replica is a full copy of an index and needs the same amount of disk space. By default, each Elasticsearch index has one replica. We recommend at least one to prevent against data loss. Replicas also improve search performance, so you might want more if you have a read-heavy workload.

2. Elasticsearch indexing overhead: The on-disk size of an index varies, but is often 10% larger than the source data. After indexing your data, you can use the `_cat/indices` API and `pri.store.size` value to calculate the exact overhead. The `_cat/allocation` API also provides a useful summary.

3. Operating system reserved space: By default, Linux reserves 5% of the file system for the `root` user for critical processes, system recovery, and to safeguard against disk fragmentation problems.

4. Amazon ES overhead: Amazon ES reserves 20% of the storage space of each instance (up to 20 GB) for segment merges, logs, and other internal operations.

   Because of this 20 GB maximum, the total amount of reserved space can vary dramatically depending on the number of instances in your domain. For example, a domain might have three `m4.xlarge.elasticsearch` instances, each with 500 GB of storage space, for a total of 1.5 TB. In this case, the total reserved space is only 60 GB. Another domain might have 10 `m3.medium.elasticsearch` instances, each with 100 GB of storage space, for a total of 1 TB. Here, the total reserved space is 200 GB, even though the first domain is 50% larger.

   In the following formula, we apply a "worst-case" estimate for overhead that is accurate for domains with less than 100 GB of storage space per instance and over-allocates for larger instances.

In summary, if you have 67 GB of data at any given time and want one replica, your *minimum* storage requirement is closer to 67 * 2 * 1.1 / 0.95 / 0.8 = 194 GB. You can generalize this calculation as follows:

Source Data * (1 + Number of Replicas) * (1 + Indexing Overhead) / (1 - Linux Reserved Space) / (1 - Amazon ES Overhead) = Minimum Storage Requirement

Or you can use this simplified version:

Source Data * (1 + Number of Replicas) * 1.45 = Minimum Storage Requirement

Insufficient storage space is one of the most common causes of cluster instability, so you should cross-check the numbers when you choose instance types, instance counts, and storage volumes.

Note
If your minimum storage requirement exceeds 1 PB, see Petabyte Scale for Amazon Elasticsearch Service.

Choosing the Number of Shards

After you understand your storage requirements, you can investigate your indexing strategy. Each Elasticsearch index is split into some number of shards. Because you can't easily change the number of primary shards for an existing index, you should decide about shard count *before* indexing your first document.

The overarching goal of choosing a number of shards is to distribute an index evenly across all data nodes in the cluster. However, these shards shouldn't be too large or too numerous. A good rule of thumb is to try to keep shard size between 10–50 GB. Large shards can make it difficult for Elasticsearch to recover from failure, but because each shard uses some amount of CPU and memory, having too many small shards can cause performance issues and out of memory errors. In other words, shards should be small enough that the underlying Amazon ES instance can handle them, but not so small that they place needless strain on the hardware.

For example, suppose you have 67 GB of data. You don't expect that number to increase over time, and you want to keep your shards around 30 GB each. Your number of shards therefore should be approximately 67 * 1.1 / 30 = 3. You can generalize this calculation as follows:

(Source Data + Room to Grow) * (1 + Indexing Overhead) / Desired Shard Size = Approximate Number of Primary Shards

This equation helps compensate for growth over time. If you expect those same 67 GB of data to quadruple over the next year, the approximate number of shards is (67 + 201) * 1.1 / 30 = 10. Remember, though, you don't have those extra 201 GB of data *yet*. Check to make sure this preparation for the future doesn't create unnecessarily tiny shards that consume huge amounts of CPU and memory in the present. In this case, 67 * 1.1 / 10 shards = 7.4 GB per shard, which will consume extra resources and is below the recommended size range. You might consider the more middle-of-the-road approach of six shards, which leaves you with 12 GB shards today and 49 GB shards in the future. Then again, you might prefer to start with three 30 GB shards and reindex your data when the shards exceed 50 GB.

Note
By default, Elasticsearch indices are split into five primary shards. You can specify different settings when you create an index.

Choosing Instance Types and Testing

After you calculate your storage requirements and choose the number of shards that you need, you can start to make hardware decisions. Hardware requirements vary dramatically by workload, but we can still offer some basic recommendations.

In general, the storage limits for each instance type map to the amount of CPU and memory you might need for light workloads. For example, an `m4.large.elasticsearch` instance has a maximum EBS volume size of 512 GB, 2 vCPU cores, and 8 GB of memory. If your cluster has many shards, performs taxing aggregations, updates documents frequently, or processes a large number of queries, those resources might be insufficient for your needs. If you believe your cluster falls into one of these categories, try starting with a configuration closer to 2 vCPU cores and 8 GB of memory for every 100 GB of your storage requirement.

Tip

For a summary of the hardware resources that are allocated to each instance type, see Amazon Elasticsearch Service Pricing.

Still, even those resources might be insufficient. Some Elasticsearch users report that they need many times those resources to fulfill their requirements. Finding the right hardware for your workload means making an educated initial estimate, testing with representative workloads, adjusting, and testing again:

1. To start, we recommend a minimum of three instances to avoid potential Elasticsearch issues, such as the split brain issue. If you have three dedicated master nodes, we still recommend a minimum of two data nodes for replication.

2. If you have a 184 GB storage requirement and the recommended minimum number of three instances, you use the equation 184 / 3 = 61 GB to find the amount of storage that each instance needs. In this example, you might select three `m3.medium.elasticsearch` instances for your cluster, each using a 90 GB EBS storage volume so that you have a safety net and some room for growth over time. This configuration provides 3 vCPU cores and 12 GB of memory, so it's suited to lighter workloads.

   For a more substantial example, consider a 14 TB storage requirement and a heavy workload. In this case, you might choose to begin testing with 2 * 140 = 280 vCPU cores and 8 * 140 = 1120 GB of memory. These numbers work out to approximately 18 `i3.4xlarge.elasticsearch` instances. If you don't need the fast, local storage or extra RAM, you could also test 18 `m4.4xlarge.elasticsearch` instances, each using a 900 GB EBS storage volume.

3. After configuring the cluster, you can add your index, perform some representative client testing using a realistic dataset, and monitor CloudWatch metrics to see how the cluster handles the workload.

4. If performance satisfies your needs, tests succeed, and CloudWatch metrics are normal, the cluster is ready to use. Remember to set CloudWatch alarms to detect unhealthy resource usage.

   If performance isn't acceptable, tests fail, or `CPUUtilization` or `JVMMemoryPressure` are high, you might need to choose a different instance type (or add instances) and continue testing. As you add instances, Elasticsearch automatically rebalances the distribution of shards throughout the cluster.

   Because it is easier to measure the excess capacity in an overpowered cluster than the deficit in an underpowered one, we recommend starting with a larger cluster than you think you need, testing, and scaling down to an efficient cluster that has the extra resources to ensure stable operations during periods of increased activity.

Production clusters or clusters with complex states benefit from dedicated master nodes, which improve performance and cluster reliability.

Dedicated Master Nodes

Amazon Elasticsearch Service uses *dedicated master nodes* to increase cluster stability. A dedicated master node performs cluster management tasks, but does not hold data or respond to data upload requests. This offloading of cluster management tasks increases the stability of your domain.

We recommend that you allocate **three** dedicated master nodes for each production Amazon ES domain:

1. One dedicated master node means that you have no backup in the event of a failure.

2. Two dedicated master nodes means that your cluster does not have the necessary quorum of nodes to elect a new master node in the event of a failure.

   A quorum is Number of Dedicated Master Nodes / 2 + 1 (rounded down to the nearest whole number), which Amazon ES sets to `discovery.zen.minimum_master_nodes` when you create your domain.

   In this case, 2 / 2 + 1 = 2. Because one dedicated master node has failed and only one backup exists, the cluster does not have a quorum and cannot elect a new master.

3. Three dedicated master nodes, the recommended number, provides two backup nodes in the event of a master node failure and the necessary quorum (2) to elect a new master.

4. Four dedicated master nodes is no better than three and can cause issues if you use zone awareness.

   - If one master node fails, you have the quorum (3) to elect a new master. If two nodes fail, you lose that quorum, just as you do with three dedicated master nodes.
   - If each Availability Zone has two dedicated master nodes and the zones are unable to communicate with each other, neither zone has the quorum to elect a new master.

5. Having five dedicated master nodes works as well as three and allows you to lose two nodes while maintaining a quorum, but because only one dedicated master node is active at any given time, this configuration means paying for four idle nodes. Many customers find this level of failover protection excessive.

Note

If your cluster does not have does not have the necessary quorum to elect a new master node, write *and* read requests to the cluster both fail. This behavior differs from the Elasticsearch default.

Dedicated master nodes perform the following cluster management tasks:

- Track all nodes in the cluster
- Track the number of indices in the cluster
- Track the number of shards belonging to each index
- Maintain routing information for nodes in the cluster
- Update the cluster state after state changes, such as creating an index and adding or removing nodes in the cluster
- Replicate changes to the cluster state across all nodes in the cluster
- Monitor the health of all cluster nodes by sending *heartbeat signals*, periodic signals that monitor the availability of the data nodes in the cluster

The following illustration shows an Amazon ES domain with ten instances. Seven of the instances are data nodes and three are dedicated master nodes. Only one of the dedicated master nodes is active; the two gray dedicated master nodes wait as backup in case the active dedicated master node fails. All data upload requests are served by the seven data nodes, and all cluster management tasks are offloaded to the active dedicated master node.

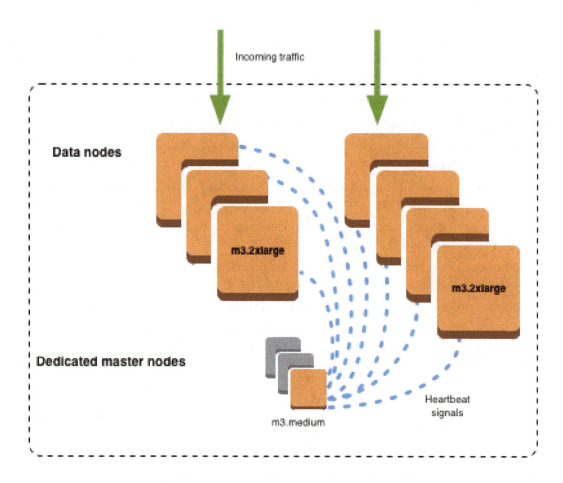

Although dedicated master nodes do not process search and query requests, their size is highly correlated with the number of instances, indices, and shards that they can manage. For production clusters, we recommend the following instance types for dedicated master nodes. These recommendations are based on typical workloads and can vary based on your needs.

Instance Count	Recommended Minimum Dedicated Master Instance Type
5–10	`m3.medium.elasticsearch`
10–20	`m4.large.elasticsearch`
20–50	`c4.xlarge.elasticsearch`
50–100	`c4.2xlarge.elasticsearch`

- For recommendations on dedicated master nodes for large clusters, see Petabyte Scale for Amazon Elasticsearch Service.
- For information about how certain configuration changes can affect dedicated master nodes, see About Configuration Changes.
- For clarification on instance count limits, see Cluster and Instance Limits.
- For more information about specific instance types, including vCPU, memory, and pricing, see Amazon Elasticsearch Instance Prices.

Recommended CloudWatch Alarms

CloudWatch alarms perform an action when a CloudWatch metric exceeds a specified value for some amount of time. For example, you might want AWS to email you if your cluster health status is `red` for longer than one minute. This section includes some recommended alarms and how to respond to them.

For more information about setting alarms, see Creating Amazon CloudWatch Alarms in the *Amazon CloudWatch User Guide*.

[See the AWS documentation website for more details]

Note
If you just want to *view* metrics, see Monitoring CloudWatch Metrics.

Petabyte Scale for Amazon Elasticsearch Service

Amazon Elasticsearch Service offers domain storage of up to 1.5 PB. You can configure a domain with 100 `i3.16xlarge.elasticsearch` instance types, each with 15 TB of storage. Because of the sheer difference in scale, recommendations for domains of this size differ from our general recommendations. This section discusses considerations for creating domains, costs, storage, shard size, and dedicated master nodes. Despite frequent references to the `i3` instance types, the shard size and dedicated master node recommendations in this section apply to any domain approaching petabyte scale.

Creating domains
Domains of this size exceed the default limit of 20 instances per domain. To request a service limit increase of up to 100 instances per domain, open a case at the AWS Support Center.

Pricing
Before creating a domain of this size, check the Amazon Elasticsearch Service Pricing page to ensure that the associated costs match your expectations.

Storage
The `i3` instance types are specifically designed to provide fast, local non-volatile memory express (NVMe) storage. Because this local storage tends to offer considerable performance benefits when compared to Amazon Elastic Block Store, EBS volumes are not an option when you select these instance types in Amazon ES.

Shard size
A common Elasticsearch guideline is not to exceed 50 GB per shard. Given the number of shards necessary to accommodate a 1.5 PB storage requirement, we recommend a shard size of *at least* 100 GB.

For example, if you have 450 TB of source data and want one replica, your *minimum* storage requirement is closer to 450 TB * 2 * 1.1 / 0.95 = 1.04 PB. For an explanation of this calculation, see Calculating Storage Requirements. Although 1.04 PB / 15 TB = 70 instances, you might select 77 or more `i3.16xlarge.elasticsearch` instances to give yourself a storage safety net and account for some variance in the amount of data over time. Each instance adds another 20 GB to your minimum storage requirement, but for disks of this size, those 20 GB are almost negligible.

To calculate the number of primary shards, use this formula: 450,000 GB * 1.1 / 150 GB per shard = 3,300 shards. As always, the most important step of sizing and configuring your domain is to perform representative client testing using a realistic data set.

Dedicated master nodes
We recommend that you allocate three dedicated master nodes to each production Amazon ES domain. Rather than our usual guidelines for dedicated master nodes, however, we recommend more powerful instance types for domains of this size. The following table shows recommended instance types for dedicated master nodes for large domains.

[See the AWS documentation website for more details]

126

VPC Support for Amazon Elasticsearch Service Domains

A *virtual private cloud* (VPC) is a virtual network that is dedicated to your AWS account. It's logically isolated from other virtual networks in the AWS Cloud. You can launch AWS resources, such as Amazon ES domains, into your VPC.

Placing an Amazon ES domain within a VPC enables secure communication between Amazon ES and other services within the VPC without the need for an internet gateway, NAT device, or VPN connection. All traffic remains securely within the AWS Cloud. Because of their logical isolation, domains that reside within a VPC have an extra layer of security when compared to domains that use public endpoints.

To support VPCs, Amazon ES places an endpoint into either one or two subnets of your VPC. A *subnet* is a range of IP addresses in your VPC. If you enable zone awareness for your domain, Amazon ES places an endpoint into two subnets. The subnets must be in different Availability Zones in the same region. If you don't enable zone awareness, Amazon ES places an endpoint into only one subnet.

The following illustration shows the VPC architecture if zone awareness is not enabled.

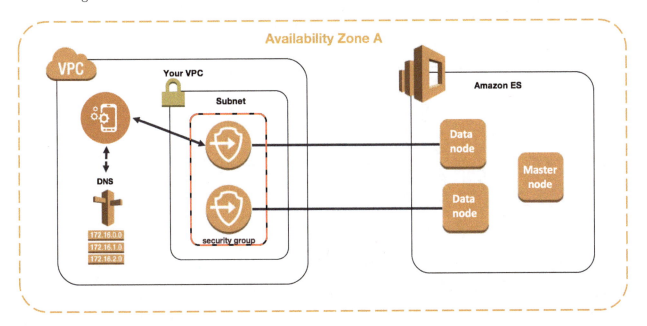

The following illustration shows the VPC architecture if zone awareness is enabled.

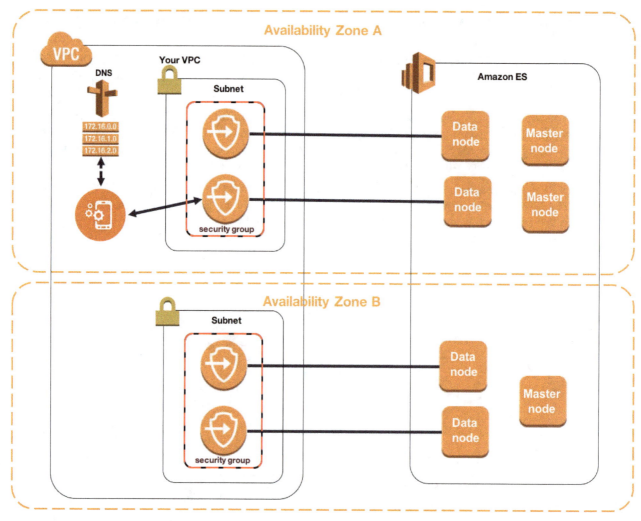

Amazon ES also places an *elastic network interface* (ENI) in the VPC for each of your data nodes. Amazon ES assigns each ENI a private IP address from the IPv4 address range of your subnet. The service also assigns a public DNS hostname (which is the domain endpoint) for the IP addresses. You must use a public DNS service to resolve the endpoint (which is a DNS hostname) to the appropriate IP addresses for the data nodes:

- If your VPC uses the Amazon-provided DNS server by setting the `enableDnsSupport` option to `true` (the default value), resolution for the Amazon ES endpoint will succeed.
- If your VPC uses a private DNS server and the server can reach the public authoritative DNS servers to resolve DNS hostnames, resolution for the Amazon ES endpoint will also succeed.

Because the IP addresses might change, you should resolve the domain endpoint periodically so that you can always access the correct data nodes. We recommend that you set the DNS resolution interval to one minute. If you're using a client, you should also ensure that the DNS cache in the client is cleared.

Note
Amazon ES doesn't support IPv6 addresses with a VPC. You can use a VPC that has IPv6 enabled, but the domain will use IPv4 addresses.

Topics

- Limitations
- About Access Policies on VPC Domains
- Before You Begin: Prerequisites for VPC Access
- Creating a VPC
- Reserving IP Addresses in a VPC Subnet

- Service-Linked Role for VPC Access
- Migrating from Public Access to VPC Access
- Amazon VPC Documentation

Limitations

Currently, operating an Amazon ES domain within a VPC has the following limitations:

- You can either launch your domain within a VPC or use a public endpoint, but you can't do both. You must choose one or the other when you create your domain.
- If you launch a new domain within a VPC, you can't later switch it to use a public endpoint. The reverse is also true: If you create a domain with a public endpoint, you can't later place it within a VPC. Instead, you must create a new domain and migrate your data.
- You can't launch your domain within a VPC that uses dedicated tenancy. You must use a VPC with tenancy set to **Default**.
- After you place a domain within a VPC, you can't move it to a different VPC. However, you can change the subnets and security group settings.
- Compared to public domains, VPC domains display less information in the Amazon ES console. Specifically, the **Cluster health** tab does not include shard information, and the **Indices** tab is not present at all.
- Currently, Amazon ES does not support integration with Amazon Kinesis Data Firehose for domains that reside within a VPC. To use this service with Amazon ES, you must use a domain with public access.
- To access the default installation of Kibana for a domain that resides within a VPC, users must have access to the VPC. This process varies by network configuration, but likely involves connecting to a VPN or managed network or using a proxy server. To learn more, see About Access Policies on VPC Domains, the Amazon VPC User Guide, and Controlling Access to Kibana.

About Access Policies on VPC Domains

Placing your Amazon ES domain within a VPC provides an inherent, strong layer of security. When you create a domain with public access, the endpoint takes the following form:

```
1 https://search-domain-name-identifier.region.es.amazonaws.com
```

As the "public" label suggests, this endpoint is accessible from any internet-connected device, though you can (and should) control access to it. If you access the endpoint in a web browser, you might receive a `Not Authorized` message, but the request reaches the domain.

When you create a domain with VPC access, the endpoint *looks* similar to a public endpoint:

```
1 https://vpc-domain-name-identifier.region.es.amazonaws.com
```

If you try to access the endpoint in a web browser, however, you might find that the request times out. To perform even basic `GET` requests, your computer must be able to connect to the VPC. This connection often takes the form of an internet gateway, VPN server, or proxy server. For details on the various forms it can take, see Scenarios and Examples in the *Amazon VPC User Guide.*

In addition to this connectivity requirement, VPCs let you manage access to the domain through security groups. For many use cases, this combination of security features is sufficient, and you might feel comfortable applying an open access policy to the domain.

Operating with an open access policy does *not* mean that anyone on the internet can access the Amazon ES domain. Rather, it means that if a request reaches the Amazon ES domain and the associated security groups permit it, the domain accepts the request without further security checks.

For an additional layer of security, we recommend using access policies that specify IAM users or roles. Applying these policies means that, for the domain to accept a request, the security groups must permit it *and* it must be signed with valid credentials.

Note

Because security groups already enforce IP-based access policies, you can't apply IP-based access policies to Amazon ES domains that reside within a VPC. If you use public access, IP-based policies are still available.

Before You Begin: Prerequisites for VPC Access

Before you can enable a connection between a VPC and your new Amazon ES domain, you must do the following:

- **Create a VPC**

  To create your VPC, you can use the Amazon VPC console, the AWS CLI, or one of the AWS SDKs. You must create a subnet in the VPC, or two subnets if you enable zone awareness. For more information, see Creating A VPC. If you already have a VPC, you can skip this step.

- ****Reserve IP addresses ****

  Amazon ES enables the connection of a VPC to a domain by placing network interfaces in a subnet of the VPC. Each network interface is associated with an IP address. You must reserve a sufficient number of IP addresses in the subnet for the network interfaces. For more information, see Reserving IP Addresses in a VPC Subnet.

Creating a VPC

To create your VPC, you can use one of the following: the Amazon VPC console, the AWS CLI, or one of the AWS SDKs. The VPC must have a subnet, or two subnets if you enable zone awareness. The two subnets must be in different Availability Zones in the same region.

The following procedure shows how to use the Amazon VPC console to create a VPC with a public subnet, reserve IP addresses for the subnet, and create a security group to control access to your Amazon ES domain. For other VPC configurations, see Scenarios and Examples in the *Amazon VPC User Guide*.

To create a VPC (console)

1. Sign in to the AWS Management Console, and open the Amazon VPC console at https://console.aws.amazon.com/vpc/.

2. In the navigation pane, choose **VPC Dashboard**.

3. Choose **Start VPC Wizard**.

4. On the **Select a VPC Configuration** page, select **VPC with a Single Public Subnet**.

5. On the **VPC with a Single Public Subnet** page, keep the default options, and then choose **Create VPC**.

6. In the confirmation message that appears, choose **Close**.

7. If you intend to enable zone awareness for your Amazon ES domain, you must create a second subnet in a different Availability Zone in the same region. If you don't intend to enable zone awareness, skip to step 8.

    1. In the navigation pane, choose **Subnets**.

    2. Choose **Create Subnet**.

    3. In the **Create Subnet** dialog box, optionally create a name tag to help you identify the subnet later.

    4. For **VPC**, choose the VPC that you just created.

    5. For **Availability Zone**, choose an Availability Zone that differs from that of the first subnet. The Availability Zones for both subnets must be in the same region.

6. For **IPv4 CIDR block**, configure a CIDR block large enough to provide sufficient IP addresses for Amazon ES to use during maintenance activities. For more information, see Reserving IP Addresses in a VPC Subnet. **Note**
   Amazon ES domains using VPC access don't support IPv6 addresses. You can use a VPC that has IPv6 enabled, but the ENIs will have IPv4 addresses.

7. Choose **Yes, Create**.

8. In the navigation pane, choose **Subnets**.

9. In the list of subnets, find your subnet (or subnets, if you created a second subnet in step 7). In the **Available IPv4** column, confirm that you have a sufficient number of IPv4 addresses.

10. Make a note of the subnet ID and Availability Zone. You need this information later when you launch your Amazon ES domain and add an Amazon EC2 instance to your VPC.

11. Create an Amazon VPC security group. You use this security group to control access to your Amazon ES domain.

    1. In the navigation pane, choose **Security Groups**.

    2. Choose **Create Security Group**.

    3. In the **Create Security Group** dialog box, type a name tag, a group name, and a description. For **VPC**, choose the ID of your VPC.

    4. Choose **Yes, Create**.

12. Define a network ingress rule for your security group. This rule allows you to connect to your Amazon ES domain.

    1. In the navigation pane, choose **Security Groups**, and then select the security group that you just created.

    2. At the bottom of the page, choose the **Inbound Rules** tab.

    3. Choose **Edit**, and then choose **HTTPS (443)**.

    4. Choose **Save**.

Now you are ready to launch an Amazon ES domain in your Amazon VPC.

Reserving IP Addresses in a VPC Subnet

Amazon ES connects a domain to a VPC by placing network interfaces in a subnet of the VPC (or two subnets of the VPC if you enable zone awareness). Each network interface is associated with an IP address. Before you create your Amazon ES domain, you must have a sufficient number of IP addresses available in the VPC subnet to accommodate the network interfaces.

The number of IP addresses that Amazon ES requires depends on the following:

- Number of data nodes in your domain. (Master nodes are not included in the number.)
- Whether you enable zone awareness. If you enable zone awareness, you need only half the number of IP addresses per subnet that you need if you don't enable zone awareness.

Here is the basic formula: The number of IP addresses reserved in each subnet is three times the number of nodes, divided by two if zone awareness is enabled.

Examples

- If a domain has 10 data nodes and zone awareness is enabled, the IP count is 10 / 2 * 3 = 15.
- If a domain has 10 data nodes and zone awareness is disabled, the IP count is 10 * 3 = 30.

When you create the domain, Amazon ES reserves the IP addresses. You can see the network interfaces and their associated IP addresses in the **Network Interfaces** section of the Amazon EC2 console at https://console.aws.amazon.com/ec2/. The **Description** column shows which Amazon ES domain the network interface is associated with.

Tip

We recommend that you create dedicated subnets for the Amazon ES reserved IP addresses. By using dedicated subnets, you avoid overlap with other applications and services and ensure that you can reserve additional IP addresses if you need to scale your cluster in the future. To learn more, see Creating a Subnet in Your VPC.

Service-Linked Role for VPC Access

A service-linked role is a unique type of IAM role that delegates permissions to a service so that it can create and manage resources on your behalf. Amazon ES requires a service-linked role to access your VPC, create the domain endpoint, and place network interfaces in a subnet of your VPC.

Amazon ES automatically creates the role when you use the Amazon ES console to create a domain within a VPC. For this automatic creation to succeed, you must have permissions for the `iam:CreateServiceLinkedRole` action. To learn more, see Service-Linked Role Permissions in the *IAM User Guide*.

After Amazon ES creates the role, you can view it (`AWSServiceRoleForAmazonElasticsearchService`) using the IAM console.

Note

If you create a domain that uses a public endpoint, Amazon ES doesn't need the service-linked role and doesn't create it.

For full information on this role's permissions and how to delete it, see Using Service-Linked Roles for Amazon ES.

Migrating from Public Access to VPC Access

When you create a domain, you specify whether it should have a public endpoint or reside within a VPC. Once created, you cannot switch from one to the other. Instead, you must create a new domain and either manually reindex or migrate your data. Snapshots offer a convenient means of migrating data. For information about taking and restoring snapshots, see Working with Amazon Elasticsearch Service Index Snapshots.

Amazon VPC Documentation

Amazon VPC has its own set of documentation to describe how to create and use your Amazon VPC. The following table provides links to the Amazon VPC guides.

Description	Documentation
How to get started using Amazon VPC	Amazon VPC Getting Started Guide
How to use Amazon VPC through the AWS Management Console	Amazon VPC User Guide
Complete descriptions of all the Amazon VPC commands	Amazon EC2 Command Line Reference (The Amazon VPC commands are part of the Amazon EC2 reference.)
Complete descriptions of the Amazon VPC API actions, data types, and errors	Amazon EC2 API Reference (The Amazon VPC API actions are part of the Amazon EC2 reference.)

Description	Documentation
Information for the network administrator who configures the gateway at your end of an optional IPsec VPN connection	Amazon VPC Network Administrator Guide

For more detailed information about Amazon Virtual Private Cloud, see Amazon Virtual Private Cloud.

Encryption of Data at Rest for Amazon Elasticsearch Service

Amazon ES domains offer encryption of data at rest, a security feature that helps prevent unauthorized access to your data. The feature uses AWS Key Management Service (KMS) to store and manage your encryption keys. If enabled, it encrypts the following aspects of a domain:

- Indices
- Automated snapshots
- Elasticsearch logs
- Swap files
- All other data in the application directory

The following are *not* encrypted when you enable encryption of data at rest, but you can take additional steps to protect them:

- Manual snapshots: Currently, you can't use KMS master keys to encrypt manual snapshots. You can, however, use server-side encryption with S3-managed keys to encrypt the bucket that you use as a snapshot repository. For instructions, see Registering a Manual Snapshot Repository.
- Slow logs: If you publish slow logs and want to encrypt them, you can encrypt their CloudWatch Logs log group using the same KMS master key as the Amazon ES domain. To learn more, see Encrypt Log Data in CloudWatch Logs Using AWS KMS in the Amazon CloudWatch Logs User Guide.

To learn how to create KMS master keys, see Creating Keys in the *AWS Key Management Service Developer Guide*.

Enabling Encryption of Data at Rest

By default, domains do not encrypt data at rest, and you can't configure existing domains to use the feature. To enable the feature, you must create another domain and migrate your data. Encryption of data at rest requires Elasticsearch 5.1 or newer.

In order to use the Amazon ES console to create a domain that encrypts data at rest, you must have read-only permissions to KMS, such as the following identity-based policy:

```
1  {
2    "Version": "2012-10-17",
3    "Statement": [
4      {
5        "Effect": "Allow",
6        "Action": [
7          "kms:List*",
8          "kms:Describe*"
9        ],
10       "Resource": "*"
11     }
12   ]
13 }
```

If you want to use a key other than **(Default) aws/es**, you must also have permissions to create grants for the key. These permissions typically take the form of a resource-based policy that you specify when you create the key. To learn more, see Using Key Policies in AWS KMS in the *AWS Key Management Service Developer Guide*.

Disabling Encryption of Data at Rest

After you configure a domain to encrypt data at rest, you can't disable the setting. Instead, you can take a manual snapshot of the existing domain, create another domain, migrate your data, and delete the old domain.

Monitoring Domains That Encrypt Data at Rest

Domains that encrypt data at rest have two additional metrics: `KMSKeyError` and `KMSKeyInaccessible`. For full descriptions of these metrics, see Cluster Metrics. You can view them using the Amazon ES console or Amazon CloudWatch.

Tip
Each metric represents a significant problem for a domain, so we recommend that you create CloudWatch alarms for both. For more information, see Recommended CloudWatch Alarms.

Other Considerations

- If you delete the key that you used to encrypt a domain, the domain becomes inaccessible. The Amazon ES team can't help you recover your data. AWS Key Management Service deletes master keys only after a waiting period of at least seven days, so the Amazon ES team might contact you if they detect that your domain is at risk.

- Automatic key rotation preserves the properties of your KMS master keys, so the rotation has no effect on your ability to access your Elasticsearch data. Encrypted Amazon ES domains do not support manual key rotation, which involves creating a new master key and updating any references to the old key. To learn more, see Rotating Customer Master Keys in the *AWS Key Management Service Developer Guide*.

- Certain instance types do not support encryption of data at rest. For details, see Supported Instance Types.

- Encryption of data at rest is not available in the cn-northwest-1 (Ningxia) region.

- Kibana still works on domains that encrypt data at rest.

- Domains that encrypt data at rest use a different repository name for their automated snapshots. To learn more, see Restoring Snapshots.

- Encrypting an Amazon ES domain requires two grants, and each encryption key has a limit of 500 grants per principal. This limit means that the maximum number of Amazon ES domains you can encrypt using a single key is 250. At present, Amazon ES supports a maximum of 100 domains per account, so this grant limit is of no consequence. If the domain limit per account increases, however, the grant limit might become relevant.

  If you need to encrypt more than 250 domains at that time, you can create additional keys. Keys are regional, not global, so if you operate in more than one region, you already need multiple keys.

Using Curator to Rotate Data in Amazon Elasticsearch Service

This chapter has sample code for using AWS Lambda and Curator to manage indices and snapshots. Curator offers numerous filters to help you identity indices and snapshots that meet certain criteria, such as indices created more than 60 days ago or snapshots that failed to complete.

Although Curator is often used as a command line interface (CLI), it also features a Python API, which means that you can use it within Lambda functions.

For information about configuring Lambda functions and creating deployment packages, see Loading Streaming Data into Amazon ES from Amazon S3. For even more information, see the AWS Lambda Developer Guide. This chapter contains only sample code, basic settings, triggers, and permissions.

Topics

- Sample Code
- Basic Settings
- Triggers
- Permissions

Sample Code

The following sample code uses Curator and the official Python Elasticsearch client to delete any index whose name contains a time stamp indicating that the data is more than 30 days old. For example, if an index name is `my-logs-2014.03.02`, the index is deleted. Deletion occurs even if you create the index today, because this filter uses the name of the index to determine its age.

The code also contains some commented-out examples of other common filters, including one that determines age by creation date. The AWS SDK for Python (Boto 3) and requests-aws4auth library sign the requests to Amazon ES.

Warning

Both code samples in this section delete data—potentially a lot of data. Modify and test each sample on a non-critical domain until you're satisfied with its behavior.

Index Deletion

```
1  import boto3
2  from requests_aws4auth import AWS4Auth
3  from elasticsearch import Elasticsearch, RequestsHttpConnection
4  import curator
5
6  host = '' # For example, search-my-domain.region.es.amazonaws.com
7  region = '' # For example, us-west-1
8  service = 'es'
9  credentials = boto3.Session().get_credentials()
10 awsauth = AWS4Auth(credentials.access_key, credentials.secret_key, region, service,
       session_token=credentials.token)
11
12 # Lambda execution starts here.
13 def lambda_handler(event, context):
14
15     # Build the Elasticsearch client.
16     es = Elasticsearch(
17         hosts = [{'host': host, 'port': 443}],
18         http_auth = awsauth,
19         use_ssl = True,
```

```
20        verify_certs = True,
21        connection_class = RequestsHttpConnection
22    )
23
24    # A test document.
25    document = {
26        "title": "Moneyball",
27        "director": "Bennett Miller",
28        "year": "2011"
29    }
30
31    # Index the test document so that we have an index that matches the timestring pattern.
32    # You can delete this line and the test document if you already created some test indices.
33    es.index(index="movies-2017.01.31", doc_type="movie", id="1", body=document)
34
35    index_list = curator.IndexList(es)
36
37    # Filters by age, anything with a time stamp older than 30 days in the index name.
38    index_list.filter_by_age(source='name', direction='older', timestring='%Y.%m.%d', unit='days
          ', unit_count=30)
39
40    # Filters by naming prefix.
41    # index_list.filter_by_regex(kind='prefix', value='my-logs-2017')
42
43    # Filters by age, anything created more than one month ago.
44    # index_list.filter_by_age(source='creation_date', direction='older', unit='months',
          unit_count=1)
45
46    # Delete all indices in the filtered list.
47    curator.DeleteIndices(index_list).do_action()
```

You must update the values for host and region.

The next code sample deletes any snapshot that is more than two weeks old. It also takes a new snapshot.

Snapshot Deletion

```
1 import boto3
2 from datetime import datetime
3 from requests_aws4auth import AWS4Auth
4 from elasticsearch import Elasticsearch, RequestsHttpConnection
5 import logging
6 import curator
7
8 # Adding a logger isn't strictly required, but helps with understanding Curator's requests and
       debugging.
9 logger = logging.getLogger('curator')
10 logger.addHandler(logging.StreamHandler())
11 logger.setLevel(logging.INFO)
12
13 host = ''  # For example, search-my-domain.region.es.amazonaws.com
14 region = ''  # For example, us-west-1
15 service = 'es'
16 credentials = boto3.Session().get_credentials()
17 awsauth = AWS4Auth(credentials.access_key, credentials.secret_key, region, service,
       session_token=credentials.token)
```

```
18
19 now = datetime.now()
20 # Clunky, but this approach keeps colons out of the URL.
21 date_string = '-'.join((str(now.year), str(now.month), str(now.day), str(now.hour), str(now.
      second)))
22
23 snapshot_name = 'my-snapshot-prefix-' + date_string
24 repository_name = 'my-repo'
25
26 # Lambda execution starts here.
27 def lambda_handler(event, context):
28
29     # Build the Elasticsearch client.
30     es = Elasticsearch(
31         hosts = [{'host': host, 'port': 443}],
32         http_auth = awsauth,
33         use_ssl = True,
34         verify_certs = True,
35         connection_class = RequestsHttpConnection,
36         timeout = 120 # Deleting snapshots can take a while, so keep the connection open for
            long enough to get a response.
37     )
38
39     try:
40         # Get all snapshots in the repository.
41         snapshot_list = curator.SnapshotList(es, repository=repository_name)
42
43         # Filter by age, any snapshot older than two weeks.
44         # snapshot_list.filter_by_age(source='creation_date', direction='older', unit='weeks',
            unit_count=2)
45
46         # Delete the old snapshots.
47         curator.DeleteSnapshots(snapshot_list, retry_interval=30, retry_count=3).do_action()
48     except (curator.exceptions.SnapshotInProgress, curator.exceptions.NoSnapshots, curator.
        exceptions.FailedExecution) as e:
49         print(e)
50
51     # Split into two try blocks. We still want to try and take a snapshot if deletion failed.
52     try:
53         # Get the list of indexes.
54         # You can filter this list if you didn't want to snapshot all indexes.
55         index_list = curator.IndexList(es)
56
57         # Take a new snapshot. This operation can take a while, so we don't want to wait for it
            to complete.
58         curator.Snapshot(index_list, repository=repository_name, name=snapshot_name,
            wait_for_completion=False).do_action()
59     except (curator.exceptions.SnapshotInProgress, curator.exceptions.FailedExecution) as e:
60         print(e)
```

You must update the values for host, region, snapshot_name, and repository_name. If the output is too verbose for your taste, you can change logging.INFO to logging.WARN.

Because taking and deleting snapshots can take a while, this code is more sensitive to connection and Lambda timeouts—hence the extra logging code. In the Elasticsearch client, you can see that we set the timeout to 120 seconds. If the `DeleteSnapshots` function takes longer to get a response from the Amazon ES domain, you might need to increase this value. You must also increase the Lambda function timeout from its default value of three seconds. For a recommended value, see Basic Settings.

Basic Settings

We recommend the following settings for the code samples in this chapter.

Sample Code	Memory	Timeout
Index Deletion	128 MB	10 seconds
Snapshot Deletion	128 MB	3 minutes

Triggers

Rather than reacting to some event (such as a file upload to Amazon S3), these functions are meant to be scheduled. You might prefer to run these functions more or less frequently.

Sample Code	Service	Rule Type	Example Expression
Index Deletion	CloudWatch Events	Schedule expression	rate(1 day)
Snapshot Deletion	CloudWatch Events	Schedule expression	rate(4 hours)

Permissions

Both Lambda functions in this chapter need the basic logging permissions that all Lambda functions need, plus HTTP method permissions for the Amazon ES domain:

```
1  {
2    "Version": "2012-10-17",
3    "Statement": [
4      {
5        "Effect": "Allow",
6        "Action": "logs:CreateLogGroup",
7        "Resource": "arn:aws:logs:us-west-1:123456789012:*"
8      },
9      {
10       "Effect": "Allow",
11       "Action": [
12         "logs:CreateLogStream",
13         "logs:PutLogEvents"
14       ],
15       "Resource": [
16         "arn:aws:logs:us-west-1:123456789012:log-group:/aws/lambda/your-lambda-function:*"
17       ]
18     },
19     {
20       "Effect": "Allow",
21       "Action": [
22         "es:ESHttpPost",
23         "es:ESHttpGet",
24         "es:ESHttpPut",
```

```
25        "es:ESHttpDelete"
26      ],
27      "Resource": "arn:aws:es:us-west-1:123456789012:domain/my-domain/*"
28    }
29  ]
30 }
```

Handling AWS Service Errors

This section describes how to respond to common AWS service errors. Consult the information in this section before contacting AWS Support.

Failed Cluster Nodes

Amazon EC2 instances might experience unexpected terminations and restarts. Typically, Amazon ES restarts the nodes for you. However, it's possible for one or more nodes in an Elasticsearch cluster to remain in a failed condition.

To check for this condition, open your domain dashboard on the Amazon ES console. Choose the **Monitoring** tab, and then choose the **Nodes** metric. See if the reported number of nodes is fewer than the number that you configured for your cluster. If the metric shows that one or more nodes is down for more than one day, contact AWS Support.

You can also set a CloudWatch alarm to notify you when this issue occurs.

Note
The **Nodes** metric is not accurate during changes to your cluster configuration and during routine maintenance for the service. This behavior is expected. The metric will report the correct number of cluster nodes soon. To learn more, see About Configuration Changes.

To protect your clusters from unexpected node terminations and restarts, create at least one replica for each index in your Amazon ES domain.

Red Cluster Status

A red cluster status means that at least one primary shard and its replicas are not allocated to a node. Amazon ES stops taking automatic snapshots, even of healthy indices, while the red cluster status persists.

The most common causes of a red cluster status are failed cluster nodes and the Elasticsearch process crashing due to a continuous heavy processing load.

Note
Amazon ES stores up to 14 daily automated snapshots for 30 days, so if the red cluster status persists for more than 16 days, permanent data loss can occur. If your Amazon ES domain enters a red cluster status, AWS Support might contact you to ask whether you want to address the problem yourself or you want the support team to assist. You can set a CloudWatch alarm to notify you when a red cluster status occurs.

Ultimately, red shards cause red clusters, and red indices cause red shards. To identity the indices causing the red cluster status, Elasticsearch has some helpful APIs.

- `GET /_cluster/allocation/explain` chooses the first unassigned shard that it finds and explains why it cannot be allocated to a node:

```
1 {
2     "index": "test4",
3     "shard": 0,
4     "primary": true,
5     "current_state": "unassigned",
6     "can_allocate": "no",
7     "allocate_explanation": "cannot allocate because allocation is not permitted to any of
            the nodes"
8 }
```

- `GET /_cat/indices?v` shows the health status, number of documents, and disk usage for each index:

```
1 health status index              uuid                   pri rep docs.count docs.deleted store
    .size pri.store.size
2 green  open   test1              30h1EiMvS5uAFr2t5CEVoQ   5   0       820             0
            14mb            14mb
3 green  open   test2              sdIxs_WDT56afFGu5KPbFQ   1   0         0             0
            233b            233b
4 green  open   test3              GGRZp_TBRZuSaZpAGk2pmw   1   1         2             0
        14.7kb         7.3kb
5 red    open   test4              BJxfAErbTtu5HBjIXJV_7A   1   0
6 green  open   test5              _8C6MIXOSxCqVYicH3jsEA   1   0         7             0
        24.3kb         24.3kb
```

Deleting red indices is the fastest way to fix a red cluster status. Depending on the reason for the red cluster status, you might then scale your Amazon ES domain to use larger instance types, more instances, or more EBS-based storage and try to recreate the problematic indices.

If deleting a problematic index isn't feasible, you can restore a snapshot, delete documents from the index, change the index settings, reduce the number of replicas, or delete other indices to free up disk space. The important step is to resolve the red cluster status *before* reconfiguring your Amazon ES domain. Reconfiguring a domain with a red cluster status can compound the problem and lead to the domain being stuck in a configuration state of **Processing** until you resolve the status.

Recovering from a Continuous Heavy Processing Load

To determine if a red cluster status is due to a continuous heavy processing load on a data node, monitor the following cluster metrics.

Relevant Metric	Description	Recovery
JVMMemoryPressure	Specifies the percentage of the Java heap used for all data nodes in a cluster. View the **Maximum** statistic for this metric, and look for smaller and smaller drops in memory pressure as the Java garbage collector fails to reclaim sufficient memory. This pattern likely is due to complex queries or large data fields. At 75% memory usage, Elasticsearch triggers the Concurrent Mark Sweep (CMS) garbage collector, which runs alongside other processes to keep pauses and disruptions to a minimum. If CMS fails to reclaim enough memory and usage remains above 75%, Elasticsearch triggers a different garbage collection algorithm that halts or slows other processes in order to free up sufficient memory to prevent an out of memory error. At 95% memory usage, Elasticsearch kills processes that attempt to allocate memory. It might kill a critical process and bring down one or more nodes in the cluster. The `_nodes/stats/jvm` API offers a useful summary of JVM statistics, memory pool usage, and garbage collection information: GET elasticsearch_domain_endpoint/_nodes/stats/jvm?pretty	Set memory circuit breakers for the JVM. For more information, see JVM OutOfMemoryError. If the problem persists, delete unnecessary indices, reduce the number or complexity of requests to the domain, add instances, or use larger instance types.
CPUUtilization	Specifies the percentage of CPU resources used for data nodes in a cluster. View the Maximum statistic for this metric, and look for a continuous pattern of high usage.	Add data nodes or increase the size of the instance types of existing data nodes. For more information, see Configuring Amazon ES Domains.
Nodes	Specifies the number of nodes in a cluster. View the Minimum statistic for this metric. This value fluctuates when the service deploys a new fleet of instances for a cluster.	Add data nodes. For more information, see Configuring Amazon ES Domains.

Yellow Cluster Status

A yellow cluster status means that the primary shards for all indices are allocated to nodes in a cluster, but the replica shards for at least one index are not. Single-node clusters always initialize with a yellow cluster status because there is no other node to which Amazon ES can assign a replica. To achieve green cluster status, increase your node count. For more information, see Sizing Amazon ES Domains and Configuring Amazon ES Domains.

ClusterBlockException

You might receive a `ClusterBlockException` error for the following reasons.

Lack of Available Storage Space

If no nodes have enough storage space to accommodate shard relocation, basic write operations like adding documents and creating indices can begin to fail. Calculating Storage Requirements provides a summary of how Amazon ES uses disk space.

To avoid issues, monitor the `FreeStorageSpace` metric in the Amazon ES console and create CloudWatch alarms to trigger when `FreeStorageSpace` drops below a certain threshold. `GET /_cat/allocation?v` also provides a useful summary of shard allocation and disk usage. To resolve issues associated with a lack of storage space, scale your Amazon ES domain to use larger instance types, more instances, or more EBS-based storage. For instructions, see Configuring Amazon ES Domains.

Block Disks Due to Low Memory

When the **JVMMemoryPressure** metric exceeds 92% for 30 minutes, Amazon ES triggers a protection mechanism and blocks all write operations to prevent the cluster from reaching red status. When the protection is on, write operations fail with a `ClusterBlockException` error, new indexes can't be created, and the `IndexCreateBlockException` error is thrown.

When the **JVMMemoryPressure** metric returns to 88% or lower for five minutes, the protection is disabled, and write operations to the cluster are unblocked.

JVM OutOfMemoryError

A JVM `OutOfMemoryError` typically means that one of the following JVM circuit breakers was reached.

Circuit Breaker	Description	Cluster Setting Property
Parent Breaker	Total percentage of JVM heap memory allowed for all circuit breakers. The default value is 70%.	indices.breaker.total.limit
Field Data Breaker	Percentage of JVM heap memory allowed to load a single data field into memory. The default value is 60%. If you upload data with large fields, we recommend raising this limit.	indices.breaker.fielddata.limit

Circuit Breaker	Description	Cluster Setting Property
Request Breaker	Percentage of JVM heap memory allowed for data structures used to respond to a service request. The default value is 40%. If your service requests involve calculating aggregations, we recommend raising this limit.	indices.breaker.request.limit

Troubleshooting

The following sections offer solutions to common problems that you might encounter when you use services and products that integrate with Amazon Elasticsearch Service (Amazon ES):

Topics

- Kibana: I Can't Access Kibana
- Kibana: I Get a Browser Error When I Use Kibana to View My Data
- Domain Creation: Unauthorized Operation When Selecting VPC Access
- Domain Creation: Stuck at Loading After Choosing VPC Access
- SDKs: I Get Certificate Errors When I Try to Use an SDK

For information about service-specific errors, see Handling AWS Service Errors in this guide.

Kibana: I Can't Access Kibana

The Kibana endpoint doesn't support signed requests. If the access control policy for your domain only grants access to certain IAM users or roles, you might receive the following error when you attempt to access Kibana:

```
1  "User: anonymous is not authorized to perform: es:ESHttpGet"
```

If your Amazon ES domain uses VPC access, you might not receive that error. Instead, the request might time out. To learn more about correcting this issue and the various configuration options available to you, see Controlling Access to Kibana, About Access Policies on VPC Domains, and Amazon Elasticsearch Service Access Control.

Kibana: I Get a Browser Error When I Use Kibana to View My Data

Your browser wraps service error messages in HTTP response objects when you use Kibana to view data in your Amazon ES domain. You can use developer tools commonly available in web browsers, such as Developer Mode in Chrome, to view the underlying service errors and assist your debugging efforts.

To view service errors in Chrome

1. From the menu, choose **View, Developer, Developer Tools**.

2. Choose the **Network** tab.

3. In the **Status** column, choose any HTTP session with a status of 500.

   For example, the following service error message indicates that a search request likely failed for one of the reasons shown in the following table:

   ```
   "Request to Elasticsearch failed: {"error":"SearchPbe larger than limit of
   [5143501209/4.7gb]]; }]"}"
   ```

[See the AWS documentation website for more details]

To view service errors in Firefox

1. From the menu, choose **Tools, Web Developer, Network**.

2. Choose any HTTP session with a status of 500.

3. Choose the **Response** tab to view the service response.

Domain Creation: Unauthorized Operation When Selecting VPC Access

When you create a new domain using the Amazon ES console, you have the option to select public access or VPC access. If you select **VPC access**, Amazon ES queries for VPC information and fails if you don't have the right policies associated with your user credentials. The error message follows:

```
1 You are not authorized to perform this operation. (Service: AmazonEC2; Status Code: 403; Error
     Code: UnauthorizedOperation
```

To enable this query, you must have access to the `ec2:DescribeVpcs`, `ec2:DescribeSubnets`, and `ec2:DescribeSecurityGroups` operations. This requirement is only for the console. If you use the AWS CLI to create and configure a domain with a VPC endpoint, you don't need access to those operations.

Domain Creation: Stuck at Loading After Choosing VPC Access

After creating a new domain that uses VPC access, the domain's **Configuration state** might never progress beyond **Loading**. If this issue occurs, you likely have AWS Security Token Service (AWS STS) *disabled* for your region.

To add VPC endpoints to your VPC, Amazon ES needs to assume the `AWSServiceRoleForAmazonElasticsearchService` role. Thus, AWS STS must be enabled to create new domains that use VPC access in a given region. To learn more about enabling and disabling AWS STS, see the IAM User Guide.

SDKs: I Get Certificate Errors When I Try to Use an SDK

Because AWS SDKs use the CA certificates from your computer, changes to the certificates on the AWS servers can cause connection failures when you attempt to use an SDK. Error messages vary, but typically contain the following text:

```
1 Failed to query Elasticsearch
2 ...
3 SSL3_GET_SERVER_CERTIFICATE:certificate verify failed
```

You can prevent these failures by keeping your computer's CA certificates and operating system up-to-date. If you encounter this issue in a corporate environment and do not manage your own computer, you might need to ask an administrator to assist with the update process.

The following list shows minimum operating system and Java versions:

- Microsoft Windows versions that have updates from January 2005 or later installed contain at least one of the required CAs in their trust list.
- Mac OS X 10.4 with Java for Mac OS X 10.4 Release 5 (February 2007), Mac OS X 10.5 (October 2007), and later versions contain at least one of the required CAs in their trust list.
- Red Hat Enterprise Linux 5 (March 2007), 6, and 7 and CentOS 5, 6, and 7 all contain at least one of the required CAs in their default trusted CA list.
- Java 1.4.2_12 (May 2006), 5 Update 2 (March 2005), and all later versions, including Java 6 (December 2006), 7, and 8, contain at least one of the required CAs in their default trusted CA list.

The three certificate authorities are:

- Amazon Root CA 1
- Starfield Services Root Certificate Authority - G2
- Starfield Class 2 Certification Authority

Root certificates from the first two authorities are available from Amazon Trust Services, but keeping your computer up-to-date is the more straightforward solution. To learn more about ACM-provided certificates, see AWS Certificate Manager FAQs.

Note

Currently, Amazon ES domains in the us-east-1 region use certificates from a different authority. We plan to update the region to use these new certificate authorities in the near future.

Amazon Elasticsearch Service General Reference

Amazon Elasticsearch Service (Amazon ES) supports a variety of instances, operations, plugins, and other resources.

Topics

- Supported Instance Types
- Supported Elasticsearch Operations
- Supported Plugins
- Other Supported Resources

Supported Instance Types

An *instance* is a virtual computing environment. An *instance type* is a specific configuration of CPU, memory, storage, and networking capacity. Choose an instance type for your Amazon ES domain that is based on the requirements of the application or software that you plan to run on your instance. If you have enabled dedicated master nodes, you can choose an instance type for the master nodes that differs from the instance type that you choose for the data nodes.

To learn more, see Sizing Amazon ES Domains, Cluster and Instance Limits, and EBS Volume Size Limits.

Amazon ES supports the following instance types.

T2 Instance Types

- t2.micro.elasticsearch
- t2.small.elasticsearch
- t2.medium.elasticsearch

Note

You can use the t2 instance types only if the instance count for your domain is 10 or fewer. The t2.micro. elasticsearch instance type supports only Elasticsearch 2.3 and 1.5. The t2 instance types do not support encryption of data at rest.

M3 Instance Types

- m3.medium.elasticsearch
- m3.large.elasticsearch
- m3.xlarge.elasticsearch
- m3.2xlarge.elasticsearch

Note

The m3 instance types are not available in the us-east-2, ca-central-1, eu-west-2, eu-west-3, ap-northeast-2, ap-south-1, and cn-northwest-1 regions. The m3 instance types do not support encryption of data at rest.

M4 Instance Types

- m4.large.elasticsearch
- m4.xlarge.elasticsearch
- m4.2xlarge.elasticsearch
- m4.4xlarge.elasticsearch
- m4.10xlarge.elasticsearch

Note

The m4 instance types are not available in the eu-west-3 region.

C4 Instance Types

- c4.large.elasticsearch
- c4.xlarge.elasticsearch
- c4.2xlarge.elasticsearch
- c4.4xlarge.elasticsearch
- c4.8xlarge.elasticsearch

Note

The c4 instance types are not available in the eu-west-3 region.

R3 Instance Types

- r3.large.elasticsearch
- r3.xlarge.elasticsearch
- r3.2xlarge.elasticsearch
- r3.4xlarge.elasticsearch

- `r3.8xlarge.elasticsearch`

Note

The `r3` instance types are not available in the ca-central-1, eu-west-2, eu-west-3, sa-east-1, and cn-northwest-1 regions. The `r3` instance types do not support encryption of data at rest.

R4 Instance Types

- `r4.large.elasticsearch`
- `r4.xlarge.elasticsearch`
- `r4.2xlarge.elasticsearch`
- `r4.4xlarge.elasticsearch`
- `r4.8xlarge.elasticsearch`
- `r4.16xlarge.elasticsearch`

I2 Instance Types

- `i2.xlarge.elasticsearch`
- `i2.2xlarge.elasticsearch`

Note

The `i2` instance types are not available in the sa-east-1, ca-central-1, eu-west-2, eu-west-3, us-east-2, and cn-northwest-1 regions.

I3 Instance Types

- `i3.large.elasticsearch`
- `i3.xlarge.elasticsearch`
- `i3.2xlarge.elasticsearch`
- `i3.4xlarge.elasticsearch`
- `i3.8xlarge.elasticsearch`
- `i3.16xlarge.elasticsearch`

Note

The `i3` instance types do not support EBS storage volumes. The `i3` instance types do not support Elasticsearch 2.3 or 1.5.

Supported Elasticsearch Operations

Amazon ES supports many versions of Elasticsearch. The following topics show the operations that Amazon ES supports for each version.

Topics

- Notable API Differences
- Version 6.2
- Version 6.0
- Version 5.5
- Version 5.3
- Version 5.1
- Version 2.3
- Version 1.5

Notable API Differences

Prior to Elasticsearch 5.3, the `_cluster/settings` API on Amazon ES domains supported only the HTTP `PUT` method, not the `GET` method. Newer versions support the `GET` method, as shown in the following example:

```
1  curl -XGET 'https://domain.region.es.amazonaws.com/_cluster/settings?pretty'
```

A sample return follows:

```
1  {
2    "persistent" : {
3      "cluster" : {
4        "routing" : {
5          "allocation" : {
6            "cluster_concurrent_rebalance" : "2"
7          }
8        }
9      },
10     "indices" : {
11       "recovery" : {
12         "max_bytes_per_sec" : "20mb"
13       }
14     }
15   },
16   "transient" : {
17     "cluster" : {
18       "routing" : {
19         "allocation" : {
20           "exclude" : {
21             "di_number" : "2"
22           }
23         }
24       }
25     }
26   }
27 }
```

- `cluster_concurrent_rebalance` specifies the number of shards that can be relocated to new nodes at any given time.

- `max_bytes_per_sec` is the maximum data transfer speed that Elasticsearch uses during a recovery event.
- `di_number` is an internal Amazon ES value that is used to copy shards to new *domain instances* after configuration changes.

Version 6.2

For Elasticsearch 6.2, Amazon ES supports the following operations.

[See the AWS documentation website for more details]	[See the AWS documentation website for more details]	[See the AWS documentation website for more details]

1. Cluster configuration changes might interrupt these operations before completion. We recommend that you use the `/_tasks` operation along with these operations to verify that the requests completed successfully.

2. DELETE requests to `/_search/scroll` with a message body must specify `"Content-Length"` in the HTTP header. Most clients add this header by default. To avoid a problem with = characters in `scroll_id` values, use the request body, not the query string, to pass `scroll_id` values to Amazon ES.

3. For considerations about using scripts, see Other Supported Resources.

4. Refers to the `PUT` method. For information about the `GET` method, see Notable API Differences.

Version 6.0

For Elasticsearch 6.0, Amazon ES supports the following operations.

[See the AWS documentation website for more details]	[See the AWS documentation website for more details]	[See the AWS documentation website for more details]

1. Cluster configuration changes might interrupt these operations before completion. We recommend that you use the `/_tasks` operation along with these operations to verify that the requests completed successfully.

2. DELETE requests to `/_search/scroll` with a message body must specify `"Content-Length"` in the HTTP header. Most clients add this header by default. To avoid a problem with = characters in `scroll_id` values, use the request body, not the query string, to pass `scroll_id` values to Amazon ES.

3. For considerations about using scripts, see Other Supported Resources.

4. Refers to the `PUT` method. For information about the `GET` method, see Notable API Differences.

Version 5.5

For Elasticsearch 5.5, Amazon ES supports the following operations.

[See the AWS documentation website for more details]	[See the AWS documentation website for more details]	[See the AWS documentation website for more details]

1. Cluster configuration changes might interrupt these operations before completion. We recommend that you use the `/_tasks` operation along with these operations to verify that the requests completed successfully.

2. DELETE requests to `/_search/scroll` with a message body must specify `"Content-Length"` in the HTTP header. Most clients add this header by default. To avoid a problem with = characters in `scroll_id` values, use the request body, not the query string, to pass `scroll_id` values to Amazon ES.

3. For considerations about using scripts, see Other Supported Resources.

4. Refers to the PUT method. For information about the GET method, see Notable API Differences.

Version 5.3

For Elasticsearch 5.3, Amazon ES supports the following operations.

[See the AWS documentation website for more details]	[See the AWS documentation website for more details]	[See the AWS documentation website for more details]

1. Cluster configuration changes might interrupt these operations before completion. We recommend that you use the /_tasks operation along with these operations to verify that the requests completed successfully.

2. DELETE requests to /_search/scroll with a message body must specify "Content-Length" in the HTTP header. Most clients add this header by default. To avoid a problem with = characters in scroll_id values, use the request body, not the query string, to pass scroll_id values to Amazon ES.

3. For considerations about using scripts, see Other Supported Resources.

4. Refers to the PUT method. For information about the GET method, see Notable API Differences.

Version 5.1

For Elasticsearch 5.1, Amazon ES supports the following operations.

[See the AWS documentation website for more details] [See the AWS documentation website for more details]	[See the AWS documentation website for more details]	[See the AWS documentation website for more details]

1. Cluster configuration changes might interrupt these operations before completion. We recommend that you use the /_tasks operation along with these operations to verify that the requests completed successfully.

2. DELETE requests to /_search/scroll with a message body must specify "Content-Length" in the HTTP header. Most clients add this header by default. To avoid a problem with = characters in scroll_id values, use the request body, not the query string, to pass scroll_id values to Amazon ES.

3. For considerations about using scripts, see Other Supported Resources.

Version 2.3

For Elasticsearch 2.3, Amazon ES supports the following operations.

[See the AWS documentation website for more details]	[See the AWS documentation website for more details]	[See the AWS documentation website for more details]

Version 1.5

For Elasticsearch 1.5, Amazon ES supports the following operations.

[See the AWS documentation website for more details]	[See the AWS documentation website for more details]	[See the AWS documentation website for more details]

Supported Plugins

Amazon ES domains come prepackaged with plugins that are available from the Elasticsearch community. The service automatically deploys and manages plugins for you.

Note
Kibana is a plugin in older versions of Amazon ES and a Node.js application in newer versions. All Amazon ES domains include a preinstalled version of Kibana.

Elasticsearch Version	Plugins
6.2	[See the AWS documentation website for more details]
6.0	[See the AWS documentation website for more details]
5.5	[See the AWS documentation website for more details]
5.3	[See the AWS documentation website for more details]
5.1	[See the AWS documentation website for more details]
2.3	[See the AWS documentation website for more details]
1.5	[See the AWS documentation website for more details]

Output Plugins

Amazon ES supports two Logstash output plugins to stream data into Amazon ES: the standard Elasticsearch output plugin and the logstash-output-amazon-es plugin, which signs and exports Logstash events to Amazon ES.

For more information about Logstash, see Loading Bulk Data with the Logstash Plugin.

Other Supported Resources

bootstrap.mlockall

The service enables `bootstrap.mlockall` in `elasticsearch.yml`, which locks JVM memory and prevents the operating system from swapping it to disk. This applies to all supported instance types except for the following:

- `t2.micro.elasticsearch`
- `t2.small.elasticsearch`
- `t2.medium.elasticsearch`

Scripting module

The service supports scripting for Elasticsearch 5.x and newer domains. The service does not support scripting for 1.5 or 2.3.

Supported scripting options include the following:

- Painless
- Lucene Expressions
- Mustache For Elasticsearch 5.5 and newer domains, Amazon ES supports stored scripts using the `_scripts` endpoint. Elasticsearch 5.3 and 5.1 domains only support inline scripts.

TCP transport

The service supports HTTP on port 80, but does not support TCP transport.

Amazon Elasticsearch Service Configuration API Reference

This reference describes the actions, data types, and errors in the Amazon Elasticsearch Service Configuration API. The Configuration API is a REST API that you can use to create and configure Amazon ES domains over HTTP. You also can use the AWS CLI and the console to configure Amazon ES domains. For more information, see Creating and Configuring Amazon ES Domains.

- Actions
- Data Types
- Errors

Actions

The following table provides a quick reference to the HTTP method required for each operation for the REST interface to the Amazon Elasticsearch Service Configuration API. The description of each operation also includes the required HTTP method.

Note
All configuration service requests must be signed. For more information, see Signing Amazon Elasticsearch Service Requests in this guide and Signature Version 4 Signing Process in the *AWS General Reference*.

Action	HTTP Method
AddTags	POST
CreateElasticsearchDomain	POST
DeleteElasticsearchDomain	DELETE
DeleteElasticsearchServiceRole	DELETE
DescribeElasticsearchDomain	GET
DescribeElasticsearchDomainConfig	GET
DescribeElasticsearchDomains	POST
DescribeElasticsearchInstanceTypeLimit	GET
DescribeReservedElasticsearchInstanceO	GET
DescribeReservedElasticsearchInstances	GET
ListDomainNames	GET
ListElasticsearchInstanceTypes	GET
ListElasticsearchVersions	GET
ListTags	GET
PurchaseReservedElasticsearchInstance	POST
RemoveTags	POST
UpdateElasticsearchDomainConfig	POST

AddTags

Attaches resource tags to an Amazon ES domain. For more information, see Tagging Amazon ES Domains.

Syntax

```
1 POST /2015-01-01/tags
```

```
 2 {
 3     "ARN": "<DOMAIN_ARN>",
 4     "TagList": [
 5         {
 6             "Key": "<TAG_KEY>",
 7             "Value": "<TAG_VALUE>"
 8         }
 9     ]
10 }
```

Request Parameters

This operation does not use request parameters.

Request Body

Parameter	Data Type	Required?	Description
TagList	TagList	Yes	List of resource tags
ARN	ARN	Yes	Amazon Resource Name (ARN) for the Amazon ES domain to which you want to attach resource tags.

Response Elements

Not applicable. The `AddTags` operation does not return a data structure.

Errors

The `AddTags` operation can return any of the following errors:

- `BaseException`
- `LimitExceededException`
- `ValidationException`
- `InternalException`

Example

The following example attaches a single resource tag with a tag key of `project` to the `logs` Amazon ES domain:

Request

```
1 POST es.<AWS_REGION>.amazonaws.com/2015-01-01/tags
2 {
3     "ARN": "<DOMAIN_ARN>",
4     "TagList": [
5         {
6             "Key": "project",
7             "Value": "trident"
8         }
9     ]
```

```
10 }
```

Response

```
1 HTTP/1.1 200 OK
2 x-amzn-RequestId: 5a6a5790-536c-11e5-9cd2-b36dbf43d89e
3 Content-Type: application/json
4 Content-Length: 0
5 Date: Sat, 05 Sep 2015 01:20:55 GMT
```

CreateElasticsearchDomain

Creates a new Amazon ES domain. For more information, see Creating Amazon ES Domains.

Note
If you attempt to create an Amazon ES domain and a domain with the same name already exists, the API does not report an error. Instead, it returns details for the existing domain.

Syntax

```
1  POST /2015-01-01/es/domain
2  {
3      "DomainName": "<DOMAIN_NAME>",
4      "ElasticsearchVersion": "<VERSION>",
5      "ElasticsearchClusterConfig": {
6          "InstanceType": "<INSTANCE_TYPE>",
7          "InstanceCount": <INSTANCE_COUNT>,
8          "DedicatedMasterEnabled": "<TRUE|FALSE>",
9          "DedicatedMasterCount": <INSTANCE_COUNT>,
10         "DedicatedMasterType": "<INSTANCE_TYPE>",
11         "ZoneAwarenessEnabled": "<TRUE|FALSE>"
12     },
13     "EBSOptions": {
14         "EBSEnabled": "<TRUE|FALSE>",
15         "VolumeType": "<VOLUME_TYPE>",
16         "VolumeSize": "<VOLUME_SIZE>",
17         "Iops": "<VALUE>"
18     },
19     "VPCOptions": {
20         "SubnetIds": [
21             "<SUBNET_ID>"
22         ],
23         "SecurityGroupIds": [
24             "<SECURITY_GROUP_ID>"
25         ]
26     },
27     "CognitoOptions": {
28         "IdentityPoolId": "us-west-1:12345678-1234-1234-1234-123456789012",
29         "RoleArn": "arn:aws:iam::123456789012:role/my-kibana-role",
30         "Enabled": true,
31         "UserPoolId": "us-west-1_121234567"
32     },
33     "AccessPolicies": "<ACCESS_POLICY_DOCUMENT>",
34     "SnapshotOptions": {
```

```
35      "AutomatedSnapshotStartHour": <START_HOUR>
36    },
37    "LogPublishingOptions": {
38        "SEARCH_SLOW_LOGS": {
39            "CloudWatchLogsLogGroupArn":"<ARN>",
40            "Enabled":true
41        },
42        "INDEX_SLOW_LOGS": {
43            "CloudWatchLogsLogGroupArn":"<ARN>",
44            "Enabled":true
45        }
46    },
47    "EncryptionAtRestOptions": {
48        "Enabled": true,
49        "KmsKeyId": "<KEY_ID>"
50    },
51    "AdvancedOptions": {
52            "rest.action.multi.allow_explicit_index": "<TRUE|FALSE>",
53            "indices.fielddata.cache.size": "<PERCENTAGE_OF_HEAP>"
54    }
55 }
```

Request Parameters

This operation does not use HTTP request parameters.

Request Body

Parameter	Data Type	Required?	Description
DomainName	DomainName	Yes	Name of the Amazon ES domain to create.
ElasticsearchVersion	String	No	Version of Elasticsearch. If not specified, 1.5 is used as the default. For the full list of supported versions, see Supported Elasticsearch Versions.
ElasticsearchCluster-Config	ElasticsearchCluster	No	Container for the cluster configuration of an Amazon ES domain.
EBSOptions	EBSOptions	No	Container for the parameters required to enable EBS-based storage for an Amazon ES domain. For more information, see Configuring EBS-based Storage.

Parameter	Data Type	Required?	Description
VPCOptions	`VPCOptions`	No	Container for the values required to configure Amazon ES to work with a VPC. To learn more, see VPC Support for Amazon Elasticsearch Service Domains.
CognitoOptions	`CognitoOptions`	No	Key-value pairs to configure Amazon ES to use Amazon Cognito authentication for Kibana.
AccessPolicies	String	No	IAM policy document specifying the access policies for the new Amazon ES domain. For more information, see Amazon Elasticsearch Service Access Control.
SnapshotOptions	`SnapshotOptions`	No	Container for parameters required to configure automated snapshots of domain indices. For more information, see Configuring Snapshots.
AdvancedOptions	`AdvancedOptions`	No	Key-value pairs to specify advanced configuration options. For more information, see Configuring Advanced Options.
LogPublishingOptions	`LogPublishingOptions`	No	Key-value pairs to configure slow log publishing.
EncryptionAtRestOptions	`EncryptionAtRestOpti`	No	Key-value pairs to enable encryption at rest.

Response Elements

Field	Data Type	Description
DomainStatus	ElasticsearchDomainStatus	Specifies the status and configuration of a new Amazon ES domain.

Errors

`CreateElasticsearchDomain` can return any of the following errors:

- `BaseException`
- `DisabledOperationException`
- `InternalException`
- `InvalidTypeException`
- `LimitExceededException`
- `ResourceAlreadyExistsException`
- `ValidationException`

Example

This example demonstrates the following:

- Creates an Amazon ES domain named `streaming-logs`
- Configures a cluster with six instances of the m3.medium.elasticsearch instance type and three dedicated master nodes of the same type
- Enables zone awareness
- Configures VPC endpoints for the domain

Request

```
1 POST es.<AWS_REGION>.amazonaws.com/2015-01-01/es/domain
2 {
3     "DomainName": "streaming-logs",
4     "ElasticsearchVersion": "5.5",
5     "ElasticsearchClusterConfig": {
6         "InstanceType": "m3.medium.elasticsearch",
7         "InstanceCount": 6,
8         "DedicatedMasterEnabled": "true",
9         "DedicatedMasterCount": 3,
10        "DedicatedMasterType": "m3.medium.elasticsearch",
11        "ZoneAwarenessEnabled": "true"
12    },
13    "VPCOptions": {
14        "SubnetIds": [
15            "subnet-87654321",
16            "subnet-12345678"
17        ]
18    },
19    "EncryptionAtRestOptions": {
20        "Enabled": true,
21        "KmsKeyId": "1a2a3a4-1a2a-3a4a-5a6a-1a2a3a4a5a6a"
22    }
23 }
```

Response

```
1 HTTP/1.1 200 OK
2 x-amzn-RequestId: 30b03e92-536f-11e5-9cd2-b36dbf43d89e
3 Content-Type: application/json
4 Content-Length: 645
5 Date: Sat, 05 Sep 2015 01:41:15 GMT
6 {
7     "DomainStatus": {
8         "ARN": "arn:aws:es:us-west-1:123456789012:domain/streaming-logs",
9         "AccessPolicies": "",
```

```
10        "AdvancedOptions": {
11            "rest.action.multi.allow_explicit_index": "true"
12        },
13        "Created": true,
14        "Deleted": false,
15        "DomainId": "123456789012/streaming-logs",
16        "DomainName": "streaming-logs",
17        "EBSOptions": {
18            "EBSEnabled": false,
19            "EncryptionEnabled": null,
20            "Iops": null,
21            "VolumeSize": null,
22            "VolumeType": null
23        },
24        "ElasticsearchClusterConfig": {
25            "DedicatedMasterCount": 3,
26            "DedicatedMasterEnabled": true,
27            "DedicatedMasterType": "m3.medium.elasticsearch",
28            "InstanceCount": 6,
29            "InstanceType": "m3.medium.elasticsearch",
30            "ZoneAwarenessEnabled": true
31        },
32        "ElasticsearchVersion": "5.5",
33        "EncryptionAtRestOptions": {
34            "Enabled": true,
35            "KmsKeyId": "arn:aws:kms:us-west-1:123456789012:key/1a2a3a4-1a2a-3a4a-5a6a-1
                a2a3a4a5a6a"
36        },
37        "Endpoint": null,
38        "Endpoints": null,
39        "Processing": true,
40        "SnapshotOptions": {
41            "AutomatedSnapshotStartHour": 0
42        },
43        "VPCOptions": {
44            "AvailabilityZones": [
45                "us-west-1b",
46                "us-west-1c"
47            ],
48            "SecurityGroupIds": [
49                "sg-12345678"
50            ],
51            "SubnetIds": [
52                "subnet-87654321",
53                "subnet-12345678"
54            ],
55            "VPCId": "vpc-12345678"
56        }
57    }
58 }
```

DeleteElasticsearchDomain

Deletes an Amazon ES domain and all of its data. A domain cannot be recovered after it is deleted.

Syntax

```
1  DELETE /2015-01-01/es/domain/<DOMAIN_NAME>
```

Request Parameters

Parameter	Data Type	Required?	Description
DomainName	DomainName	Yes	Name of the Amazon ES domain that you want to delete.

Request Body

This operation does not use the HTTP request body.

Response Elements

Field	Data Type	Description
DomainStatus	ElasticsearchDomainStatus	Specifies the configuration of the specified Amazon ES domain.

Errors

The `DeleteElasticsearchDomain` operation can return any of the following errors:

- `BaseException`
- `InternalException`
- `ResourceNotFoundException`
- `ValidationException`

Example

The following example deletes the `weblogs` domain:

Request

```
1  DELETE es.<AWS_REGION>.amazonaws.com/2015-01-01/es/domain/weblogs
```

Response

```
1  HTTP/1.1 200 OK
2  {
3      "DomainStatus": {
4          "ARN": "arn:aws:es:us-west-1:123456789012:domain/weblogs",
5          "AccessPolicies": "",
6          "AdvancedOptions": {
7              "rest.action.multi.allow_explicit_index": "true"
8          },
9          "Created": true,
```

```
10          "Deleted": true,
11          "DomainId": "123456789012/weblogs",
12          "DomainName": "weblogs",
13          "EBSOptions": {
14              "EBSEnabled": false,
15              "EncryptionEnabled": null,
16              "Iops": null,
17              "VolumeSize": null,
18              "VolumeType": null
19          },
20          "ElasticsearchClusterConfig": {
21              "DedicatedMasterCount": 3,
22              "DedicatedMasterEnabled": true,
23              "DedicatedMasterType": "m3.medium.elasticsearch",
24              "InstanceCount": 6,
25              "InstanceType": "m3.medium.elasticsearch",
26              "ZoneAwarenessEnabled": true
27          },
28          "ElasticsearchVersion": "5.5",
29          "EncryptionAtRestOptions": {
30              "Enabled": true,
31              "KmsKeyId": "arn:aws:kms:us-west-1:123456789012:key/1a2a3a4-1a2a-3a4a-5a6a-1
                  a2a3a4a5a6a"
32          },
33          "Endpoint": null,
34          "Endpoints": null,
35          "Processing": true,
36          "SnapshotOptions": {
37              "AutomatedSnapshotStartHour": 0
38          },
39          "VPCOptions": {
40              "AvailabilityZones": [
41                  "us-west-1b",
42                  "us-west-1c"
43              ],
44              "SecurityGroupIds": [
45                  "sg-12345678"
46              ],
47              "SubnetIds": [
48                  "subnet-87654321",
49                  "subnet-12345678"
50              ],
51              "VPCId": "vpc-12345678"
52          }
53      }
54 }
```

DeleteElasticsearchServiceRole

Deletes the service-linked role between Amazon ES and Amazon EC2. This role gives Amazon ES permissions to place VPC endpoints into your VPC. A service-linked role must be in place for domains with VPC endpoints to be created or function properly.

Note

This action only succeeds if no domains are using the service-linked role.

Syntax

```
1 DELETE /2015-01-01/es/role
```

Request Parameters

This operation does not use request parameters.

Request Body

This operation does not use the HTTP request body.

Response Elements

Not applicable. The `DeleteElasticsearchServiceRole` operation does not return a data structure.

Errors

`DeleteElasticsearchServiceRole` can return any of the following errors:

- `BaseException`
- `InternalException`
- `ValidationException`

Example

The following example demonstrates deletion of the service-linked role:

Request

```
1 DELETE es.<AWS_REGION>.amazonaws.com/2015-01-01/es/role
```

Response

If successful, this action provides no response.

DescribeElasticsearchDomain

Describes the domain configuration for the specified Amazon ES domain, including the domain ID, domain service endpoint, and domain ARN.

Syntax

```
1 GET /2015-01-01/es/domain/<DOMAIN_NAME>
```

Request Parameters

Parameter	Data Type	Required?	Description
DomainName	DomainName	Yes	Name of the Amazon ES domain that you want to describe.

Request Body

This operation does not use the HTTP request body.

Response Elements

Field	Data Type	Description
DomainStatus	ElasticsearchDomainStatus	Configuration of the specified Amazon ES domain.

Errors

DescribeElasticsearchDomain can return any of the following errors:

- BaseException
- InternalException
- ResourceNotFoundException
- ValidationException

Example

The following example returns a description of the streaming-logs domain:

Request

```
1 GET es.<AWS_REGION>.amazonaws.com/2015-01-01/es/domain/streaming-logs
```

Response

```
1  {
2      "DomainStatus": {
3          "ARN": "arn:aws:es:us-west-1:123456789012:domain/streaming-logs",
4          "AccessPolicies": "{\"Version\":\"2012-10-17\",\"Statement\":[{\"Effect\":\"Allow\",\"
               Principal\":{\"AWS\":\"*\"},\"Action\":\"es:*\",\"Resource\":\"arn:aws:es:us-west
               -1:123456789012:domain/streaming-logs/*\",\"Condition\":{\"IpAddress\":{\"aws:
               SourceIp
               \":[\"11.222.333.11\",\"11.222.333.12\",\"11.222.333.13\",\"11.222.333.14\",\"11.222.333.
5          "AdvancedOptions": {
6              "rest.action.multi.allow_explicit_index": "true"
7          },
8          "Created": true,
9          "Deleted": false,
10         "DomainId": "123456789012/streaming-logs",
11         "DomainName": "streaming-logs",
12         "EBSOptions": {
13             "EBSEnabled": true,
```

```
14        "EncryptionEnabled": false,
15        "Iops": null,
16        "VolumeSize": 11,
17        "VolumeType": "gp2"
18    },
19    "ElasticsearchClusterConfig": {
20        "DedicatedMasterCount": 2,
21        "DedicatedMasterEnabled": false,
22        "DedicatedMasterType": "m4.large.elasticsearch",
23        "InstanceCount": 2,
24        "InstanceType": "t2.small.elasticsearch",
25        "ZoneAwarenessEnabled": false
26    },
27    "ElasticsearchVersion": "5.5",
28    "EncryptionAtRestOptions": {
29        "Enabled": true,
30        "KmsKeyId": "arn:aws:kms:us-west-1:123456789012:key/1a2a3a4-1a2a-3a4a-5a6a-1
               a2a3a4a5a6a"
31    },
32    "CognitoOptions": {
33        "IdentityPoolId": "us-west-1:12345678-1234-1234-1234-123456789012",
34        "RoleArn": "arn:aws:iam::123456789012:role/my-kibana-role",
35        "Enabled": true,
36        "UserPoolId": "us-west-1_121234567"
37    },
38    "Endpoint": "search-streaming-logs-oojmrbhufr27n44zdri52wukdy.us-west-1.es.amazonaws.com
            ",
39    "Endpoints": null,
40    "Processing": false,
41    "SnapshotOptions": {
42        "AutomatedSnapshotStartHour": 8
43    },
44    "VPCOptions": null
45    }
46 }
```

DescribeElasticsearchDomainConfig

Displays the configuration of an Amazon ES domain.

Syntax

```
1 GET /2015-01-01/es/domain/<DOMAIN_NAME>/config
```

Request Parameters

Parameter	Data Type	Required?	Description
DomainName	DomainName	Yes	Name of the Amazon ES domain.

Request Body

This operation does not use the HTTP request body.

Response Elements

Field	Data Type	Description
DomainConfig	ElasticsearchDomainConfig	Configuration of the Amazon ES domain.

Errors

The `DescribeElasticsearchDomainConfig` operation can return any of the following errors:

- `BaseException`
- `InternalException`
- `ResourceNotFoundException`

Example

The following example returns a description of the configuration of the `logs` domain:

Request

```
1 GET es.<AWS_REGION>.amazonaws.com/2015-01-01/es/domain/logs/config
```

Response

```
1  HTTP/1.1 200 OK
2  {
3      "DomainConfig": {
4          "AccessPolicies": {
5              "Options": "{\"Version\":\"2012-10-17\",\"Statement\":[{\"Effect\":\"Allow\",\"
                   Principal\":{\"AWS\":\"arn:aws:iam::123456789012:root\"},\"Action\":\"es:*\",\"
                   Resource\":\"arn:aws:es:us-west-1:123456789012:domain/logs/*\"}]}",
6              "Status": {
7                  "CreationDate": 1499817484.04,
8                  "PendingDeletion": false,
9                  "State": "Active",
10                 "UpdateDate": 1500308955.652,
11                 "UpdateVersion": 17
12             }
13         },
14         "AdvancedOptions": {
15             "Options": {
16                 "indices.fielddata.cache.size": "",
17                 "rest.action.multi.allow_explicit_index": "true"
18             },
19             "Status": {
20                 "CreationDate": 1499817484.04,
21                 "PendingDeletion": false,
22                 "State": "Active",
23                 "UpdateDate": 1499818054.108,
24                 "UpdateVersion": 5
```

```
25              }
26          },
27          "EBSOptions": {
28              "Options": {
29                  "EBSEnabled": true,
30                  "EncryptionEnabled": false,
31                  "Iops": 0,
32                  "VolumeSize": 10,
33                  "VolumeType": "gp2"
34              },
35              "Status": {
36                  "CreationDate": 1499817484.04,
37                  "PendingDeletion": false,
38                  "State": "Active",
39                  "UpdateDate": 1499818054.108,
40                  "UpdateVersion": 5
41              }
42          },
43          "ElasticsearchClusterConfig": {
44              "Options": {
45                  "DedicatedMasterCount": 2,
46                  "DedicatedMasterEnabled": false,
47                  "DedicatedMasterType": "m4.large.elasticsearch",
48                  "InstanceCount": 2,
49                  "InstanceType": "m4.large.elasticsearch",
50                  "ZoneAwarenessEnabled": false
51              },
52              "Status": {
53                  "CreationDate": 1499817484.04,
54                  "PendingDeletion": false,
55                  "State": "Active",
56                  "UpdateDate": 1499966854.612,
57                  "UpdateVersion": 13
58              }
59          },
60          "ElasticsearchVersion": {
61              "Options": "5.5",
62              "Status": {
63                  "PendingDeletion": false,
64                  "State": "Active",
65                  "CreationDate": 1436913638.995,
66                  "UpdateVersion": 6,
67                  "UpdateDate": 1436914324.278
68              },
69              "Options": "{\"Version\":\"2012-10-17\",\"Statement\":[{\"Sid\":\"\",\"Effect\":\"
                  Allow\",\"Principal\":{\"AWS\":\"*\"},\"Action\":\"es:*\",\"Resource\":\"arn:aws
                  :es:us-east-1:123456789012:domain/logs/*\"}]}"
70          },
71          "EncryptionAtRestOptions": {
72              "Options": {
73                  "Enabled": true,
74                  "KmsKeyId": "arn:aws:kms:us-west-1:123456789012:key/1a2a3a4-1a2a-3a4a-5a6a-1
                      a2a3a4a5a6a"
75              },
```

171

```
76          "Status": {
77              "CreationDate": 1509490412.757,
78              "PendingDeletion": false,
79              "State": "Active",
80              "UpdateDate": 1509490953.717,
81              "UpdateVersion": 6
82          }
83      },
84      "LogPublishingOptions":{
85          "Status":{
86              "CreationDate":1502774634.546,
87              "PendingDeletion":false,
88              "State":"Processing",
89              "UpdateDate":1502779590.448,
90              "UpdateVersion":60
91          },
92          "Options":{
93              "INDEX_SLOW_LOGS":{
94                  "CloudWatchLogsLogGroupArn":"arn:aws:logs:us-east-1:123456789012:log-group:
                        sample-domain",
95                  "Enabled":true
96              },
97              "SEARCH_SLOW_LOGS":{
98                  "CloudWatchLogsLogGroupArn":"arn:aws:logs:us-east-1:123456789012:log-group:
                        sample-domain",
99                  "Enabled":true
100             }
101         }
102     },
103     "SnapshotOptions": {
104         "Options": {
105             "AutomatedSnapshotStartHour": 6
106         },
107         "Status": {
108             "CreationDate": 1499817484.04,
109             "PendingDeletion": false,
110             "State": "Active",
111             "UpdateDate": 1499818054.108,
112             "UpdateVersion": 5
113         }
114     },
115     "VPCOptions": {
116         "Options": {
117             "AvailabilityZones": [
118                 "us-west-1b"
119             ],
120             "SecurityGroupIds": [
121                 "sg-12345678"
122             ],
123             "SubnetIds": [
124                 "subnet-12345678"
125             ],
126             "VPCId": "vpc-12345678"
127         },
```

```
128        "Status": {
129            "CreationDate": 1499817484.04,
130            "PendingDeletion": false,
131            "State": "Active",
132            "UpdateDate": 1499818054.108,
133            "UpdateVersion": 5
134        }
135    }
136  }
137 }
```

DescribeElasticsearchDomains

Describes the domain configuration for up to five specified Amazon ES domains. Information includes the domain ID, domain service endpoint, and domain ARN.

Syntax

```
1 POST /2015-01-01/es/domain-info
2 {
3    "DomainNames": [
4        "<DOMAIN_NAME>",
5        "<DOMAIN_NAME>",
6    ]
7 }
```

Request Parameters

This operation does not use HTTP request parameters.

Request Body

Field	Data Type	Required?	Description
DomainNames	DomainNameList	Yes	Array of Amazon ES domains in the following format:`{"DomainNames":["<Domain_Name>","<Domain_Name>"...]`

Response Elements

Field	Data Type	Description
DomainStatusList	ElasticsearchDomainStatusL	List that contains the status of each requested Amazon ES domain.

Errors

The `DescribeElasticsearchDomains` operation can return any of the following errors:

- `BaseException`
- `InternalException`
- `ValidationException`

Example

The following example returns a description of the `logs` and `streaming-logs` domains:

Request

```
1  POST es.<AWS_REGION>.amazonaws.com/2015-01-01/es/domain-info/
2  {
3      "DomainNames": [
4          "logs",
5          "streaming-logs"
6      ]
7  }
```

Response

```
1  HTTP/1.1 200 OK
2  {
3      "DomainStatusList": [
4          {
5              "ElasticsearchClusterConfig": {
6                  "DedicatedMasterEnabled": true,
7                  "InstanceCount": 3,
8                  "ZoneAwarenessEnabled": false,
9                  "DedicatedMasterType": "m3.medium.elasticsearch",
10                 "InstanceType": "m3.medium.elasticsearch",
11                 "DedicatedMasterCount": 3
12             },
13             "ElasticsearchVersion": "5.5",
14             "EncryptionAtRestOptions": {
15                 "Enabled": true,
16                 "KmsKeyId": "arn:aws:kms:us-west-1:123456789012:key/1a2a3a4-1a2a-3a4a-5a6a-1
                       a2a3a4a5a6a"
17             },
18             "Endpoint": "search-streaming-logs-okga24ftzsbz2a2hzhsqw73jpy.us-east-1.es.example.
                   com",
19             "Created": true,
20             "Deleted": false,
21             "DomainName": "streaming-logs",
22             "EBSOptions": {
23                 "EBSEnabled": false
24             },
25             "VPCOptions": {
26                 "SubnetIds": [
27                     "subnet-d1234567"
28                 ],
29                 "VPCId": "vpc-12345678",
30                 "SecurityGroupIds": [
31                     "sg-123456789"
```

174

```
32              ],
33              "AvailabilityZones": [
34                  "us-east-1"
35              ]
36          },
37          "SnapshotOptions": {
38              "AutomatedSnapshotStartHour": 0
39          },
40          "DomainId": "123456789012/streaming-logs",
41          "AccessPolicies": "",
42          "Processing": false,
43          "AdvancedOptions": {
44              "rest.action.multi.allow_explicit_index": "true",
45              "indices.fielddata.cache.size": ""
46          },
47          "ARN": "arn:aws:es:us-east-1:123456789012:domain/streaming-logs"
48      },
49      {
50          "ElasticsearchClusterConfig": {
51              "DedicatedMasterEnabled": true,
52              "InstanceCount": 1,
53              "ZoneAwarenessEnabled": false,
54              "DedicatedMasterType": "search.m3.medium",
55              "InstanceType": "search.m3.xlarge",
56              "DedicatedMasterCount": 3
57          },
58          "ElasticsearchVersion": "5.5",
59          "EncryptionAtRestOptions": {
60              "Enabled": true,
61              "KmsKeyId": "arn:aws:kms:us-west-1:123456789012:key/1a2a3a4-1a2a-3a4a-5a6a-1
                  a2a3a4a5a6a"
62          },
63          "Endpoint": "search-logs-p5st2kbt77diuihoqi6omd7jiu.us-east-1.es.example.com",
64          "Created": true,
65          "Deleted": false,
66          "DomainName": "logs",
67          "EBSOptions": {
68              "Iops": 4000,
69              "VolumeSize": 512,
70              "VolumeType": "io1",
71              "EBSEnabled": true
72          },
73          "VPCOptions": {
74              "SubnetIds": [
75                  "subnet-d1234567"
76              ],
77              "VPCId": "vpc-12345678",
78              "SecurityGroupIds": [
79                  "sg-123456789"
80              ],
81              "AvailabilityZones": [
82                  "us-east-1"
83              ]
84          },
```

```
85        "SnapshotOptions": {
86            "AutomatedSnapshotStartHour": 0
87        },
88        "DomainId": "123456789012/logs",
89        "AccessPolicies": "{\"Version\":\"2012-10-17\",\"Statement\":[{\"Sid\":\"\",\"Effect
          \":\"Allow\",\"Principal\":{\"AWS\":\"*\"},\"Action\":\"es:*\",\"Resource\":\"
          arn:aws:es:us-east-1:123456789012:domain/logs/*\"}]}",
90        "Processing": false,
91        "AdvancedOptions": {
92            "rest.action.multi.allow_explicit_index": "true"
93        },
94        "ARN": "arn:aws:es:us-east-1:123456789012:domain/logs"
95     }
96   ]
97 }
```

DescribeElasticsearchInstanceTypeLimits

Describes the instance count, storage, and master node limits for a given Elasticsearch version and instance type.

Syntax

```
1 GET 2015-01-01/es/instanceTypeLimits/{ElasticsearchVersion}/{InstanceType}?domainName={
    DomainName}
```

Request Parameters

Parameter	Data Type	Required?	Description
ElasticsearchVersion	String	Yes	Elasticsearch version. For a list of supported versions, see Supported Elasticsearch Versions.
InstanceType	String	Yes	Instance type. To view instance types by region, see Amazon Elasticsearch Service Pricing.
DomainName	DomainName	No	The name of an existing domain. Only specify if you need the limits for an existing domain.

Request Body

This operation does not use the HTTP request body.

Response Elements

Field	Data Type	Description
LimitsByRole	Map	Map containing all applicable instance type limits. "data" refers to data nodes. "master" refers to dedicated master nodes.

Errors

The `DescribeElasticsearchInstanceTypeLimits` operation can return any of the following errors:

- `BaseException`
- `InternalException`
- `InvalidTypeException`
- `LimitExceededException`
- `ResourceNotFoundException`
- `ValidationException`

Example

The following example returns a description of the `logs` and `streaming-logs` domains:

Request

```
1 GET es.<AWS_REGION>.amazonaws.com/2015-01-01/es/instanceTypeLimits/6.0/m4.large.elasticsearch
```

Response

```
1  HTTP/1.1 200 OK
2  {
3      "LimitsByRole": {
4          "data": {
5              "AdditionalLimits": [
6                  {
7                      "LimitName": "MaximumNumberOfDataNodesWithoutMasterNode",
8                      "LimitValues": [
9                          "10"
10                     ]
11                 }
12             ],
13             "InstanceLimits": {
14                 "InstanceCountLimits": {
15                     "MaximumInstanceCount": 20,
16                     "MinimumInstanceCount": 1
17                 }
18             },
19             "StorageTypes": [
20                 {
21                     "StorageSubTypeName": "standard",
22                     "StorageTypeLimits": [
23                         {
24                             "LimitName": "MaximumVolumeSize",
25                             "LimitValues": [
```

```
26                      "100"
27                  ]
28              },
29              {
30                  "LimitName": "MinimumVolumeSize",
31                  "LimitValues": [
32                      "10"
33                  ]
34              }
35          ],
36          "StorageTypeName": "ebs"
37      },
38      {
39          "StorageSubTypeName": "io1",
40          "StorageTypeLimits": [
41              {
42                  "LimitName": "MaximumVolumeSize",
43                  "LimitValues": [
44                      "512"
45                  ]
46              },
47              {
48                  "LimitName": "MinimumVolumeSize",
49                  "LimitValues": [
50                      "35"
51                  ]
52              },
53              {
54                  "LimitName": "MaximumIops",
55                  "LimitValues": [
56                      "16000"
57                  ]
58              },
59              {
60                  "LimitName": "MinimumIops",
61                  "LimitValues": [
62                      "1000"
63                  ]
64              }
65          ],
66          "StorageTypeName": "ebs"
67      },
68      {
69          "StorageSubTypeName": "gp2",
70          "StorageTypeLimits": [
71              {
72                  "LimitName": "MaximumVolumeSize",
73                  "LimitValues": [
74                      "512"
75                  ]
76              },
77              {
78                  "LimitName": "MinimumVolumeSize",
79                  "LimitValues": [
```

178

```
80                              "10"
81                          ]
82                      }
83                  ],
84                  "StorageTypeName": "ebs"
85              }
86          ]
87      },
88      "master": {
89          "AdditionalLimits": [
90              {
91                  "LimitName": "MaximumNumberOfDataNodesSupported",
92                  "LimitValues": [
93                      "100"
94                  ]
95              }
96          ],
97          "InstanceLimits": {
98              "InstanceCountLimits": {
99                  "MaximumInstanceCount": 5,
100                 "MinimumInstanceCount": 2
101             }
102         },
103         "StorageTypes": null
104     }
105 }
106 }
```

DescribeReservedElasticsearchInstanceOfferings

Describes the available reserved instance offerings for a given region.

Syntax

```
1 GET /2015-01-01/es/reservedInstanceOfferings?offeringId={OfferingId}&maxResults={MaxResults}&
    nextToken={NextToken}
```

Request Parameters

Parameter	Data Type	Required?	Description
OfferingId	String	No	The offering ID.
MaxResults	Integer	No	Limits the number of results. Must be between 30 and 100.

Parameter	Data Type	Required?	Description
NextToken	String	No	Used for pagination. Only necessary if a previous API call produced a result containing NextToken. Accepts a next-token input to return results for the next page and provides a next-token output in the response, which clients can use to retrieve more results.

Request Body

This operation does not use the HTTP request body.

Response Elements

Field	Data Type	Description
ReservedElasticsearchInstanceOfferings	ReservedElasticsearchInstanceOfferings	Container for all information on a reserved instance offering. To learn more, see Purchasing Reserved Instances (AWS CLI).

Errors

The `DescribeReservedElasticsearchInstanceOfferings` operation can return any of the following errors:

- `DisabledOperationException`
- `InternalException`
- `ResourceNotFoundException`
- `ValidationException`

Example

Request

```
1 GET es.<AWS_REGION>.amazonaws.com/2015-01-01/es/reservedInstanceOfferings
```

Response

```
1 {
2   "ReservedElasticsearchInstanceOfferings": [
3     {
4       "FixedPrice": 100.0,
5       "ReservedElasticsearchInstanceOfferingId": "1a2a3a4a5-1a2a-3a4a-5a6a-1a2a3a4a5a6a",
6       "RecurringCharges": [
7         {
```

```
 8        "RecurringChargeAmount": 0.603,
 9        "RecurringChargeFrequency": "Hourly"
10      }
11    ],
12    "UsagePrice": 0.0,
13    "PaymentOption": "PARTIAL_UPFRONT",
14    "Duration": 31536000,
15    "ElasticsearchInstanceType": "m4.2xlarge.elasticsearch",
16    "CurrencyCode": "USD"
17  }
18  ]
19 }
```

DescribeReservedElasticsearchInstances

Describes the instances you have reserved in a given region.

Syntax

```
1 GET 2015-01-01/es/reservedInstances?reservationId={ReservationId}&maxResults={PageSize}&
    nextToken={NextToken}
```

Request Parameters

Parameter	Data Type	Required?	Description
ReservationId	String	No	The reservation ID, assigned after you purchase a reservation.
MaxResults	Integer	No	Limits the number of results. Must be between 30 and 100.
NextToken	String	No	Used for pagination. Only necessary if a previous API call produced a result containing NextToken. Accepts a next-token input to return results for the next page and provides a next-token output in the response, which clients can use to retrieve more results.

Request Body

This operation does not use the HTTP request body.

Response Elements

Field	Data Type	Description
ReservedElasticsearchInstances	ReservedElasticsearchInsta	Container for all information on the instance you have reserved. To learn more, see Purchasing Reserved Instances (AWS CLI).

Errors

The `DescribeReservedElasticsearchInstances` operation can return any of the following errors:

- `DisabledOperationException`
- `InternalException`
- `ResourceNotFoundException`
- `ValidationException`

Example

Request

```
1 GET es.<AWS_REGION>.amazonaws.com/2015-01-01/es/reservedInstances
```

Response

```
1  {
2    "ReservedElasticsearchInstances": [
3      {
4        "FixedPrice": 100.0,
5        "ReservedElasticsearchInstanceOfferingId": "1a2a3a4a5-1a2a-3a4a-5a6a-1a2a3a4a5a6a",
6        "ReservationName": "my-reservation",
7        "PaymentOption": "PARTIAL_UPFRONT",
8        "UsagePrice": 0.0,
9        "ReservedElasticsearchInstanceId": "9a8a7a6a-5a4a-3a2a-1a0a-9a8a7a6a5a4a",
10       "RecurringCharges": [
11         {
12           "RecurringChargeAmount": 0.603,
13           "RecurringChargeFrequency": "Hourly"
14         }
15       ],
16       "State": "payment-pending",
17       "StartTime": 1522872571.229,
18       "ElasticsearchInstanceCount": 3,
19       "Duration": 31536000,
20       "ElasticsearchInstanceType": "m4.2xlarge.elasticsearch",
21       "CurrencyCode": "USD"
22     }
23   ]
24 }
```

ListDomainNames

Displays the names of all Amazon ES domains owned by the current user *in the active region.*

Syntax

```
1 GET /2015-01-01/domain
```

Request Parameters

This operation does not use request parameters.

Request Body

This operation does not use the HTTP request body.

Response Elements

Field	Data Type	Description
DomainNameList	DomainNameList	The names of all Amazon ES domains owned by the current user.

Errors

The `ListDomainNames` operation can return any of the following errors:

- BaseException
- ValidationException

Example

The following example lists all three domains owned by the current user:

Request

```
1 GET es.<AWS_REGION>.amazonaws.com/2015-01-01/domain
```

Response

```
1  {
2      "DomainNames": [
3          {
4              "DomainName": "logs"
5          },
6          {
7              "DomainName": "streaming-logs"
8          }
9      ]
10 }
```

ListElasticsearchInstanceTypes

Lists all Elasticsearch instance types that are supported for a given Elasticsearch version.

Syntax

```
1 GET 2015-01-01/es/instanceTypes/{ElasticsearchVersion}?domainName={DomainName}&maxResults={
    MaxResults}&nextToken={NextToken}
```

Request Parameters

Parameter	Data Type	Required?	Description
ElasticsearchVersion	String	Yes	The Elasticsearch version.
DomainName	String	No	The Amazon ES domain name.
MaxResults	Integer	No	Limits the number of results. Must be between 30 and 100.
NextToken	String	No	Used for pagination. Only necessary if a previous API call produced a result containing NextToken. Accepts a next-token input to return results for the next page and provides a next-token output in the response, which clients can use to retrieve more results.

Request Body

This operation does not use the HTTP request body.

Response Elements

Field	Data Type	Description
ElasticsearchInstanceTypes	List	List of supported instance types for the given Elasticsearch version.

Field	Data Type	Description
NextToken	String	Used for pagination. Only necessary if a previous API call produced a result containing NextToken. Accepts a next-token input to return results for the next page and provides a next-token output in the response, which clients can use to retrieve more results.

Errors

ListElasticsearchInstanceTypes can return any of the following errors:

- BaseException
- InternalException
- ResourceNotFoundException
- ValidationException

Example

Request

```
1 GET es.<AWS_REGION>.amazonaws.com/2015-01-01/es/instanceTypes/6.0
```

Response

```
1  {
2      "ElasticsearchInstanceTypes": [
3          "t2.small.elasticsearch",
4          "t2.medium.elasticsearch",
5          "r4.large.elasticsearch",
6          "r4.xlarge.elasticsearch",
7          "r4.2xlarge.elasticsearch",
8          "r4.4xlarge.elasticsearch",
9          "r4.8xlarge.elasticsearch",
10         "r4.16xlarge.elasticsearch",
11         "m4.large.elasticsearch",
12         "m4.xlarge.elasticsearch",
13         "m4.2xlarge.elasticsearch",
14         "m4.4xlarge.elasticsearch",
15         "m4.10xlarge.elasticsearch",
16         "c4.large.elasticsearch",
17         "c4.xlarge.elasticsearch",
18         "c4.2xlarge.elasticsearch",
19         "c4.4xlarge.elasticsearch",
20         "c4.8xlarge.elasticsearch"
21     ],
22     "NextToken": null
23  }
```

ListElasticsearchVersions

Lists all supported Elasticsearch versions on Amazon ES.

Syntax

```
1 GET 2015-01-01/es/versions?maxResults={MaxResults}&nextToken={NextToken}
```

Request Parameters

Parameter	Data Type	Required?	Description
MaxResults	Integer	No	Limits the number of results. Must be between 30 and 100.
NextToken	String	No	Used for pagination. Only necessary if a previous API call produced a result containing NextToken. Accepts a next-token input to return results for the next page and provides a next-token output in the response, which clients can use to retrieve more results.

Request Body

This operation does not use the HTTP request body.

Response Elements

Field	Data Type	Description
ElasticsearchVersions	List	Lists all supported Elasticsearch versions.
NextToken	String	Used for pagination. Only necessary if a previous API call produced a result containing NextToken. Accepts a next-token input to return results for the next page and provides a next-token output in the response, which clients can use to retrieve more results.

Errors

`ListElasticsearchVersions` can return any of the following errors:

- `BaseException`
- `InternalException`
- `ResourceNotFoundException`
- `ValidationException`

Example

Request

```
1 GET es.<AWS_REGION>.amazonaws.com/2015-01-01/es/versions
```

Response

```
1  {
2      "ElasticsearchVersions": [
3          "6.0",
4          "5.5",
5          "5.3",
6          "5.1",
7          "2.3",
8          "1.5"
9      ],
10     "NextToken": null
11 }
```

ListTags

Displays all resource tags for an Amazon ES domain.

Syntax

```
1 GET /2015-01-01/tags?arn=<DOMAIN_ARN>
```

Request Parameters

Parameter	Data Type	Required?	Description
ARN	ARN	Yes	Amazon Resource Name (ARN) for the Amazon ES domain.

Request Body

This operation does not use the HTTP request body.

Response Elements

Field	Data Type	Description
TagList	TagList	List of resource tags. For more information, see Tagging Amazon Elasticsearch Service Domains.

Errors

The `ListTags` operation can return any of the following errors:

- `BaseException`
- `ResourceNotFoundException`
- `ValidationException`
- `InternalException`

Example

The following example lists the tags attached to the `logs` domain:

Request

```
1 GET es.<AWS_REGION>.amazonaws.com/2015-01-01/tags?arn=arn:aws:es:us-west-1:123456789012:domain/
    logs
```

Response

```
1 HTTP/1.1 200 OK
2 {
3     "TagList": [
4         {
5             "Key": "Environment",
6             "Value": "MacOS"
7         },
8         {
9             "Key": "project",
10            "Value": "trident"
11        }
12    ]
13 }
```

PurchaseReservedElasticsearchInstance

Purchase a reserved instance.

Syntax

```
1 POST /2015-01-01/es/purchaseReservedInstanceOffering
```

Request Parameters

This operation does not use HTTP request parameters.

Request Body

Name	Data Type	Required?	Description
ReservationName	String	Yes	A descriptive name for your reservation.
ReservedElastic-searchInstanceOf-feringId	String	Yes	The offering ID.
InstanceCount	Integer	Yes	The number of instances you want to reserve.

Response Elements

Field	Data Type	Description
ReservationName	String	The name of your reservation.
ReservedElasticsearchInstan-ceId	String	The reservation ID.

Errors

The `PurchaseReservedElasticsearchInstance` operation can return any of the following errors:

- `DisabledOperationException`
- `InternalException`
- `ResourceNotFoundException`
- `ValidationException`
- `LimitExceededException`
- `ResourceAlreadyExistsException`

Example

Request

```
1 POST es.<AWS_REGION>.amazonaws.com/2015-01-01/es/purchaseReservedInstanceOffering
2 {
3   "ReservationName" : "my-reservation",
4   "ReservedElasticsearchInstanceOfferingId" : "1a2a3a4a5-1a2a-3a4a-5a6a-1a2a3a4a5a6a",
5   "InstanceCount" : 3
6 }
```

Response

```
1 {
2   "ReservationName": "my-reservation",
3   "ReservedElasticsearchInstanceId": "9a8a7a6a-5a4a-3a2a-1a0a-9a8a7a6a5a4a"
4 }
```

RemoveTags

Removes the specified resource tags from an Amazon ES domain.

Syntax

```
1 POST es.<AWS_REGION>.amazonaws.com/2015-01-01/tags-removal
2 {
3     "ARN": "<DOMAIN_ARN>",
4     "TagKeys": [
5         "<TAG_KEY>",
6         "<TAG_KEY>",
7         ...
8     ]
9 }
```

Request Parameters

This operation does not use HTTP request parameters.

Request Body

Parameter	Data Type	Required?	Description
ARN	ARN	Yes	Amazon Resource Name (ARN) of an Amazon ES domain. For more information, see Identifiers for IAM Entities in Using AWS Identity and Access Management.
TagKeys	TagKey	Yes	List of tag keys for resource tags that you want to remove from an Amazon ES domain.

Response Elements

Not applicable. The `RemoveTags` operation does not return a response element.

Errors

The `RemoveTags` operation can return any of the following errors:

- `BaseException`
- `ValidationException`
- `InternalException`

Example

The following example deletes a resource tag with a tag key of `project` from the Amazon ES domain:

Request

```
1  POST /2015-01-01/tags-removal
2  {
3      "ARN": "<DOMAIN_ARN>",
4      "TagKeys": [
5          "project"
6      ]
7  }
```

This operation does not return a response element.

UpdateElasticsearchDomainConfig

Modifies the configuration of an Amazon ES domain, such as the instance type and the number of instances. You only need to specify the values that you want to update.

Syntax

```
1   POST /2015-01-01/es/domain/<DOMAIN_NAME>/config
2   {
3       "ElasticsearchClusterConfig": {
4           "InstanceType": "<INSTANCE_TYPE>",
5           "Instance_Count": <INSTANCE_COUNT>,
6           "DedicatedMasterEnabled": "<TRUE|FALSE>",
7           "DedicatedMasterCount": <INSTANCE_COUNT>,
8           "DedicatedMasterType": "<INSTANCE_COUNT>",
9           "ZoneAwarenessEnabled": "<TRUE|FALSE>"
10      },
11      "EBSOptions": {
12          "EBSEnabled": "<TRUE|FALSE>",
13          "VolumeType": "<VOLUME_TYPE>",
14          "VolumeSize": "<VOLUME_SIZE>",
15          "Iops": "<VALUE>"
16      },
17      "VPCOptions": {
18          "SubnetIds": [
19              "<SUBNET_ID>"
20          ],
21          "SecurityGroupIds": [
22              "<SECURITY_GROUP_ID>"
23          ]
24      },
25      "AccessPolicies": "<ACCESS_POLICY_DOCUMENT>",
26      "SnapshotOptions": {
27          "AutomatedSnapshotStartHour": <START_HOUR>,
28          "AdvancedOptions": {
29              "rest.action.multi.allow_explicit_index": "<TRUE|FALSE>",
30              "indices.fielddata.cache.size": "<PERCENTAGE_OF_HEAP>"
31          }
32      },
33      "LogPublishingOptions": {
34          "SEARCH_SLOW_LOGS": {
```

191

```
35        "CloudWatchLogsLogGroupArn":"<ARN>",
36        "Enabled":true
37      },
38      "INDEX_SLOW_LOGS": {
39        "CloudWatchLogsLogGroupArn":"<ARN>",
40        "Enabled":true
41      }
42    }
43 }
```

Request Parameters

This operation does not use HTTP request parameters.

Request Body

Parameter	Data Type	Required?	Description
DomainName	DomainName	Yes	Name of the Amazon ES domain for which you want to update the configuration.
ElasticsearchCluster-Config	ElasticsearchCluster	No	Desired changes to the cluster configuration, such as the instance type and number of EC2 instances.
EBSOptions	EBSOptions	No	Type and size of EBS volumes attached to data nodes.
VPCOptions	VPCOptions	No	Container for the values required to configure Amazon ES to work with a VPC. To learn more, see VPC Support for Amazon Elasticsearch Service Domains.
SnapshotOptions	SnapshotOptions	No	Hour during which the service takes an automated daily snapshot of the indices in the Amazon ES domain.
AdvancedOptions	AdvancedOptions	No	Key-value pairs to specify advanced configuration options. For more information, see Configuring Advanced Options.

Parameter	Data Type	Required?	Description
AccessPolicies	String	No	Specifies the access policies for the Amazon ES domain. For more information, see Configuring Access Policies.
LogPublishingOptions	LogPublishingOptions	No	Key-value string pairs to configure slow log publishing.
CognitoOptions	CognitoOptions	No	Key-value pairs to configure Amazon ES to use Amazon Cognito authentication for Kibana.

Response Elements

Field	Data Type	Description
DomainConfig	String	Status of the Amazon ES domain after updating its configuration.

Errors

UpdateElasticsearchDomainConfig can return any of the following errors:

- BaseException
- InternalException
- InvalidTypeException
- LimitExceededException
- ValidationException

Example

The following example configures the daily automatic snapshot for the streaming-logs domain to occur during the hour starting at 3:00 AM GMT:

Request

```
1 POST es.<AWS_REGION>.amazonaws.com/2015-01-01/es/domain/streaming-logs/config
2 {
3     "SnapshotOptions": {
4         "AutomatedSnapshotStartHour": 3
5     }
6 }
```

Response

```
1 {
2     "DomainConfig": {
3         "AccessPolicies": {
```

```
4        "Options": "{\"Version\":\"2012-10-17\",\"Statement\":[{\"Effect\":\"Allow\",\"
             Principal\":{\"AWS\":\"*\"},\"Action\":\"es:*\",\"Resource\":\"arn:aws:es:us-
             west-1:123456789012:domain/streaming-logs/*\",\"Condition\":{\"IpAddress\":{\"
             aws:SourceIp
             \":[\"11.222.333.11\",\"11.222.333.12\",\"11.222.333.13\",\"11.222.333.14\",\"11.222.

5        "Status": {
6            "CreationDate": 1502213150.329,
7            "PendingDeletion": false,
8            "State": "Active",
9            "UpdateDate": 1502213466.93,
10           "UpdateVersion": 6
11       }
12   },
13   "AdvancedOptions": {
14       "Options": {
15           "rest.action.multi.allow_explicit_index": "true"
16       },
17       "Status": {
18           "CreationDate": 1502213150.329,
19           "PendingDeletion": false,
20           "State": "Active",
21           "UpdateDate": 1502213466.93,
22           "UpdateVersion": 6
23       }
24   },
25   "EBSOptions": {
26       "Options": {
27           "EBSEnabled": true,
28           "EncryptionEnabled": false,
29           "Iops": null,
30           "VolumeSize": 11,
31           "VolumeType": "gp2"
32       },
33       "Status": {
34           "CreationDate": 1502213150.329,
35           "PendingDeletion": false,
36           "State": "Active",
37           "UpdateDate": 1502929669.653,
38           "UpdateVersion": 23
39       }
40   },
41   "ElasticsearchClusterConfig": {
42       "Options": {
43           "DedicatedMasterCount": 2,
44           "DedicatedMasterEnabled": false,
45           "DedicatedMasterType": "m4.large.elasticsearch",
46           "InstanceCount": 2,
47           "InstanceType": "t2.small.elasticsearch",
48           "ZoneAwarenessEnabled": false
49       },
50       "Status": {
51           "CreationDate": 1502213150.329,
52           "PendingDeletion": false,
```

```
 53            "State": "Active",
 54            "UpdateDate": 1502929669.653,
 55            "UpdateVersion": 23
 56        }
 57    },
 58    "ElasticsearchVersion": {
 59        "Options": "5.5",
 60        "Status": {
 61            "CreationDate": 1502213150.329,
 62            "PendingDeletion": false,
 63            "State": "Active",
 64            "UpdateDate": 1502213466.93,
 65            "UpdateVersion": 6
 66        }
 67    },
 68    "EncryptionAtRestOptions": {
 69        "Options": {
 70            "Enabled": true,
 71            "KmsKeyId": "arn:aws:kms:us-west-1:123456789012:key/1a2a3a4-1a2a-3a4a-5a6a-1
                a2a3a4a5a6a"
 72        },
 73        "Status": {
 74            "CreationDate": 1509490412.757,
 75            "PendingDeletion": false,
 76            "State": "Active",
 77            "UpdateDate": 1509490953.717,
 78            "UpdateVersion": 6
 79        }
 80    },
 81    "LogPublishingOptions":{
 82        "Options":{
 83            "INDEX_SLOW_LOGS":{
 84                "CloudWatchLogsLogGroupArn":"arn:aws:logs:us-east-1:123456789012:log-group:
                    sample-domain",
 85                "Enabled":true
 86            },
 87            "SEARCH_SLOW_LOGS":{
 88                "CloudWatchLogsLogGroupArn":"arn:aws:logs:us-east-1:123456789012:log-group:
                    sample-domain",
 89                "Enabled":true
 90            }
 91        },
 92        "Status":{
 93            "CreationDate":1502774634.546,
 94            "PendingDeletion":false,
 95            "State":"Processing",
 96            "UpdateDate":1502779590.448,
 97            "UpdateVersion":60
 98        }
 99    },
100    "SnapshotOptions": {
101        "Options": {
102            "AutomatedSnapshotStartHour": 3
103        },
```

```
104        "Status": {
105            "CreationDate": 1502213150.329,
106            "PendingDeletion": false,
107            "State": "Active",
108            "UpdateDate": 1503093165.447,
109            "UpdateVersion": 25
110        }
111    },
112    "VPCOptions": {
113        "Options": {
114            "AvailabilityZones": null,
115            "SecurityGroupIds": null,
116            "SubnetIds": null,
117            "VPCId": null
118        },
119        "Status": {
120            "CreationDate": 1503093165.597,
121            "PendingDeletion": false,
122            "State": "Active",
123            "UpdateDate": 1503093165.597,
124            "UpdateVersion": 25
125        }
126    }
127    }
128 }
```

Data Types

This section describes the data types used by the REST Configuration API.

AdvancedOptions

Key-value string pairs to specify advanced Elasticsearch configuration options.

Field	Data Type	Description
rest.action.multi.allow_explicit_index	Key-value pair:rest .action.multi. allow_explicit_index =<true|false>	Specifies whether explicit references to indices are allowed inside the body of HTTP requests. If you want to configure access policies for domain sub-resources, such as specific indices and domain APIs, you must disable this property. For more information, see URL-based Access Control. For more information about access policies for sub-resources, see Configuring Access Policies.

Field	Data Type	Description
indices.fielddata.cache.size	Key-value pair:`indices.fielddata.cache.size=<percentage_of_heap>`	Specifies the percentage of Java heap space that is allocated to field data. By default, this setting is unbounded.
indices.query.bool.max_clause_c	Key-value pair:`indices.query.bool.max_clause_count=<int>`	Specifies the maximum number of clauses allowed in a Lucene boolean query. 1024 is the default. Queries with more than the permitted number of clauses result in a TooManyClauses error. To learn more, see the Lucene documentation.

AdvancedOptionsStatus

Status of an update to advanced configuration options for an Amazon ES domain.

Field	Data Type	Description
Options	AdvancedOptions	Key-value pairs to specify advanced Elasticsearch configuration options.
Status	OptionStatus	Status of an update to advanced configuration options for an Amazon ES domain.

ARN

Field	Data Type	Description
ARN	String	Amazon Resource Name (ARN) of an Amazon ES domain. For more information, see IAM ARNs in the AWS Identity and Access Management documentation.

CognitoOptions

Field	Data Type	Description
Enabled	Boolean	Whether to enable or disable Amazon Cognito authentication for Kibana. See Amazon Cognito Authentication for Kibana.
UserPoolId	String	The Amazon Cognito user pool ID that you want Amazon ES to use for Kibana authentication.
IdentityPoolId	String	The Amazon Cognito identity pool ID that you want Amazon ES to use for Kibana authentication.
RoleArn	String	The AmazonESCognitoAccess role that allows Amazon ES to configure your user pool and identity pool.

CognitoOptionsStatus

Field	Data Type	Description
Options	CognitoOptions	Key-value pairs to configure Amazon ES to use Amazon Cognito authentication for Kibana.
Status	OptionStatus	Status of an update to the Cognito configuration options for an Amazon ES domain.

CreateElasticsearchDomainRequest

Container for the parameters required by the `CreateElasticsearchDomain` service operation.

Field	Data Type	Description
DomainName	DomainName	Name of the Amazon ES domain to create.
ElasticsearchClusterConfig	ElasticsearchClusterConfig	Container for the cluster configuration of an Amazon ES domain.
EBSOptions	EBSOptions	Container for the parameters required to enable EBS-based storage for an Amazon ES domain. For more information, see Configuring EBS-based Storage.

Field	Data Type	Description
AccessPolicies	String	IAM policy document specifying the access policies for the new Amazon ES domain. For more information, see Configuring Access Policies.
SnapshotOptions	SnapshotOptionsStatus	Container for parameters required to configure automated snapshots of domain indices. For more information, see Configuring Snapshots.
VPCOptions	VPCOptions	Container for the values required to configure Amazon ES to work with a VPC.
LogPublishingOptions	LogPublishingOptions	Key-value string pairs to configure slow log publishing.
SnapshotOptions	SnapshotOptionsStatus	Container for parameters required to configure automated snapshots of domain indices. For more information, see Configuring Snapshots.
AdvancedOptions	AdvancedOptionsStatus	Key-value pairs to specify advanced configuration options.
CognitoOptions	CognitoOptions	Key-value pairs to configure Amazon ES to use Amazon Cognito authentication for Kibana.

DomainID

Data Type	Description
String	Unique identifier for an Amazon ES domain

DomainName

Name of an Amazon ES domain.

Data Type	Description
String	Name of an Amazon ES domain. Domain names are unique across all domains owned by the same account within an AWS region. Domain names must start with a lowercase letter and must be between 3 and 28 characters. Valid characters are a-z (lowercase only), 0-9, and − (hyphen).

DomainNameList

String of Amazon ES domain names.

Data Type	Description
String Array	Array of Amazon ES domains in the following format:["<Domain_Name>","<Domain_Name>"...]

EBSOptions

Container for the parameters required to enable EBS-based storage for an Amazon ES domain. For more information, see Configuring EBS-based Storage.

Field	Data Type	Description
EBSEnabled	Boolean	Indicates whether EBS volumes are attached to data nodes in an Amazon ES domain.
VolumeType	String	Specifies the type of EBS volumes attached to data nodes.
VolumeSize	String	Specifies the size of EBS volumes attached to data nodes.
Iops	String	Specifies the baseline input/output (I/O) performance of EBS volumes attached to data nodes. Applicable only for the Provisioned IOPS EBS volume type.

ElasticsearchClusterConfig

Container for the cluster configuration of an Amazon ES domain.

Field	Data Type	Description
InstanceType	String	Instance type of data nodes in the cluster.
InstanceCount	Integer	Number of instances in the cluster.

Field	Data Type	Description
DedicatedMasterEnabled	Boolean	Indicates whether dedicated master nodes are enabled for the cluster. True if the cluster will use a dedicated master node. False if the cluster will not. For more information, see About Dedicated Master Nodes.
DedicatedMasterType	String	Amazon ES instance type of the dedicated master nodes in the cluster.
DedicatedMasterCount	Integer	Number of dedicated master nodes in the cluster.
ZoneAwarenessEnabled	Boolean	Indicates whether zone awareness is enabled. Zone awareness allocates the nodes and replica index shards belonging to a cluster across two Availability Zones in the same region.If you enable zone awareness, you must have an even number of instances in the instance count, and you also must use the Amazon ES Configuration API to replicate your data for your Elasticsearch cluster. For more information, see Enabling Zone Awareness.

ElasticsearchDomainConfig

Container for the configuration of an Amazon ES domain.

Field	Data Type	Description
ElasticsearchVersion	String	Elasticsearch version.
ElasticsearchClusterConfig	`ElasticsearchClusterConfig`	Container for the cluster configuration of an Amazon ES domain.
EBSOptions	`EBSOptions`	Container for EBS options configured for an Amazon ES domain.
AccessPolicies	String	Specifies the access policies for the Amazon ES domain. For more information, see Configuring Access Policies.

Field	Data Type	Description
SnapshotOptions	SnapshotOptionsStatus	Hour during which the service takes an automated daily snapshot of the indices in the Amazon ES domain. For more information, see Configuring Snapshots.
VPCOptions	VPCDerivedInfoStatus	The current VPCOptions for the domain and the status of any updates to their configuration.
LogPublishingOptions	LogPublishingOptions	Key-value pairs to configure slow log publishing.
AdvancedOptions	AdvancedOptionsStatus	Key-value pairs to specify advanced configuration options.
EncryptionAtRestOptions	EncryptionAtRestOptionsSta	Key-value pairs to enable encryption at rest.

ElasticsearchDomainStatus

Container for the contents of a DomainStatus data structure.

Field	Data Type	Description
DomainID	DomainID	Unique identifier for an Amazon ES domain.
DomainName	DomainName	Name of an Amazon ES domain. Domain names are unique across all domains owned by the same account within an AWS Region. Domain names must start with a lowercase letter and must be between 3 and 28 characters. Valid characters are a-z (lowercase only), 0-9, and – (hyphen).
ARN	ARN	Amazon Resource Name (ARN) of an Amazon ES domain. For more information, see Identifiers for IAM Entities in Using AWS Identity and Access Management.
Created	Boolean	Status of the creation of an Amazon ES domain. True if creation of the domain is complete. False if domain creation is still in progress.

Field	Data Type	Description
Deleted	Boolean	Status of the deletion of an Amazon ES domain. True if deletion of the domain is complete. False if domain deletion is still in progress.
Endpoint	ServiceUrl	Domain-specific endpoint used to submit index, search, and data upload requests to an Amazon ES domain.
Endpoints	EndpointsMap	The key-value pair that exists if the Amazon ES domain uses VPC endpoints.
Processing	Boolean	Status of a change in the configuration of an Amazon ES domain. True if the service is still processing the configuration changes. False if the configuration change is active. You must wait for a domain to reach active status before submitting index, search, and data upload requests.
ElasticsearchVersion	String	Elasticsearch version.
ElasticsearchClusterConfig	ElasticsearchClusterConfig	Container for the cluster configuration of an Amazon ES domain.
EBSOptions	EBSOptions	Container for the parameters required to enable EBS-based storage for an Amazon ES domain. For more information, see Configuring EBS-based Storage.
AccessPolicies	String	IAM policy document specifying the access policies for the new Amazon ES domain. For more information, see Configuring Access Policies.
SnapshotOptions	SnapshotOptions	Container for parameters required to configure the time of daily automated snapshots of Amazon ES domain indices.
VPCOptions	VPCDerivedInfo	Information that Amazon ES derives based on VPCOptions for the domain.
LogPublishingOptions	LogPublishingOptions	Key-value pairs to configure slow log publishing.
AdvancedOptions	AdvancedOptions	Key-value pairs to specify advanced configuration options.
EncryptionAtRestOptions	EncryptionAtRestOptions	Key-value pairs to enable encryption at rest.

Field	Data Type	Description
CognitoOptions	CognitoOptions	Key-value pairs to configure Amazon ES to use Amazon Cognito authentication for Kibana.

ElasticsearchDomainStatusList

List that contains the status of each specified Amazon ES domain.

Field	Data Type	Description
DomainStatusList	ElasticsearchDomainStatus	List that contains the status of each specified Amazon ES domain.

EncryptionAtRestOptions

Specifies whether the domain should encrypt data at rest, and if so, the AWS Key Management Service (KMS) key to use. Can only be used to create a new domain, not update an existing one.

Field	Data Type	Description
Enabled	Boolean	Specify true to enable encryption at rest.
KmsKeyId	String	The KMS key ID. Takes the form 1a2a3a4-1a2a-3a4a-5a6a-1a2a3a4a5a6a.

EncryptionAtRestOptionsStatus

Status of the domain's encryption at rest options.

Field	Data Type	Description
Options	EncryptionAtRestOptions	Encryption at rest options for the domain.
Status	OptionStatus	Status of the domain's encryption at rest options.

EndpointsMap

The key-value pair that contains the VPC endpoint. Only exists if the Amazon ES domain resides in a VPC.

Field	Data Type	Description
Endpoints	Key-value string pair: "vpc": "<VPC_ENDPOINT>"	The VPC endpoint for the domain.

LogPublishingOptions

Specifies whether the Amazon ES domain publishes the Elasticsearch slow logs to Amazon CloudWatch. You still have to enable the *collection* of slow logs using the Elasticsearch REST API. To learn more, see Setting Elasticsearch Logging Thresholds.

Field	Data Type	Description
INDEX_SLOW_LOGS	Key-value	Two key-value pairs that define the CloudWatch log group and whether or not the Elasticsearch index slow log should be published there: "CloudWatchLogsLogGroupArn":"arn:aws:logs:us-east-1:264071961897:log-group:sample-domain","Enabled":true
SEARCH_SLOW_LOGS	Key-value	Two key-value pairs that define the CloudWatch log group and whether or not the Elasticsearch search slow log should be published there: "CloudWatchLogsLogGroupArn":"arn:aws:logs:us-east-1:264071961897:log-group:sample-domain","Enabled":true

LogPublishingOptionsStatus

Status of an update to the configuration of the slow log publishing options for the Amazon ES domain.

Field	Data Type	Description
Options	LogPublishingOptions	Slow log publishing options for the domain
Status	OptionStatus	Status of an update to snapshot options for an Amazon ES domain

OptionState

State of an update to advanced options for an Amazon ES domain.

Field	Data Type	Description
OptionStatus	String	One of three valid values:[See the AWS documentation website for more details]

OptionStatus

Status of an update to configuration options for an Amazon ES domain.

Field	Data Type	Description
CreationDate	Timestamp	Date and time when the Amazon ES domain was created
UpdateDate	Timestamp	Date and time when the Amazon ES domain was updated
UpdateVersion	Integer	Whole number that specifies the latest version for the entity
State	OptionState	State of an update to configuration options for an Amazon ES domain
PendingDeletion	Boolean	Indicates whether the service is processing a request to permanently delete the Amazon ES domain and all of its resources

ServiceURL

Domain-specific endpoint used to submit index, search, and data upload requests to an Amazon ES domain.

Field	Data Type	Description
ServiceURL	String	Domain-specific endpoint used to submit index, search, and data upload requests to an Amazon ES domain

SnapshotOptions

Container for parameters required to configure the time of daily automated snapshots of the indices in an Amazon ES domain.

Field	Data Type	Description
AutomatedSnapshot-StartHour	Integer	Hour during which the service takes an automated daily snapshot of the indices in the Amazon ES domain

SnapshotOptionsStatus

Status of an update to the configuration of the daily automated snapshot for an Amazon ES domain.

Field	Data Type	Description
Options	SnapshotOptions	Container for parameters required to configure the time of daily automated snapshots of indices in an Amazon ES domain
Status	OptionStatus	Status of an update to snapshot options for an Amazon ES domain

Tag

Field	Data Type	Description
Key	TagKey	Required name of the tag. Tag keys must be unique for the Amazon ES domain to which they are attached. For more information, see Tagging Amazon Elasticsearch Service Domains.
Value	TagValue	Optional string value of the tag. Tag values can be null and do not have to be unique in a tag set. For example, you can have a key-value pair in a tag set of project/Trinity and cost-center/Trinity.

TagKey

Field	Data Type	Description
Key	String	Name of the tag. String can have up to 128 characters.

TagList

Field	Data Type	Description
Tag	Tag	Resource tag attached to an Amazon ES domain.

TagValue

Field	Data Type	Description
Value	String	Holds the value for a TagKey. String can have up to 256 characters.

VPCDerivedInfo

Field	Data Type	Description
VPCId	String	The ID for your VPC. Amazon VPC generates this value when you create a VPC.
SubnetIds	StringList	A list of subnet IDs associated with the VPC endpoints for the domain. To learn more, see VPCs and Subnets in the Amazon VPC User Guide.
AvailabilityZones	StringList	The list of availability zones associated with the VPC subnets. To learn more, see VPC and Subnet Basics in the Amazon VPC User Guide.
SecurityGroupIds	StringList	The list of security group IDs associated with the VPC endpoints for the domain. To learn more, see Security Groups for your VPC in the Amazon VPC User Guide.

VPCDerivedInfoStatus

Field	Data Type	Description
Options	VPCDerivedInfo	Information that Amazon ES derives based on VPCOptions for the domain.

Field	Data Type	Description
Status	OptionStatus	Status of an update to VPC configuration options for an Amazon ES domain.

VPCOptions

Field	Data Type	Description
SubnetIds	StringList	A list of subnet IDs associated with the VPC endpoints for the domain. If your domain has zone awareness enabled, you need to provide two subnet IDs, one per zone. Otherwise, you only need to provide one. To learn more, see VPCs and Subnets in the Amazon VPC User Guide.
SecurityGroupIds	StringList	The list of security group IDs associated with the VPC endpoints for the domain. If you do not provide a security group ID, Amazon ES uses the default security group for the VPC. To learn more, see Security Groups for your VPC in the Amazon VPC User Guide.

VPCOptionsStatus

Field	Data Type	Description
Options	VPCOptions	Container for the values required to configure Amazon ES to work with a VPC.
Status	OptionStatus	Status of an update to VPC configuration options for an Amazon ES domain.

Errors

Amazon ES throws the following errors:

Exception	Description
BaseException	Thrown for all service errors. Contains the HTTP status code of the error.
ValidationException	Thrown when the HTTP request contains invalid input or is missing required input. Returns HTTP status code 400.
DisabledOperationException	Thrown when the client attempts to perform an unsupported operation. Returns HTTP status code 409.
InternalException	Thrown when an error internal to the service occurs while processing a request. Returns HTTP status code 500.
InvalidTypeException	Thrown when trying to create or access an Amazon ES domain sub-resource that is either invalid or not supported. Returns HTTP status code 409.
LimitExceededException	Thrown when trying to create more than the allowed number and type of Amazon ES domain resources and sub-resources. Returns HTTP status code 409.
ResourceNotFoundException	Thrown when accessing or deleting a resource that does not exist. Returns HTTP status code 400.
ResourceAlreadyExistsException	Thrown when a client attempts to create a resource that already exists in an Amazon ES domain. Returns HTTP status code 400.

Amazon Elasticsearch Service Limits

The following tables show limits for Amazon ES resources, including the number of instances per cluster, the minimum and maximum sizes for EBS volumes, and network limits.

Cluster and Instance Limits

The following table shows Amazon ES limits for clusters and instances.

Clusters and Instances	Limit
Maximum Number of Instances (Instance Count) per Cluster	20 (except for T2 instance types, which have a maximum of 10) The default limit is 20 instances per domain. To request an increase up to 100 instances per domain (for Elasticsearch 2.3 or later), create a case with the AWS Support Center. For more information about requesting an increase, see AWS Service Limits.
Maximum Number of Dedicated Master Nodes	5 You can use a T2 instance type as a dedicated master node only if the instance count is 10 or fewer.
Smallest Instance Type Supported by Elasticsearch Version	t2.micro.elasticsearch (versions 1.5 and 2.3) and t2.small.elasticsearch (version 5.x and 6.x).

For a list of the instance types that Amazon ES supports, see Supported Instance Types.

EBS Volume Size Limits

The following table shows the minimum and maximum sizes for EBS volumes for each instance type that Amazon ES supports. See Amazon Elasticsearch Service Pricing for information on which instance types offer instance storage.

Note
If you select magnetic storage under **EBS volume type** when creating your domain, maximum volume size is 100 GB for all instance types except t2.micro, t2.small, and t2.medium. For the maximum sizes listed in the following table, select one of the SSD options.

Instance Type	Minimum EBS Size	Maximum EBS Size
t2.micro.elasticsearch	10 GB	35 GB
t2.small.elasticsearch	10 GB	35 GB
t2.medium.elasticsearch	10 GB	35 GB
m3.medium.elasticsearch	10 GB	100 GB
m3.large.elasticsearch	10 GB	512 GB
m3.xlarge.elasticsearch	10 GB	512 GB
m3.2xlarge.elasticsearch	10 GB	512 GB
m4.large.elasticsearch	10 GB	512 GB
m4.xlarge.elasticsearch	10 GB	1 TB*
m4.2xlarge.elasticsearch	10 GB	1.5 TB*

Instance Type	Minimum EBS Size	Maximum EBS Size
m4.4xlarge.elasticsearch	10 GB	1.5 TB*
m4.10xlarge.elasticsearch	10 GB	1.5 TB*
c4.large.elasticsearch	10 GB	100 GB
c4.xlarge.elasticsearch	10 GB	512 GB
c4.2xlarge.elasticsearch	10 GB	1 TB*
c4.4xlarge.elasticsearch	10 GB	1.5 TB*
c4.8xlarge.elasticsearch	10 GB	1.5 TB*
r3.large.elasticsearch	10 GB	512 GB
r3.xlarge.elasticsearch	10 GB	512 GB
r3.2xlarge.elasticsearch	10 GB	512 GB
r3.4xlarge.elasticsearch	10 GB	512 GB
r3.8xlarge.elasticsearch	10 GB	512 GB
r4.large.elasticsearch	10 GB	1 TB*
r4.xlarge.elasticsearch	10 GB	1.5 TB*
r4.2xlarge.elasticsearch	10 GB	1.5 TB*
r4.4xlarge.elasticsearch	10 GB	1.5 TB*
r4.8xlarge.elasticsearch	10 GB	1.5 TB*
r4.16xlarge.elasticsearch	10 GB	1.5 TB*
i2.xlarge.elasticsearch	10 GB	512 GB
i2.2xlarge.elasticsearch	10 GB	512 GB
i3.large.elasticsearch	N/A	N/A
i3.xlarge.elasticsearch	N/A	N/A
i3.2xlarge.elasticsearch	N/A	N/A
i3.4xlarge.elasticsearch	N/A	N/A
i3.8xlarge.elasticsearch	N/A	N/A
i3.16xlarge.elasticsearch	N/A	N/A

* 512 GB is the maximum volume size that is supported with Elasticsearch version 1.5.

Network Limits

The following table shows the maximum size of HTTP request payloads.

Instance Type	Maximum Size of HTTP Request Payloads
t2.micro.elasticsearch	10 MB
t2.small.elasticsearch	10 MB
t2.medium.elasticsearch	10 MB
m3.medium.elasticsearch	10 MB
m3.large.elasticsearch	10 MB
m3.xlarge.elasticsearch	100 MB
m3.2xlarge.elasticsearch	100 MB
m4.large.elasticsearch	10 MB
m4.xlarge.elasticsearch	100 MB
m4.2xlarge.elasticsearch	100 MB
m4.4xlarge.elasticsearch	100 MB
m4.10xlarge.elasticsearch	100 MB
c4.large.elasticsearch	10 MB
c4.xlarge.elasticsearch	100 MB
c4.2xlarge.elasticsearch	100 MB

Instance Type	Maximum Size of HTTP Request Payloads
c4.4xlarge.elasticsearch	100 MB
c4.8xlarge.elasticsearch	100 MB
r3.large.elasticsearch	10 MB
r3.xlarge.elasticsearch	100 MB
r3.2xlarge.elasticsearch	100 MB
r3.4xlarge.elasticsearch	100 MB
r3.8xlarge.elasticsearch	100 MB
r4.large.elasticsearch	100 MB
r4.xlarge.elasticsearch	100 MB
r4.2xlarge.elasticsearch	100 MB
r4.4xlarge.elasticsearch	100 MB
r4.8xlarge.elasticsearch	100 MB
r4.16xlarge.elasticsearch	100 MB
i2.xlarge.elasticsearch	100 MB
i2.2xlarge.elasticsearch	100 MB
`i3.large.elasticsearch`	100 MB
i3.xlarge.elasticsearch	100 MB
i3.2xlarge.elasticsearch	100 MB
i3.4xlarge.elasticsearch	100 MB
i3.8xlarge.elasticsearch	100 MB
i3.16xlarge.elasticsearch	100 MB

Java Process Limit

Amazon ES limits Java processes to a heap size of 32 GB. Advanced users can specify the percentage of the heap used for field data. For more information, see Configuring Advanced Options and JVM OutOfMemoryError.

Amazon Elasticsearch Service Reserved Instances

Amazon Elasticsearch Service Reserved Instances (RIs) offer significant discounts compared to standard On-Demand Instances. The instances themselves are identical; RIs are just a billing discount applied to On-Demand Instances in your account. For long-lived applications with predictable usage, RIs can provide considerable savings over time.

Amazon ES RIs require one- or three-year terms and have three payment options that affect the discount rate:

- **No Upfront** – You pay nothing upfront. You pay a discounted hourly rate for every hour within the term.
- **Partial Upfront** – You pay a portion of the cost upfront, and you pay a discounted hourly rate for every hour within the term.
- **All Upfront** – You pay the entirety of the cost upfront. You don't pay an hourly rate for the term.

Generally speaking, a larger upfront payment means a larger discount. You can't cancel Reserved Instances—when you reserve them, you commit to paying for the entire term—and upfront payments are nonrefundable. For full details, see Amazon Elasticsearch Service Pricing and FAQ.

Topics

- Purchasing Reserved Instances (Console)
- Purchasing Reserved Instances (AWS CLI)
- Purchasing Reserved Instances (AWS SDKs)
- Examining Costs

Purchasing Reserved Instances (Console)

The console lets you view your existing Reserved Instances and purchase new ones.

To purchase a reservation

1. Go to https://aws.amazon.com, and then choose **Sign In to the Console**.

2. Under **Analytics**, choose **Elasticsearch Service**.

3. Choose **Reserved Instances**.

   On this page, you can view your existing reservations. If you have many reservations, you can filter them to more easily identify and view a particular reservation.

4. Choose **Purchase Reserved Instance**.

5. For **Reservation Name**, type a unique, descriptive name.

6. Choose an instance type, size, and number of instances. For guidance, see Sizing Amazon ES Domains.

7. Choose a term length and payment option.

8. Review the payment details carefully.

9. Choose **Submit**.

10. Review the purchase summary carefully. Purchases of Reserved Instances are non-refundable.

11. Choose **Purchase**.

Purchasing Reserved Instances (AWS CLI)

The AWS CLI has commands for viewing offerings, purchasing a reservation, and viewing your reservations. The following command and sample response show the offerings for a given AWS Region:

```
1 aws es describe-reserved-elasticsearch-instance-offerings --region us-east-1
2 {
3   "ReservedElasticsearchInstanceOfferings": [
4     {
5       "FixedPrice": x,
6       "ReservedElasticsearchInstanceOfferingId": "1a2a3a4a5-1a2a-3a4a-5a6a-1a2a3a4a5a6a",
7       "RecurringCharges": [
8         {
9           "RecurringChargeAmount": y,
10          "RecurringChargeFrequency": "Hourly"
11        }
12      ],
13      "UsagePrice": 0.0,
14      "PaymentOption": "PARTIAL_UPFRONT",
15      "Duration": 31536000,
16      "ElasticsearchInstanceType": "m4.2xlarge.elasticsearch",
17      "CurrencyCode": "USD"
18    }
19  ]
20 }
```

For an explanation of each return value, see the following table.

Field	Description
FixedPrice	The upfront cost of the reservation.
ReservedElasticsearchInstanceOfferingId	The offering ID. Make note of this value if you want to reserve the offering.
RecurringCharges	The hourly rate for the reservation.
UsagePrice	A legacy field. For Amazon ES, this value is always 0.
PaymentOption	No Upfront, Partial Upfront, or All Upfront.
Duration	Length of the term in seconds:[See the AWS documentation website for more details]
ElasticsearchInstanceType	The instance type for the reservation. For information about the hardware resources that are allocated to each instance type, see Amazon Elasticsearch Service Pricing.
CurrencyCode	The currency for FixedPrice and RecurringChargeAmount.

This next example purchases a reservation:

```
1 aws es purchase-reserved-elasticsearch-instance-offering --reserved-elasticsearch-instance-
    offering-id 1a2a3a4a5-1a2a-3a4a-5a6a-1a2a3a4a5a6a --reservation-name my-reservation --
    instance-count 3 --region us-east-1
2 {
3   "ReservationName": "my-reservation",
4   "ReservedElasticsearchInstanceId": "9a8a7a6a-5a4a-3a2a-1a0a-9a8a7a6a5a4a"
5 }
```

Finally, you can list your reservations for a given region using the following example:

```
1 aws es describe-reserved-elasticsearch-instances --region us-east-1
```

215

```
2 {
3   "ReservedElasticsearchInstances": [
4     {
5       "FixedPrice": x,
6       "ReservedElasticsearchInstanceOfferingId": "1a2a3a4a5-1a2a-3a4a-5a6a-1a2a3a4a5a6a",
7       "ReservationName": "my-reservation",
8       "PaymentOption": "PARTIAL_UPFRONT",
9       "UsagePrice": 0.0,
10      "ReservedElasticsearchInstanceId": "9a8a7a6a-5a4a-3a2a-1a0a-9a8a7a6a5a4a",
11      "RecurringCharges": [
12        {
13          "RecurringChargeAmount": y,
14          "RecurringChargeFrequency": "Hourly"
15        }
16      ],
17      "State": "payment-pending",
18      "StartTime": 1522872571.229,
19      "ElasticsearchInstanceCount": 3,
20      "Duration": 31536000,
21      "ElasticsearchInstanceType": "m4.2xlarge.elasticsearch",
22      "CurrencyCode": "USD"
23    }
24  ]
25 }
```

Note

`StartTime` is Unix epoch time, which is the number of seconds that have passed since midnight UTC of 1 January 1970. For example, 1522872571 epoch time is 20:09:31 UTC of 4 April 2018. You can use online converters.

To learn more about the commands used in the preceding examples, see the AWS CLI Command Reference.

Purchasing Reserved Instances (AWS SDKs)

The AWS SDKs (except the Android and iOS SDKs) support all the operations that are defined in the Amazon ES Configuration API Reference, including the following:

- `DescribeReservedElasticsearchInstanceOfferings`
- `PurchaseReservedElasticsearchInstance`
- `DescribeReservedElasticsearchInstances`

For more information about installing and using the AWS SDKs, see AWS Software Development Kits.

Examining Costs

Cost Explorer is a free tool that you can use to view your spending data for the past 13 months. Analyzing this data helps you identify trends and understand if RIs fit your use case. If you already have RIs, you can group by **Purchase Option** and show amortized costs to compare that spending to your spending for On-Demand Instances. For more information, see Analyzing Your Costs with Cost Explorer in the *AWS Billing and Cost Management User Guide*.

Using Service-Linked Roles for Amazon ES

Amazon Elasticsearch Service uses AWS Identity and Access Management (IAM) service-linked roles. A service-linked role is a unique type of IAM role that is linked directly to Amazon ES. Service-linked roles are predefined by Amazon ES and include all the permissions that the service requires to call other AWS services on your behalf.

A service-linked role makes setting up Amazon ES easier because you don't have to manually add the necessary permissions. Amazon ES defines the permissions of its service-linked roles, and unless defined otherwise, only Amazon ES can assume its roles. The defined permissions include the trust policy and the permissions policy, and that permissions policy cannot be attached to any other IAM entity.

You can delete a service-linked role only after first deleting its related resources. This protects your Amazon ES resources because you can't inadvertently remove permission to access the resources.

For information about other services that support service-linked roles, see AWS Services That Work with IAM and look for the services that have **Yes **in the **Service-Linked Role** column. Choose a **Yes** with a link to view the service-linked role documentation for that service.

Service-Linked Role Permissions for Amazon ES

Amazon ES uses the service-linked role named **AWSServiceRoleForAmazonElasticsearchService**.

The AWSServiceRoleForAmazonElasticsearchService service-linked role trusts the following services to assume the role:

- `es.amazonaws.com`

The role permissions policy allows Amazon ES to complete the following actions on the specified resources:

- Action: `ec2:CreateNetworkInterface` on *
- Action: `ec2:DeleteNetworkInterface` on *
- Action: `ec2:DescribeNetworkInterfaces` on *
- Action: `ec2:ModifyNetworkInterfaceAttribute` on *
- Action: `ec2:DescribeSecurityGroups` on *
- Action: `ec2:DescribeSubnets` on *

You must configure permissions to allow an IAM entity (such as a user, group, or role) to create, edit, or delete a service-linked role. For more information, see Service-Linked Role Permissions in the *IAM User Guide.*

Creating a Service-Linked Role for Amazon ES

You don't need to manually create a service-linked role. When you create a VPC access domain using the AWS Management Console, Amazon ES creates the service-linked role for you. In order for this automatic creation to succeed, you must have permissions for the `iam:CreateServiceLinkedRole` action.

If you delete this service-linked role and then need to create it again, you can use the same process to recreate the role in your account.

You can also use the IAM console, the IAM CLI, or the IAM API to create a service-linked role manually. For more information, see Creating a Service-Linked Role in the *IAM User Guide.*

Editing a Service-Linked Role for Amazon ES

Amazon ES does not allow you to edit the AWSServiceRoleForAmazonElasticsearchService service-linked role. After you create a service-linked role, you cannot change the name of the role because various entities might reference the role. However, you can edit the description of the role using IAM. For more information, see Editing a Service-Linked Role in the *IAM User Guide*.

Deleting a Service-Linked Role for Amazon ES

If you no longer need to use a feature or service that requires a service-linked role, we recommend that you delete that role. That way you don't have an unused entity that is not actively monitored or maintained. However, you must clean up your service-linked role before you can manually delete it.

Cleaning Up a Service-Linked Role

Before you can use IAM to delete a service-linked role, you must first confirm that the role has no active sessions and remove any resources used by the role.

To check whether the service-linked role has an active session in the IAM console

1. Sign in to the AWS Management Console and open the IAM console at https://console.aws.amazon.com/iam/.

2. In the navigation pane of the IAM console, choose **Roles**. Then choose the name (not the check box) of the AWSServiceRoleForAmazonElasticsearchService role.

3. On the **Summary** page for the selected role, choose the **Access Advisor** tab.

4. On the **Access Advisor** tab, review recent activity for the service-linked role. **Note**
   If you are unsure whether Amazon ES is using the AWSServiceRoleForAmazonElasticsearchService role, you can try to delete the role. If the service is using the role, then the deletion fails and you can view the regions where the role is being used. If the role is being used, then you must wait for the session to end before you can delete the role. You cannot revoke the session for a service-linked role.

To remove Amazon ES resources used by the AWSServiceRoleForAmazonElasticsearchService

1. Sign in to the AWS Management Console and open the Amazon ES console.

2. Delete any domains that list **VPC** under the **Endpoint** column.

Manually Delete a Service-Linked Role

Use the Amazon ES configuration API to delete the AWSServiceRoleForAmazonElasticsearchService service-linked role. For more information, see DeleteElasticsearchServiceRole.

Document History for Amazon Elasticsearch Service

This topic describes important changes to the documentation for Amazon Elasticsearch Service (Amazon ES).

Relevant Dates to this History:

- **Current product version—**2015-01-01
- **Latest product release—**29 May 2018
- **Latest documentation update—**29 May 2018

Change	Description	Release Date
China (Ningxia) Reserved Instances	Amazon ES now offers Reserved Instances in the China (Ningxia) region.	29 May 2018
Reserved Instances	Amazon ES now offers Reserved Instances. To learn more, see Amazon Elasticsearch Service Reserved Instances.	7 May 2018
Amazon Cognito Authentication for Kibana	Amazon ES now offers login page protection for Kibana. To learn more, see Amazon Cognito Authentication for Kibana.	2 April 2018
Elasticsearch 6.2 Support	Amazon Elasticsearch Service now supports Elasticsearch version 6.2.	14 March 2018
Korean Analysis Plugin	Amazon ES now supports a memory-optimized version of the Seunjeon Korean analysis plugin.	13 March 2018
Instant Access Control Updates	Changes to the access control policies on Amazon ES domains now take effect instantly.	7 March 2018
Petabyte Scale	Amazon ES now supports i3 instance types and total domain storage of up to 1.5 PB. To learn more, see Petabyte Scale for Amazon Elasticsearch Service.	19 December 2017
Encryption of Data at Rest	Amazon ES now supports encryption of data at rest. To learn more, see Encryption of Data at Rest for Amazon Elasticsearch Service.	7 December 2017
Elasticsearch 6.0 Support	Amazon ES now supports Elasticsearch version 6.0. For migration considerations and instructions, see Migrating to a Different Elasticsearch Version.	6 December 2017

Change	Description	Release Date
VPC Support	Amazon ES now lets you launch domains within an Amazon Virtual Private Cloud. VPC support provides an additional layer of security and simplifies communications between Amazon ES and other services within a VPC. To learn more, see VPC Support for Amazon Elasticsearch Service Domains.	17 October 2017
Slow Logs Publishing	Amazon ES now supports the publishing of slow logs to CloudWatch Logs. To learn more, see Configuring Slow Logs.	16 October 2017
Elasticsearch 5.5 Support	Amazon ES now supports Elasticsearch version 5.5. For new feature summaries, see the Amazon announcement of availability. You can now restore automated snapshots without contacting AWS Support and store scripts using the Elasticsearch `_scripts` API.	7 September 2017
Elasticsearch 5.3 Support	Amazon ES added support for Elasticsearch version 5.3.	1 June 2017
More Instances and EBS Capacity per Cluster	Amazon ES now supports up to 100 nodes and 150 TB EBS capacity per cluster.	5 April 2017
Canada (Central) and EU (London) Support	Amazon ES added support for the following regions: Canada (Central), ca-central-1 and EU (London), eu-west-2.	20 March 2017
More Instances and Larger EBS Volumes	Amazon ES added support for more instances and larger EBS volumes.	21 February 2017
Elasticsearch 5.1 Support	Amazon ES added support for Elasticsearch version 5.1.	30 January 2017
Support for the Phonetic Analysis Plugin	Amazon ES now provides built-in integration with the Phonetic Analysis plugin, which allows you to run "sounds-like" queries on your data.	22 December 2016
US East (Ohio) Support	Amazon ES added support for the following region: US East (Ohio), us-east-2. For a list of regions supported by Amazon ES, see AWS Regions and Endpoints in the AWS General Reference.	17 October 2016

Change	Description	Release Date
New Performance Metric	Amazon ES added a performance metric, ClusterUsedSpace.	29 July 2016
Elasticsearch 2.3 Support	Amazon ES added support for Elasticsearch version 2.3.	27 July 2016
Asia Pacific (Mumbai) Support	Amazon ES added support for the following region: Asia Pacific (Mumbai), ap-south-1. For a list of regions supported by Amazon ES, see AWS Regions and Endpoints in the AWS General Reference.	27 June 2016
More Instances per Cluster	Amazon ES increased the maximum number of instances (instance count) per cluster from 10 to 20.	18 May 2016
Asia Pacific (Seoul) Support	Amazon ES added support for the following region: Asia Pacific (Seoul), ap-northeast-2. For a list of regions supported by Amazon ES, see AWS Regions and Endpoints in the AWS General Reference.	28 January 2016
Amazon ES	Initial release.	1 October 2015

AWS Glossary

For the latest AWS terminology, see the AWS Glossary in the *AWS General Reference.*